The Politics of
Labour and Development
in
Trinidad

❏

Ray Kiely

THE PRESS UNIVERSITY OF THE WEST INDIES
Barbados • Jamaica• Trinidad and Tobago

The Press University of the West Indies
1A Aqueduct Flats Kingston 7 Jamaica W I

00 99 98 97 96   5 4 3 2 1

CATALOGUING IN PUBLICATION DATA
Kiely, Ray
    The politics of labour and development in
    Trinidad / Ray Kiely.

    p. cm.
    Includes bibliographical references and index.
    ISBN 976-640-017-2
    1. Labour movement – Trinidad – History.
    2. Working class in Trinidad.
    3. Trade unions – Trinidad – Political activity.
    4. Social conflict – Trinidad.
    I. Title.
    HD8246.K53 1996   345'7298 dc–20

Book design and typesetting by Jenni Anderson & Associates,
Jamaica
Cover design by Robert Harris
Set in 10.5/13 Bodoni with Souvenir display type

Contents

◻

Acknowledgements

◻

Thanks to Economic and Social Research Council (England) for financing the research, and to the Government of Trinidad and Tobago for permission to research. Thanks to Robin Cohen (PhD supervisor), Ronaldo Munck and Bob Fine (PhD examiners). The research had significant assistance from Rudy Moonilal, Donna Coombs-Montrose, Barbara Fidely, Cecil Paul, Patrick Rabathly and Dave Ramsaran. Many thanks to all these persons.

May I also express my appreciation to the Director of the The Press University of the West Indies and to the academic reviewers of this work which, in the end, would not be what it now is without the commendable work of The Press UWI's editorial team – Jenni Anderson, Glory Robertson, Shivaun Hearne.

Ray Kiely

April 1996

List of Acronyms

❒

ABWWU	Amalgamated Building and Wood Workers' Union
ATSEFWTU	All-Trinidad Sugar Estates and Factory Workers' Trade Union
CLC	Caribbean Labour Congress
CLS	Committee for Labour Solidarity
CNLP	Caribbean National Labour Party
COLA	cost of living allowance
COSSABO	Conference of Shop Stewards and Branch Officers
CPTU	Council of Progressive Trade Unions
CSP	Caribbean Socialist Party
CSA	Civil Service Association
DLP	Democratic Labour Party
DEWD	Department of Educational Works Development
ECA	Employers' Consultative Association
FWTU	Federated Workers' Trade Union
GDP	gross domestic product
ICFTU	International Confederation of Free Trade Unions
ICFU	Islandwide Cane Farmers Trade Union
ISA	Industrial Stabilization Act
ISI	Import substitution industrialization
JTUM	Joint Trade Union Movement
LARR	Latin American Regional Report
MOTION	Movement for Social Transformation
NAMOTI	National Movement for the Total Independence of Trinidad and Tobago
NAR	National Alliance for Reconstruction
NBM	New Beginning Movement
NJAC	National Joint Action Committee
NLM	National Liberation Movement

NLM	National Liberation Movement
NWA	Negro Welfare Cultural and Social Association
NUGFW	National Union of Government and Federated Workers
ONR	Organization for National Reconstruction
OPEC	Organization for Petroleum Exporting Countries
ORIT	Inter-American Regional Organization of Workers
OWTU	Oilfields Workers' Trade Union
PDP	People's Democratic Party
PNM	People's National Movement
PPG	Political Progress Group
PSA	Public Services' Association
PSTC	Public Service Transport Corporation
PWTU	Public Workers' Trade Union
SNCC	Student Non-violent Coordinating Committee
SOPO	Summit of People's Organizations
SWWTU	Seamen and Waterfront Workers Trade Union
TICFA	Trinidad Islandwide Cane Farmers Association
TIWU	Transport and Industrial Workers' Union
TLP	Trinidad Labour Party
TTUC	Trinidad and Tobago Trades Union Congress
TUC (Britain)	Trades Union Congress
TUCo	Trinidad and Tobago Trade Union Council
TWA	Trinidad Working Men's Association
ULF	United Labour Front
UNC	United National Congress
UNIP	United National Independence Party
VAT	Value added tax
WASA	Water and Sewerage Authority
WFP	Workers and Farmers Party
WFTU	World Federation of Trade Unions
WIIP	West Indian Independence Party
WINP	West Indian National Party

Introduction

This work focuses on the politics of labour in Trinidad from 1937 to the early 1990s. It examines how historically constructed social divisions have militated against the successful development of a united working class and/or socialist party. In exploring these divisions, some pre-1937 historical detail, including the periods of slavery and indentureship, are examined.

The work employs a Marxist methodology, but one that does not believe in the inevitability of revolution or a united working class. Instead, class struggle is used to show how both.overt and covert forms of resistance have influenced the wider history and development of Trinidad. Orthodox positivist and structuralist Marxisms which posit the belief that working class political behaviour can be explained independently of the historical record are therefore rejected (as are those criticisms of such a caricature of Marxism – see chapter one).

Instead, this work examines how labour has been divided by the unevenness of capitalist development, and the particular racialized form that this development has taken in Trinidad. Previous histories of labour have focused almost exclusively on the trade union movement [Ramdin 1982], or have crudely used an inappropriate two-class model to explain periods of conflict and consensus [Rennie 1974]. This work, which is strongly influenced by the so-called new international labour studies [Cohen 1983; Munck 1988], constitutes a new approach in that it seeks to address the questions set out below (see Cohen [1988: 23]).

(a) What is the shape and character of the working class?
(b) Where do its parameters begin and end, especially in relation to other oppressed and exploited groups such as women, the peasantry, and the informal sector?
(c) What is the relationship between these different segments of the working class, and how are these reflected in working class organizations, including political parties?

My theoretical approach is examined in greater detail in the opening chapter, which is then followed by a substantive history of the politics of labour in Trinidad. In examining this history, it is hoped that this book can at least provide some of the answers to these questions.

Before moving on to the main text, three points of clarification are necessary. First, the term "Creole" is used to refer to the section of the population that is descended from African slaves. However, the term French Creole is also used, and this refers to those people born in Trinidad (and other parts of the Caribbean) who are of French descent. Secondly, the main focus of the book is on Trinidad rather than Trinidad and Tobago. As the work makes clear, patterns of labour control and resistance are very different on the two islands, and the labour history of Tobago deserves a work in its own right, and so a full treatment was beyond the scope of this work. Nevertheless, some reference is made to Tobago in so far as events on that island have had more than a local significance. Thirdly, at times the book uses the term "Third World". Although fully aware of the problems with this term, I have decided to employ it for the benefit of shorthand, and because, stereotypes notwithstanding, it is a widely recognized and reasonably clear term.

Approaches to the Study of Labour and Development in the Caribbean

We are told that free trade would create an international division of labour, and thereby give to each country the production which is most in harmony with its natural advantages.

You believe perhaps, gentlemen, that the production of coffee and sugar is the natural destiny of the West Indies.

Two centuries ago, nature, which does not trouble herself about commerce, had planted neither sugar-cane nor coffee tree there . . .

If the free-traders cannot understand how one nation can grow rich at the expense of another, we need not wonder, since these same gentlemen also refuse to understand how within one country one class can enrich itself at the expense of another.

Marx 1984

In this opening chapter, I initially examine three competing theories of Caribbean society, and relate these to the study of labour and development in the region. The three basic approaches are: first, modernization and industrial relations theory; secondly, dependency theory; thirdly, the theory of cultural pluralism. Each of these is examined both generally, and in terms of its applicability to the Caribbean region. In discussing these approaches, I argue that they are all incapable of fully illuminating the subject of my study. An alternative framework is presented, based on the notion of uneven development, which attempts to link explicitly labour and development. As a prelude to my case study, this section is completed by a brief discussion of the politics of labour organization in Third World societies.

The Political Economy and Sociology of Modernization

Introduction

This opening section examines the political economy and the sociological theory of modernization. In my discussion of the former, I concentrate on questions concerning the industrialization of the Third World, and in particular the Caribbean, from the 1940s onwards. In discussing the latter, more general questions of historical sociology are discussed, and in particular the differences between, and transition from "traditional" to "modern" societies. In discussing these two schools of thought, I show the similarities of their proposals for developing Third World societies. My discussion then moves to the question of labour and industrial relations" systems in "underdeveloped" societies. Finally, the strengths and weaknesses of this approach are analysed, and it is argued that while modernization theory constitutes a partial advance over neoclassical economic theory, its proponents still fail to comprehend the problems of economic and social development in underdeveloped societies, and therefore cannot provide a systematic analysis of labour.

Modernization Theory Outlined

Political Economy: Neoclassical Theory Amended

By the nineteenth century, an international division of labour had developed in which "advanced" countries produced manufactured goods (and some primary goods) while "backward" countries mainly produced and exported primary products. Many economists argued that this division of labour was to the mutual benefit of the countries involved; that is, each nation obtained more goods through an international division of labour in which they all specialized, and exported those goods which they produced cheaply. In other words, each nation produced the goods in which it had a natural or "comparative advantage" [Ricardo 1981: 133-41].

Even in the twentieth century, the colonial powers continued to argue that the colonies were incapable of undergoing a thorough process of industrialization. For example, the Moyne Commission of Inquiry (after the Caribbean labour riots of the 1930s) argued that various factors militated against industrial development. These included the temperament of the West Indian worker, over-population and the size of the territories. The Commission reported that the region should continue to specialize in producing those goods in which it had a natural advantage: minerals and agricultural goods [West India Royal Commission Report 1945: 426, 443; Thomas 1988: 61].

However, a number of economists began to challenge the view that unhindered "market forces" equally benefited each country in the world order. The Latin American economist Raul Prebisch [1959] argued that the Third World did not benefit from the international system of trade because of the unequal market powers involved in international transactions. Focusing his study on Latin America (where independence had been won in the nineteenth century but the region was still largely a primary good exporter), Prebisch argued that the "terms of trade" that existed between primary producers and the producers of manufactured goods were weighted in the latter's favour. Exporters of manufactured goods had a monopoly on the supply of such goods and so they could control prices. This was reinforced by the power of trade unions in industrialized countries, whose members won wage increases which in turn guaranteed that prices would remain high. On the other hand, there were many exporters of primary products and the resultant competition drove prices down. The international division of labour therefore worked to the advantage of the industrialized countries.

The proposed solution for the peripheral countries was industrialization, which would reduce the reliance on imports, and so reduce the need to export. In so doing, domestic employment would increase and the home market would expand. Prebisch therefore proposed a strategy of "import substitution industrialization" for Latin America, under which manufactured imports would be controlled by protective tariffs in the periphery.

This challenge to neoclassical economics was not as innovatory as it may initially appear. For example, the "free-trade utopia" espoused by neoclassicists hardly corresponded to the real mechanisms of the international economy in the nineteenth century as nascent industrial powers protected their domestic industry from foreign competition through high protective tariffs [Hobsbawm 1968, 1988c: 140, 39; Gamble 1985: 237]. Moreover, in Latin America itself nations such as Brazil had begun to industrialize in the 1930s (in Argentina the process started at an even earlier date) precisely through the ISI strategy advocated by Prebisch.

The work of W. Arthur Lewis on the Caribbean mirrors that of Prebisch's on Latin America. Lewis challenged the assumptions of the British Colonial Office and the Moyne Commission and argued that it was possible, indeed necessary, for the West Indies to begin to industrialize. Lewis regarded this as necessary because primary good production could not provide adequate employment. Indeed, Lewis argued that the constant factor of unemployment provided the region with a comparative advantage in cheap, "unlimited supplies of labour" [1954: 141]. This was because unemployment functioned to keep wage costs down as the supply of labour outstripped the demand. Lewis argued that this advantage would encourage investment as profits would be high. Lewis recognized, however, that domestic entrepreneurs lacked the capital to lead the investment process, so, initially at least, foreign capital would play the leading role [1950: 38].

Like Prebisch, Lewis was theorizing a process that had already begun in the region. Indeed, labourers were using advanced technology in the Caribbean region at a comparatively early period – sugar production by slave labour in Cuba used such advanced methods as the steam mill. In terms of *capitalist* industrialization, two points are relevant. First, there had been some diversification into light industries in the period of the Second World War. Secondly, and more importantly, Puerto Rico had undergone a process of industrialization from 1944. The "Puerto Rican model" was based on attracting foreign (primarily US) capital through tax incentives (such as the Industrial Incentives Law 1947), cheap labour and weak trade unions. Investment from the United States of America (USA) increased, particularly in labour intensive industries such as textiles, food processing and leather goods [Thomas 1988: 78].

So a good part of Lewis' recommendations were already in operation in Puerto Rico. Nonetheless, these proposals would influence the development strategies undertaken in the British West Indies in the 1950s, including those in Trinidad and Tobago.

Sociology's Functionalist Theory Updated

My analysis has so far concentrated on the works of development economists at a very specific time period, when Latin America and the Caribbean were beginning to industrialize. The purpose of this study is to explain the factors that determine class formation, labour control and the politics of labour both prior to and after industrial development. Of particular concern here is the "theorization" of the process of transition from a traditional, pre-industrial society to a modern, industrial society. In order to carry out this task, I now examine approaches to labour and development in the "historical sociology" tradition, and in particular the "modernization" school.

The origins of this school of thought are rooted in the works of the classical sociologist, Emile Durkheim. In his work *The Division of Labour in Society*, Durkheim contrasted traditional and modern societies in order to explain the changing nature of order (or "social solidarity"). In traditional societies, solidarity is "mechanical", in the sense that there are shared beliefs (such as religion) and community values. In modern societies, on the other hand, solidarity is based on "organic" values; in other words, "community" is no longer based on shared beliefs (for instance the modern phenomenon of secularization) but is instead "unified" by shared material interests and contractual relations, and an interdependent division of labour [Durkheim 1964: 70–110, 111 ff.].

Talcott Parsons was influenced by this contrast between traditional and modern societies when he attempted to explain how societies achieve social order. In a rather ambitious theory, Parsons argued that the basis for all societies lies in "an integrated system of generalized patterns of value orientation" [Parsons et al. 1962: 203]. In other words, Parsons argued that society is "achieved" through an agreement on beliefs and values. However, the nature of these beliefs varies from society to society. In traditional society common beliefs include an ascribed or predetermined social status, particularist or personalized social relations and collectivist values. Modern societies, by contrast, are based on achieved status (i.e., open social mobility/equality of opportunity), universalism (i.e., standards equally applicable to all, such as the rule of law), and individualist values [Parsons et al. 1962: 76–88].

Influenced by these ideas (albeit based as they are on a one-sided reading of Durkheim), sociologists began to theorize the process of development in terms of the transition from traditional to modern societies. The problem, then, for sociologists in the 1950s was to explain the causes of "backwardness" and propose appropriate solutions. Some writers argued that traditional values were the cause of "backwardness" and that the solution to this problem was to educate the traditionalists on the virtues of modern (i.e., Western) ideas [McClelland 1967: 430]. Others argued that these values may impede modernization, but they were largely a reflection (rather than a cause) of traditionalism. For instance, Walt Rostow argued that there were five stages of development through which all societies must pass: traditional, pre-conditions for take-off, take-off, drive to maturity, and high mass consumption [1960: 4-16]. Third World societies were situated at the traditional stage, which was characterized as having a basically agrarian economy, using backward technological and scientific techniques, and based on a closed system of social stratification where roles were ascribed rather than achieved. To overcome the problems of backwardness, Third World societies must pass from the traditional stage to the second stage, where the pre-conditions for the take-off to a modern, industrial society are present. These preconditions include the development of trade, the beginnings of rational, scientific ideas and the emergence of an elite group which reinvests, rather than squanders its wealth [Rostow 1960: 17-35].

In other words, the solution to the problem of backwardness was industrialization. Sociologists therefore arrived at similar conclusions to development economists, in that both schools of thought advocated industrialization. There were significant differences as well, particularly in the degree of attention paid to the international economy: development economists regarded the existing terms of trade as inequitable, even exploitative (and in this respect Prebisch was a great influence on the dependency school, discussed below), while sociologists tended to neglect existing international economic relations. Nevertheless, both schools agreed that industrialization of the periphery was necessary, and both believed that the advanced countries would (initially, at least) lead this process.

Both Latin America and the Caribbean began this process in the 1930s and 1940s (or earlier). In the 1950s, the British West Indies followed suit and impressive rates of growth were recorded. Optimism concerning the transition to "modernism" was rife. The Trinidadian sociologist Lloyd Braithwaite argued that the modernization of the Caribbean economy would lead to a modernization of the "system-goals" (social aspirations) of Caribbean society.

Trinidad was progressing "from the mere maintenance of law and order to the introduction of political and social institutions appropriate to a society in which universalistic-achievement values predominated, and to the acceptance of a system-goals corresponding to those of the United Kingdom" [Braithwaite 1975: 161].

Summary

Development economics and sociology in the 1940s to the 1960s agreed that Third World societies needed to "catch up" with advanced Western societies and that this was best achieved by the employment of Western development strategies. These could take the form of a diffusion of Western technology or Western values, or a combination of the two. In this way, the social institutions of Third World societies would be modernized, and would take on a form similar to that in the West. One of these social institutions was the arena of labour relations, and it is to this field that I now turn.

Modernization and the Modern "Industrial Man"

Development economics and sociology amended, but did not totally reject neoclassical theories of the international economy. For instance, the neoclassical argument that the Caribbean should continue to produce those goods in which it had a comparative or natural advantage was rejected, and the need to industrialize was stressed. Prebisch argued that this was due to the imperfections of "pure market forces", and their resultant inequalities. However, the "break" was only partial because the basic laws of market economies were accepted and industrialization was premised on the existence of comparative advantages other than natural resources – for instance, cheap labour.

In the field of industrial relations, sociologists in the 1950s and 1960s similarly questioned some of the premises of neoclassical economics. Free market economists saw no need for trade unions beyond their functioning as friendly societies. This was because the wage labour contract was regarded as a contract of equals, freely entered into by the concerned parties. (It was similarly argued, as I have suggested, that international trade was based on the assumption of the existence of two or more equal partners.) However, industrial relations theorists recognized that market imperfections could arise; for example, through employers paying their workers a wage lower than that which market condi-

tions alone would dictate. Therefore, trade unions could play a
proper role in society by ensuring an adequate wage for their
workers. In other words, trade unions could play a similar role
(through collective bargaining) to that of protectionist Third
World states in modifying the functioning of market forces.

In the Third World, industrial relations theorists believed that
the effect of industrialization would be to modernize the prevail-
ing system of labour relations. In other words, the radicalism of
Third World labourers would gradually diminish: "labour protest",
Kerr argued, "is on the decline as industrialization around the
world proceeds . . . The protest of today is more in favour of
industrialization than against it" [Kerr et al. 1962: 7]. This is
because industrialization "tends under any political and economic
system to raise materially the level of wages, to reduce the hours
of work, and to raise living standards as measured by such conventional means as life expectancy, health and education [Kerr et
al. 1962: 29].

West Indian industrial relations theorists such as Zin Henry put
forward the view that the Caribbean was slowly moving forward to
an "industrial relations system" [Dunlop 1975: 1–32; Craig 1975:
8–20] based on the British model; a model described as "a self-
administered system built upon principles of freedom and voluntarism where labour and management are free to regulate their
relationship, determine terms and conditions of employment, and
accommodate their problems by mutual consent" [Henry 1972:
91].

The adequacy of this theory will be examined below, but one
weakness is immediately obvious. With the benefit of hindsight, it
is clear that Kerr and his collaborators were optimistic concerning
the scope of Third World industrialization. Kerr may be correct in
his assertion that protest is for rather than against industrialization, but this in itself cannot explain why the process has been
limited. The industrialization of Haiti, Bangladesh or Burkina
Faso may lead to increased stability, but this does not address the
problem of how to proceed with such a strategy. Moreover, the
limitation of industry to certain sectors in most (or even all)
Third World countries calls into question the applicability of
Kerr's thesis to the Third World in general, as I discuss below.

These problems with Kerr's contentions have been implicitly
recognized by another mainstream industrial relations (IR) theo-
rist, Adolf Sturmthal. He recognizes that a modern IR system is
but one of a variety of systems of labour relations in the world
[Sturmthal 1973: 8]. However, he argues that the modern system

should be the only system in the world. In other words, what is required is a continued diffusion of Western ideas and technology into other areas of the world.

Modernization Theory Assessed

It is now widely recognized by sociologists that the functionalist analysis of society is inadequate. Many criticisms have been made: for instance, social equilibrium is assumed rather than explained, the existence of an institution in society does not prove its necessity, and conflict in society is underestimated [Mills 1959: 39; Mann 1987]. As a result of these weaknesses, functionalists cannot explain properly the causes of social change. The weaknesses of functionalist sociology are equally applicable in the "developed" world and the "underdeveloped" world. For my purposes, I will concentrate on the functionalist analysis of the latter.

Undoubtedly the basic weakness of modernization theory is its "dualism". Modernization theory assumes that there is a complete separation of the interrelationships between different parts of interdependent economies. This dualism occurs at two levels in modernization theory: first, there is a failure to examine properly the relationship between a particular Third World society and the wider international economy; and secondly, there is a failure to explain the relationship between the traditional and the modern sector within a Third World economy. As Frank states, "The dualist theory and the diffusionist and other theses based on it are inadequate because the supposed structural duality is contrary to both historical and contemporary reality: the entire social fabric of the underdeveloped countries has long since been penetrated and transformed by, and integrated into, the world embracing system of which it is an integral part" [1969b: 62].

An analysis which overcomes this dualism at the international level shows the inapplicability of Rostow's analysis to the Caribbean. The original traditional societies of the Arawak and Carib Indians were largely destroyed (rather than modernized) by the Europeans. Moreover, the societies that succeeded the Indian civilizations were the creations of European colonialism, but were still "traditional". So the development of "modern" society in Europe was accompanied by the reinforcement of "traditional" society in the Caribbean.

Indeed, the connection may go far deeper than this, for as Frank argues, "modern" society (or to use his phrase, the "metropolis") was a product (wholly, according to Frank, but partly in other analyses) of the exploitation of "traditional" societies (satellites). This exploitation takes place through the expropriation by the metropolis of the satellites' surplus, which in turn leads to the development of the former at the expense of the latter. In this way so-called traditional societies are not undeveloped so much as underdeveloped, due to the "lack of access to their own surplus" [Frank 1969a: 9]. The precise mechanisms (and the adequacy) of this process will be examined in sections two and three, but it should be clear that Rostow's ahistorical dichotomy between the traditional and the modern is false, and that economies do not develop in isolation from each other; indeed, one may even benefit at another's expense. It would be compatible with this analysis to argue that New World slavery promoted the industrial revolution in Europe.

The work of West Indian writers such as Lewis and Braithwaite is critical of the slave period and the period of indentured labour up to 1917 [Lewis 1950: 34-35; Lewis 1954: 149; Braithwaite 1975: 25], but is more optimistic concerning the prospects of modernization in the capitalist era. They argue that capitalist industrialization sweeps away the remnants of archaic economic practices and the particularistic values of traditional societies, and that a Western style of life will eventually emerge [Braithwaite 1975: 168].

However, industrializing Third World societies had to (and still have to) compete with countries that had a large "head-start" in industrial development. This advantage allowed the advanced countries to develop further, once again at the expense of the underdeveloped societies. Foreign dependence actually increased through industrialization, as Third World societies relied increasingly on transnational corporations. As a result, some development has taken place but critics claim that it is still largely dominated by, and for the benefit of, the "advanced" countries, or a small minority in the Third World. For instance, in Trinidad and Tobago from 1957 to 1965, foreign investment averaged $86 million a year, but over the same period average annual outflows were $111 million [McIntyre and Watson 1970: 19; Oxaal 1975: 39-40].

The dualist analysis is also inadequate in its assessment of the internal structure of Third World societies. Kerr's argument that labour protest declines as modern industry delivers a higher standard of living relies on a purely "technicist" account of industrialization, which does not account for the real contradictions of the process nor its effects on people's lives. Indeed, Rostow carried out such an analysis of the British case, arguing that the transition to an industrial society led to a uniform increase in living standards [1948: 122-25]. This view is open to question in the British case [Hobsbawm 1968: 154-71], although there may have been a slight increase in living standards from 1790 to 1840. However, this debate can become sterile if it neglects an enquiry of the very real social changes that industrialization brings [Hobsbawm 1968: 79-96]. For instance, who benefits most (and least) from the process? Moreover, the British (and any other) case was a "catastrophic experience" under which people were drawn off the land and were forced (by economic necessity) to seek employment elsewhere [Thompson 1988: 231].

In the Third World, this process has been even more uneven and "catastrophic". Rostow's analysis does not take into account the links between the "backward" and the "traditional" sectors, but instead treats them as two separate entities (thus repeating his dualist analysis, this time within the internal economy). The task of development theory is not to state that the former must simply "catch up" with the latter; instead, it should examine how the development of one sector affects the development of the other (just as it should question how the development of one country affects the development of another). Indeed, the presence of the supposedly modernizing influence of foreign capital has underlined the need for such an analysis. Capital investment in the Third World has often reinforced "archaic" labour relations (or alternatively invested in labour intensive industries and paid very low wages, as in the Puerto Rico case). For example, the British dominated sugar industry in Trinidad encouraged the development of sugar cane farming in the 1880s (see chapter two). And in Jamaica, United Fruit similarly discouraged wage labour by selling land to potential independent producers in the 1930s [Post 1978: 125]. Moreover, both national and foreign capitalists behave very differently from the expectations of modernization (and neoclassical) theory, a point to which I return below.

The more all-encompassing industrialization process that has taken place since the 1940s has been similarly uneven. Contrary to Lewis' intentions, Caribbean governments have zealously encouraged industrial development, but at the expense of the rural sector. The result has been "a growing impoverishment of rural economies" [Cross 1979: 19], unaccompanied by an "incorporation" of those forced off the land into the urban sector. This has meant that unemployment remains a constant factor, along with the growth of a large "marginal sector", selling anything from coconuts to their own bodies in order to survive. These "marginals" also perform certain functions for capital, such as reducing the social reproduction requirements of capital and acting as a reserve army of labour, which capital can draw on in a boom period and can discard in a slump. (Their existence, however, cannot be explained in terms of their "functions" to capital, and one must instead explain the origins of the "marginal" sector in terms of uneven capitalist accumulation.)

This last point is particularly important in any assessment of the role of organized labour in the Caribbean. Henry argues that "political unionism" will disappear as industrialization develops, and will be replaced by a modern IR system [1972: 83]. I discuss below how this argument neglects the unevenness of industrialization in the Third World, but for the moment a brief and more general examination of political unionism is necessary.

First, political unionism still exists, in the narrow sense of union-party relations, in the "advanced" countries – for instance, the "organic link" between the Labour Party and the trade union movement in Britain.

Secondly, mainstream industrial relations theorists regard political unionism as a sign of the "political immaturity" of a particular labour movement, but this is because they do not concern themselves with power relations (in other words, politics) at the workplace and in the wider society. Kerr, Dunlop et al. focus their attention on how conflict is contained and controlled; they regard conflict as an anomaly and consensus as the norm. The problem with this analysis is that consensus is simply assumed and there is no attempt to explain what gives rise to conflict in the first place. The question of ownership and control is "left out" of the analysis and is assumed to be a natural rather than a social phenomenon. By moving beyond this assumption, and recognizing the social character of ownership, the underlying mechanisms of the workplace are more accurately understood. As Hyman states, "industrial relations is the study of processes of control over work relations; and among these processes, those involving collective worker organization and action are of particular concern" [Hyman 1975: 12; also V.L. Allen 1975: 35]. Relations between capital and labour are therefore political by their very nature. Right wing politicians and academics denounce "political" strikes in liberal democracies on the grounds that they undermine the sovereignty of democratically elected governments. This analysis is similarly one-sided because it again "leaves out" the question of ownership and control and, therefore, the political power of capital; as Hyman states, "the power of capital is a permanent constraint on the economic and social objectives which can "realistically" be pursued" [1989: 44].

Moreover, there are good reasons why political unionism is even more overt in underdeveloped societies than in advanced capitalist countries, and these relate to the unevenness of industrialization, as I have already suggested. The collective bargaining relationship is heavily weighted in favour of the employer in the Third World who can draw on the large pool of available surplus labour; that is, the reserve army of labour. So as Cohen states, "To rely solely on collective bargaining in these circumstances is simply unproductive - not unnaturally the unions cast about for additional or alternative systems of bargaining in order to redress the imbalance between themselves and the management" [1974: 148]. Kerr and Henry are therefore incapable of developing such an analysis of political unionism in the Third World because they repeat the errors of Rostow's dualist analysis and fail to see how one sector affects, and is affected by, another.

Sturmthal's analysis is similarly one-sided. He implies that while collective bargaining is not the norm, it should at least be so. The problem with this analysis is that it is not actually attempting to understand social reality; rather, it hopes that the prescription will one day become reality. A real analysis of Third World labour is therefore precluded by a tendency to see things through Western tinted spectacles. As Cohen argues, "[d]iscussions of the relation between reproduction and production, or of the way in which the world of industry is parasitical upon or interdependent with the world of domestic and peasant labour, do not appear in traditional IR research" [1983: 4].

In short, modernization theory is too Eurocentric and weighted in favour of the capitalists' view of the world. One researcher on working class values in Trinidad and Tobago, sympathetic to this school of thought, has admitted that "[i]t seems impossible to deny that the sociological use of the word "modern" has been and still remains ethnocentric". However, she then states that "[t]he value judgement that equates "modern" with "Western" is regrettable, but nevertheless it operates" [Lengerman 1971: 152]. Such a blatantly biased approach to social science leads one to concur with Cohen when he states that "[i]n so far . . . as their ideas have provided ready ammunition for cold war warriors and the agencies of foreign policy in a powerful handful of Western nations, the extent to which comparative IR research can be seen as anything more than an ideologically limited and culturally and historically specific form of discourse must be raised" [Cohen 1987: 8].

Although the value and scientificity of theories have to be assessed in their own terms, the close association between particular political practices and advocates of modernization suggests that one cannot accept their claims to value neutrality. For example, Rostow was himself an adviser to President Johnson during the Vietnam war, and there has been a remarkably high degree of US intervention in the Caribbean Basin region this century. Intervention by the USA has taken many forms, from frequent invasions of "sovereign" territories, to covert operations (surrogate armies and dictators, illegal mining of ports) and the perhaps lesser known "trade union intervention", which includes checking the political affiliations of trade unions and specific individuals (for instance in Trinidad and Tobago in 1972 [Spalding 1988: 279]), as well as encouraging economic and political sabotage against nationalist and "socialist" regimes (for example in the Dominican Republic 1963-65 and in Grenada 1979-83 [Pearce 1982; Blum 1986; Als 1977: 1-7]). The justification for such support has often been couched in the language of modernization theory (for instance based on support for "modern" systems of collective bargaining), although the "Reagan doctrine" openly espoused a willingness to support "authoritarian" (i.e., right wing) regimes [Brenner 1984]. Needless to say, the reality has been that these same right-wing governments have not been sympathetic to organized labour or the peasantry, but have collaborated with US interests (the most notorious example being United Fruit in Guatemala in 1954 and the Dominican Republic in 1965). In this way, modernization theory is useful more as a justification for Western interests, and less as a theory that corresponds to Third World reality.

Dependency and the Theory of the Plantation Economy

Introduction

This section draws on, and extends, the critique of modernization theory outlined above. I examine dependency theory in both Latin

America and the Caribbean, and show the importance of the international economy in shaping these societies. This school of thought is criticized, however, because it lacks a sufficient analysis of internal factors in underdeveloped societies, including labour.

Outline

It should now be clear that the development process in the Caribbean was very different from that of nineteenth century Britain. Industrialization led to an increased reliance on the import of capital goods, a high capital intensity and a consequent maintenance of high unemployment. From 1951 to 1965, Jamaica's industrialization had created only 9000 jobs, while the labour force had increased by 20 000 a year; in Trinidad and Tobago from 1950 to 1963, less than 5000 jobs had been created by industrialization, whereas the total labour force had increased by 100 000 persons over the same period [Thomas 1988: 90].

In both the Caribbean and Latin America, a new theory emerged in the 1960s as a response "to the need to understand the failure of postwar economic policies to internalize the growth process, and the persistent external dependence of the economies" [Girvan 1973: 15]. The United Nations' Economic Commission for Latin America (set up in 1948 and led by Prebisch) began to radicalize and question some of Prebisch's proposals for overcoming dependence, while in the West Indies, the New World Group, an intellectual current with very similar outlooks, was set up in 1962.

The basic hypothesis of both groups was that their respective regions were unfavourably incorporated into the international economy, as Prebisch and Lewis had contested, but they went on to argue that industrialization had not overcome this problem. The Latin American economist Theotonio dos Santos summarized the basic hypothesis: "Dependence is a conditioning situation in which the economies of one group of countries are conditioned by the development and expansion of others". The "advanced" country may advance through self-impulsion, but the dependent economy can "only expand as a reflection of the expansion of the dominant countries, which may have positive or negative effects on their immediate development" (cited in O'Brien [1975: 12]).

As I showed in the previous section, one weakness of modernization theory was that it neglected an analysis of the international economy. Dependency theory stressed this "international" factor, and how one nation could develop at another's expense. Thus in Frank's theory the Caribbean had played an historical role as a "satellite" in the world capitalist economy.

One of the leading theorists of the New World Group in the 1960s was the Trinidadian, Lloyd Best. He characterized West Indian economies as plantation economies, which were basically ". . . externally propelled" and "structurally part of an overseas economy" [Best 1968: 283, 302]. Best, in partnership with Kari Levitt, argued that there were three stages of the plantation economy [Best and Levitt 1969; Levitt and Best 1975: 34-60]. First, there was the stage of the "pure plantation economy", which was the slave period (including apprenticeship, up to 1838 in the British Caribbean). The economies in this period were basically plantations, whereby Europe provided the organization, decision making, capital, transport, supplies and markets; Africa provided the labour and the Caribbean provided the land. Production (mainly sugar cane) was for export to the European market. The second period (plantation economy modified 1838-1938) starts with the abolition of slavery and apprenticeship and ends with the aforementioned Commission of Inquiry into the causes of labour unrest in the 1930s. This is a period of free trade in which British capital benefits from higher productivity and is therefore able to capture wider markets. Some changes take place in the Caribbean, such as the emergence of an independent peasantry and a system of indentured labour. However, there is no genuine transformation of society because of the legacy of pure plantation economy. Government is still run by, or on behalf of, planters, and the peasantry "carry a legacy" of tastes which require continued exports. Ultimately, the plantation sector retains the best land.

There is much in this analysis that is compatible with Lewis and Prebisch's arguments. However, Best and Levitt's characterization of the third period is critical of the actual process of industrialization in the British West Indies. This is the period of "plantation economy further modified", which dates from the late 1930s to the present. Modifications include new, high value goods and services (bauxite, petroleum, tourism and some manufacturing), and an active public sector. However, many of the features of the plantation economy still exist, primarily because of the dominance of foreign, transnational companies (TNCs), which play a similar role to that of the joint-stock trading company of the pure plantation economy, i.e., the TNC combines organization, capital, technology and entrepreneurship. Moreover, in the 1970s, licensing agreements to nationalized industries (including oil and bauxite) were often used to maintain foreign control, as the licensing of technology, management and the marketing of products were often in foreign hands [Jenkins 1987: 178; Thomas 1988: 207]. (However, these localizing factors in a sense undermine Best's analysis, as I point out in my critique below.)

The Jamaican economist, George Beckford, similarly argued that the Caribbean is made up of a number of "plantation societies". He defines the plantation system as "the totality of institutional arrangements surrounding the production and marketing of crops" [1972b: 8]. Beckford argues that all development paths are largely determined by agricultural organization, and plantation agriculture leads to distortions in the economy: persistent unemployment, low levels of national income (and its unequal distribution), and underutilization of land and underconsumption [1972b: 154–82]. This in turn means that plantation societies are underdeveloped as expansion of food supplies is inhibited, the terms of trade are unfavourable and there are few internal linkages in the economy [Beckford 1972b: 183–214].

The work of the plantation economy school is remarkably similar to that of Celso Furtado's on Latin America [Furtado 1970]. Like Best he divides the history of the region into three distinct stages: the colonial period (1600–1850), where production (of precious metals and agricultural goods) is for export; a period of externally oriented development (1850–1930), based on low wage capitalist agriculture (due to unlimited supplies of labour), and the period after 1930, based on import substitution industrialization. Furtado argues that industrialization fails to alleviate dependency because of the high import content of new investment (which leads to balance of payments problems), the capital intensity of production (which means that high unemployment persists) and the limited market for goods. Development is therefore highly uneven, and subject to stagnation.

Dependency theorists disagree on what strategies are required for Third World countries to overcome their disadvantageous situation. Frank and Wallerstein believe that only a revolutionary strategy can overcome underdevelopment and dependency, but most theorists argue that a reformist strategy is sufficient. For example, Best is not critical of Lewis' conception of capitalism; the latter's mistake was to apply a Ricardian model (albeit amended) to a "national economy", in a case where a "national economy" did not exist. Best's strategy entailed creating the conditions for the existence of a "national economy". In this respect, his outlook "did not imply a radical break from capitalism, but rather its reverse: localization would create the prerequisites for this vital engine of the capitalist dynamic to operate within Trinidad for the first time in its history" [Oxaal 1975: 43].

Best also argues that "localized development" can be achieved by a popular alliance which does not take into account class boundaries. Indeed, he argues that Caribbean societies cannot be analysed in class terms (hence the rather sketchy detailing of different forms of labour control beyond the blanket term plantation economy) for a number of reasons. Post-slave societies are said to be too flexible to have social classes; the social boundaries that exist between individuals are limited as wealthy professionals achieve their position through sacrifice and have no tradition of values separate from the rest of the population; and class solidarity is not the crucial factor in Caribbean societies, as exemplified by the phenomenon of nationalism [Best 1971a: 7-22].

Further Elaboration and Critique

Dependency theory points out some of the weaknesses of modernization theory, and begins to analyse the unequal relationship that exists between "First World" and "Third World". It also provides a powerful critique of Third World industrialization, and shows how this process has failed to overcome Third World subordination to the West. However, dependency theory contains a number of serious weaknesses, which relate to its failure to analyse labour in any significant detail.

Probably the most common criticism of dependency theory is that it analyses external forces (i.e. the international economy), at the expense of internal ones. There is some truth to this argument but it is an exaggeration. All dependency theorists incorporate internal factors into their analysis. For instance, the Caribbean dependency economist Havelock Brewster defines economic dependence as "a lack of capacity to manipulate the operative elements of an economic system. This lack of interdependence implies that the system has no internal dynamic which would enable it to function as an independent, autonomous entity" (cited in Girvan [1973: 11]). Beckford and Best similarly analysed internal factors [Beckford 1972b: xvi], and it was Best's claim that the Caribbean was a "classless society" (see above) that led him to advocate a reformist strategy of change in Trinidad and elsewhere. (Beckford later changed his position, accepting the need for an analysis of dependency based more specifically on class relations; see Beckford and Witter [1982].)

Frank also examines internal factors and, by implication, tries to link labour and development. He analyses classes in terms of groups of people located in spatial categories, in which some people benefit at the expense of others (through surplus appropriation) in the network of metropolis/satellite relations [Frank 1969b: 340-49].

The most systematic attempt to unite labour and development, however, has come from the advocates of world systems theory. Wallerstein has argued that with the development of capitalist production:

> . . . there has been the development of an ever more delineated interstate system that has enabled states within which core activities were located to develop strong state structures (in relation to those in peripheral areas), such that they could shape and reshape the world market in commodities, labor-force, and capital in ways that would maintain, in favor of large entrepreneurs located in core zones, both the capital-labor relationship as a social form and unequal exchange between core and periphery [Wallerstein 1983: 18].

The argument that countries with strong states formed the core while those with weak states became the periphery has been convincingly challenged [Skocpol 1977], but of more relevance here is Wallerstein's approach to the study of labour. In an earlier work he argued:

> . . . the relations of production that define a system are the 'relations of production' of the whole system and the system at this point in time is the European world economy. Free labour is indeed a defining feature of capitalism, but not free labour throughout the productive enterprises . . . free labour is the form of labour control used for skilled work in core countries whereas coerced labour is used for less skilled work in peripheral areas. The combination thereof is the essence of capitalism. When labour is everywhere free, we shall have socialism [Wallerstein 1974: 127].

While his focus on combinations of "free" and "unfree" labour may be useful, the particular manner in which Wallerstein attempts to unite labour and development is questionable. His basic contention is that different modes of labour control are simply the (functional) results of the requirements of the world system. However, modes of labour control are the results of human struggle and it should not be assumed *a priori* that these will always "fit the logic" of the world capitalist system. As Connell points out:

> World-systems approaches to theorizing the international dimension of class confront us with characteristic problems: a tendency to treat classes as categories of economic actors; an *a priori* cast-list of classes; the appeal to a logic-of-the-system that carries a presupposition that there is a well-formed, coherent system; and difficulty in grasping class formation other than through functionalism or through the distinction of class-in-itself from class-for-itself [Connell 1984: 182].

Wallerstein's insistence on the all-embracing nature of the world system also leads to problems of political strategy, as I discuss below.

These problems can be extended to dependency and underdevelopment theorists more generally. While it is true that dependency and underdevelopment theory does employ an analysis of internal factors, the adequacy of this analysis is questionable. Dependency theorists argue that satellite or plantation status was a product of integration into the expanding world market, and that the internal mechanisms of dependency are ultimately produced by this integration. For example, the "absence of interdependence" that Brewster refers to above is caused by the presence of transnational corporations in the economically advanced Western countries, and these in turn emerged because of the favourable conditions enjoyed by Western nations in the world market. The problem with this approach is that the division of the world into "metropolis" and "satellite" is never adequately explained. Britain and the Caribbean were both incorporated into the world market but only one developed while the other remained comparatively "underdeveloped". The transfer of surplus from the Caribbean to Britain and Europe on its own can only be a partial explanation for this process, because it does not explain how one region "became" the metropolis and the other, the satellite; in other words, "it obviously is not trade per se which accounts for whether a country or area stagnates or expands" [Mandle 1972: 53]. In order to understand the effects of trading relationships on particular regions of the world, the specific market powers of the regions involved must be explained. Internal structures, including labour, must therefore be examined prior to, rather than after, an examination of trading relationships.

A second, related problem is the ahistorical nature of dependency theory. Best's analysis of the three periods of plantation economy "portrays self enclosed movements in time and static relations which are mechanically transposed from one period to another. In addition, underlying all this is the unrealistic assumption that in the long interval between the establishment of plantations and the society of today no significant developments have taken place" [Sudama 1979: 75]. Indeed the continuing utilization of the term "plantation economy or society" is inaccurate and largely metaphorical [Craig 1982a: 149].

The consequence of such a static model is that while it may point to an important part of social reality in the Caribbean (its satellite status), it fails to specify the precise mechanisms, and the changes in them, which cause the problem. As O'Brien has written of Latin American dependency theory, "The actual mechanisms of dependency are seldom spelt out in detail . . . One looks in vain through the theories of dependency for the essential characteristics of dependency. Instead, one is given a circular argument: dependent countries are those which lack the capacity for autonomous growth and they lack this because their structures are dependent ones" [1975: 23-24].

This lack of dynamism in the dependency approach is caused by its failure to analyse properly the processes of class formation and class conflict. In Best's analysis "(t)he relationship between the international bourgeoisie through its local representatives (the managers of foreign controlled firms and the agents of international organizations) and the local bourgeoisie and petty bourgeoisie is not explored" [Sudama 1979: 79]. He argues that the professional "class" is not a capitalist class distinct from the rest of the population, but never tells us "what they do constitute, and what their relationship to local and foreign capital may be . . ." [Craig 1982b: 167].

In the cases of Frank and Wallerstein, a local/foreign capital alliance is said to exist, but their static approach militates against an analysis of the changes and contradictions in this alliance. For instance, the national/international alliance in Jamaica underwent substantial change after the abolition of slavery, and this process cannot be explained solely by the needs of the world system, as members of the old planter class declined at the expense of a wealthy and increasingly capitalist orientated peasantry [Post 1978: 36].

The faulty sociological analyses of the dependency and world system schools also lead to weak political programmes. Wallerstein's focus on an all-embracing world system leads one to question how this system can ever be replaced, beyond a rather impractical support for autarchy, or simultaneous worldwide revolution [Brenner 1977: 91; Worsley 1980: 324-25]. Best's more reformist strategy is similarly problematic. His argument that factors other than social class are considered to be important by social actors does not negate an analysis rooted in the social relations of production. Indeed, the strength of such an analysis is that it can begin to explain the "missing link" in this theory; that is the actual mechanisms of dependent situations. The argument that post-slave societies are too flexible to be considered class societies is a caricature of a class analysis, which does not deny the existence of social mobility. Indeed, one of the sources of conflict in capitalist society (both its "advanced" and "underdeveloped" varieties) is that there are limits to the number of "higher" places in society. In other words, the "exceptional" Caribbean is nothing of the sort because social mobility operates in all societies, but always within certain limits. Best's argument that foreign capital, rather than capital itself, is the problem is very weak. For example, there is no valid reason for suggesting that local capital would act (or actually has acted) any differently from foreign capital in terms of the high import content of capital goods or the export of local capital. Indeed, this vague strategy of "localizing production" through a non-class based popular alliance has in many ways already been carried out. In Trinidad and Tobago since 1956, various attempts have been made to localize production and decision making (e.g., nationalization of oil and sugar companies, and the development of an indigenous natural gas and fertilizer industry), but "there is no evidence of a commensurate degree of structural transformation" [Sudama 1979: 81].

Summary

Dependency theory constitutes a significant advance over modernization theory, because it focuses on the international economy. However, the actual focus of its analysis neglects the internal processes of "underdeveloped" societies, and the mechanisms that lead to peripheral status in the world system. Systems of labour control are one-sidedly seen as the outcome of the functioning of the world market.

The Theory of Cultural Pluralism

The Theory Outlined

While the theory of cultural pluralism is not explicitly concerned with either labour or development, its major focus has important implications for both of these factors. In the Caribbean the main exponent of this theory is M.G. Smith. The basic contention of this approach is that West Indian societies are based on conflict and not consensus, and that the root of this conflict lies in different institutional systems, which in turn are based on conflicting cultures. A population that shares a single set of institutions is deemed to be culturally and socially homogeneous, while one that shares a system of basic or compulsory institutions but practices different "alternative" institutions is heterogeneous. Finally, a population that shares neither basic nor secondary institutions is said to have a plural society. For Smith, "[c]ultural pluralism is a special form of differentiation based on institutional divergences" [1965: 770].

Smith claims that Caribbean societies are plural societies because different sections of the population practise different forms of common institutions. The two factors that unify these societies are government and the economic system. For Smith, "[g]overnment acts to limit the chances of conflict, and to limit, maintain, or increase the opportunities for acculturation; the economic system embraces the entire population, although in different degrees and different ways" [1965: 16].

The implications of this theory for a study of labour should be clear. Cultural pluralism maintains that the basic conflict in Caribbean society is between different cultural groups. Labour studies should therefore recognize the existence of this primary contradiction, rather than other alleged sources of conflict such as class or gender (the theory has nothing to say on this latter factor). Cultural pluralism is "quite distinct from other forms of social heterogeneity such as class stratification in that it consists in the coexistence of incompatible institutional systems" [Smith 1978: 774]. There is undoubtedly a need to take account of culture and ethnicity in examining Caribbean (or any) societies, and my analysis in chapters two to six emphasizes how these factors have divided the labour force in Trinidad and Tobago. However, in my critique below I show why I think that the claims of this particular theory cannot be substantiated and instead propose an alternative framework which incorporates class, ethnicity and gender, and relates these to the concept of development.

A Critique and Alternative Framework for Analysing Labour and Development

The basic strength of the plural society model is its challenge to both crude functionalist and Marxist theories of society. The contemporary reality of ethnic conflict undermines theories of society based on value consensus or purely class conflict. However, the model itself is particularly weak because it is both reductionist and lacking in explanatory power. It describes society in terms of one basic category – cultural variation – and neglects other differences in society based on gender and class. Secondly, the model is essentially static; as Cross argues, the thesis has a classificatory scheme and labels various stages in a social order, but "it does not account for how one came to change for the other . . . [T]o define a society as 'plural' and to propound a concept to cope with that society is not to understand how that society came to be 'plural' and neither is it to show that in reality we are justified in applying that particular concept" [1971: 484].

Stuart Hall has similarly argued that the theory is ahistorical because it fails to explain how the different ethnic groups arose. Furthermore, he argues that the origins of "cultural pluralism" cannot be divorced from the class relations of society and that "[f]undamentally, it is economic production which draws these two social groups into a relation of domination/subordination, conquest and the institutions of slavery which define the relations, and the 'extrinsic' composition of the two groups . . ." [Hall 1977: 160].

These criticisms seriously undermine the plural society model. As Mills has argued, "[a]n adequate explanation of the dialectics of cultural development must leave the empirical level of simple description and investigate the underlying structural forces which break up, as well as maintain, a given cultural configuration. Smith's failure to do this leaves him seriously vulnerable" [1987: 83]. However, it does not follow that a reductionist Marxist approach is more useful. As Mills states, factors such as ethnicity require investigation and should not be ignored. Contrary to the claims of Smith, I will attempt to show that class is a central category for any analysis of labour and development, but it should not necessarily be given a primacy that would lead to a neglect of ethnicity and gender.

Advocates of the plural society model share with other Caribbean critics of Marxism the belief that the latter doctrine must be based on a two-class model of inevitable polarization which ignores non-class conflict. One writer, sympathetic to the plural society thesis, has argued that "[i]n Trinidad and Tobago, it is not easy to identify a working class. This is why here, workers refuse to behave in Marxist terms" [La Guerre 1978: 27]. This view is based on a narrow, positivist Marxism which leaves no room for human beings making their own history, or for conflicts not based on social class.

Carl Stone's more subtle examination of social class in Jamaica also criticizes a particular kind of Marxist analysis. While he accepts that the capital-labour conflict exists, Stone argues that this is secondary to a wider "rich-poor" conflict. An over-emphasis on the capital-labour conflict is misconceived "because of the fragmentation of interests based on differential benefits that accrue to various categories of wage labour and the owners of property" [Stone 1973: 20]. In other words, the two-class model is too rigid because it fails to examine both wider conflicts and the uneven development of social classes.

I would accept much of Stone's analysis but this does not mean that a Marxist approach should be rejected wholesale. Instead, I will employ a conception of uneven development (outlined below), together with an analysis of the origins of gender and ethnic conflicts (outlined in chapter two), to show how the working classes in Trinidad and Tobago have remained divided. In other words, I reject the Marxist prophecy of proletarian unity but still accept the validity of much of the Marxist method.

Such an approach implies a rejection of positivist conceptions of social class (as outlined by La Guerre above) and notions of "true" or "false" class consciousness. As E.P. Thompson states, "[c]lass eventuates as men and women live their productive relations, and as they experience their determinate situations, within 'the ensemble of the social relations' . . . and [n]o actual class formation is any truer or more real than any other, and class defines itself as, in fact, it eventuates . . ." [1978: 149, 150].

This "human action" approach implies that a minimalist definition of class structure is required, especially in "Third World" societies like that of Trinidad, where class formation tends to be very uneven and fluid. Any approach that uses class as a central concept must be one "that recognizes the incomplete and embryonic character of class formation and development on the one hand, but that nonetheless attempts to derive a meaningful frame of reference for explaining a class-based act, on the other. We may thus recognize the relative infrequency and ephemerality of overt class action, but also be careful to acknowledge the existence of such acts and not underestimate their political significance" [Cohen 1972: 252]. Below, I attempt to link explicitly labour and development, and in doing so, explain the fluidity of class formation in peripheral capitalist societies.

Labour and Uneven Development in the Caribbean

In this section, I attempt to move beyond the modernization, dependency and cultural pluralist approaches by utilizing (and in some respects, going beyond) the Marxist method and more explicitly applying it to Caribbean history. The purpose of this section is to show the close linkage between labour (based on a "minimalist" class definition) and development, and how one cannot be properly analysed in isolation from the other. My argument proceeds by analysing, in individual subsections, three periods of labour control and development – slavery, indentureship and the period of "peripheral capitalist development". This is followed by a fourth subsection which attempts to draw some of the implications for my assessment of the politics of labour in Trinidad and Tobago.

Slave Labour and Development in the West Indies

Regional Political Economy: The "Origins" of Slavery in the English Caribbean

From the 1640s, a "regional political economy" [Cohen 1987: 5-6] emerged based on English merchant capital, African labour and Caribbean land. Gunder Frank's characterization of this relationship as capitalist has already been rejected, but his argument that merchant capital transforms relations of production has some plausibility. The impact of merchant capital on the Caribbean was such that it led to the creation of a "new" system of production - slavery - based on labour imported from Africa. The main commodity produced was sugar, which was then exported to the European market.

However, this increase in English trading activity had its basis, not in a "propensity to trade" (Frank's argument), but in the development of the productive forces: as more goods were produced above immediate subsistence requirements (that is, the surplus product), so there was more wealth available for trade. Moreover, this increase in the productive forces was determined by changes in the relations of production in England. Feudal relations were breaking down and capitalist relations were developing, a process that continued into the seventeenth and eighteenth centuries [Hilton 1987: 116]. The increase in merchant capital activity that had such an impact on the Caribbean therefore had its roots in the relations of production (that is, the social classes) that existed in England at the time.

Labour at the African "end" of the system was also vital to the process, because one must understand how and why the slaves from Africa were available as slaves in the first place. As Brenner points out, "Before they could be bought, the slaves had to be "produced"; more precisely, they had to appear on the market as "commodities". But this poses large questions, namely of the formation of class systems of "production" and appropriation of slaves in Africa (or elsewhere)" [Brenner 1977: 88].

The "Laws of Motion" of Slavery

The production processes that existed in England and Africa were therefore vital to the development of slavery in the New World. Once established, the precise mechanisms of production were of primary importance because it was these that explained the contradictions of slavery, and its competitive position in the world market.

Slavery was organized in such a way that the slave owner, or "planter", "gained access to the total product of the enslaved person's labour power, in return for which subsistence (or the means of subsistence) was provided" [Miles 1987: 79]. Slaves therefore entered the production process as constant rather than variable elements (as is the case with free wage labour) as they were guaranteed means of subsistence. Slaves were both producers and means of production which limited the ability of their masters to regulate the size of the labour force and burdened them with inflexible labour costs, which in turn limited their ability to reorganize the labour process on more efficient lines. As Post argues, "The masters are forced to organize the production process along the lines of closely supervised gang labour, making the only possible methods of increasing labour productivity the intensification of labour and the migration of labour to more fertile soils" [1982: 34; also 1978: 23]. This "archaic" form of labour control is also "inefficient" compared to wage labour in that there is little incentive to accumulate, as I explain below.

The slave relation of production was not as straightforward as this analysis might suggest, however. In some cases there existed a hidden wage, whereby slaves were paid in tradeable commodities, which were sometimes used as currency (for example, tobacco). In order to overcome the constant reproduction costs of slave labour, planters often allowed slaves to grow food on their own plots of land. According to Mintz, this independent subsistence production "ran entirely counter to the whole conception of how the slave mode of production was supposed to operate" [1978: 93]. This was because slaves could work in groups of their own choice, make their own calculations, and sell some of their surplus in the market-place. This last factor enabled a large number of slaves to purchase their freedom.

On the plantation itself, the labour process had similarities with that of industrial capitalism. There was a large concentration of labour working with relatively advanced technology [Moreno Fraginals 1976: 33–40]; as Mintz states, "[s]laves or no, these labourers were compelled to work in some ways that, were it not for slavery, would have been just as accurately described as the regimen of factory proletarians" [1988: xv].

However, despite the similarities, slavery cannot be accurately described as "capitalist". The "anomalies" that Mintz refers to arose out of the contradictions of the slave mode of production, and of its incorporation into a world economy that was dominated by the nascent capitalist powers of Europe, and especially England. Three points illustrate this argument: first, slave labour remained the dominant relation of production. Secondly, the non-slave relations arose out of the contradictions of slave labour

(just as wage labour in agriculture became increasingly generalized in feudal England). Thirdly, the "laws of motion" of slavery
were derived from the slave relations of production and it was
these "laws" that account for the Caribbean's unfavourable incorporation into the world market. For instance, slave relations of
production arrested technological innovation. Even though some
degree of advanced technology was utilized, especially in Cuba, it
was insufficient compared to the dynamics of capitalist production techniques; as Moreno Fraginals has argued, slavery "differed
from . . . capitalist production . . . in the form . . . of the
impossibility of constantly revolutionizing production methods, an
inherent part of capitalism" [1976: 18]. The Caribbean was
therefore incorporated into the world economy in such a way that
its market power was weak compared to parts of Europe, which
benefited from superior productive techniques.

English Capitalism and Caribbean Slavery

Capitalism emerged in Britain primarily as a result of the instabil-
ity of feudalism and the rise of a class that employed wage
labour. In other words, a qualitative change took place in English
society, culminating in the Civil War of 1640-49. However, there
was a quantitative element to the rise of British (and European)
capitalism: the plunder (of which slavery was but one form) of
the colonial world. This plunder benefited European capitalism
by extending the European market for goods such as sugar and
tobacco, providing certain raw materials (for example, cotton)
and generally increasing the amount of wealth in the economy.
This last point is important because the conversion of this wealth
into productive capital was not automatic (Frank's assumption)
but instead required the existence of capitalist relations of production. Indeed, there was no large-scale increase in investment
in Britain in the late eighteenth century (the period when slavery
was at its height). The profits acquired from slavery "increased
British income whatever the recipients of the income chose to do
with it: whether they spent it on land or coaches or wine – or on
textile machinery" [Solow and Engerman 1987: 8].

The capitalism/slavery relationship demonstrates the "uneven
and combined" development of the world economy [Trotsky 1936:
25-37]. England (and later Britain) and other European powers
"got ahead" of the rest of the world (just as the latter had before)
on the basis of "more advanced" class relations, and therefore

superior productivity. These powers were in a position to influence the development of the rest of the world, and did so by inflicting on them "backward" labour regimes. In the Anglo-Caribbean economy, the uneven development of the two regions was combined through slavery, which enabled the former to move further ahead, and left the latter "underdeveloped". Frank is therefore correct when he says that one country may develop at the expense of another, but he never explains the mechanisms that sustain the system, or which classes benefited or lost out, or what created the system in the first place.

A class-based analysis also helps to explain why slavery was abolished. As I have shown, slavery was subject to its own internal contradictions, which in turn influenced the "market power" of its products when they came to be sold on the world market. In the climate of European rivalry in the seventeenth and eighteenth centuries, each power adopted an "exclusive" policy for its colonies under which each individual colony was protected from competition. However, by the late eighteenth century Britain had emerged as the major industrial power of the world. The use of more efficient labour systems in Britain, employing more efficient technology, led to higher labour productivity, including in agriculture. The products of slave labour became increasingly unprofitable as a result. Both slavery and the monopoly system had become unnecessary expenses to Britain, because it could undersell its competitors on the world market. The gradual shift to abolition in 1834 and free trade (1846-52) reflected Britain's emergence, albeit short term, as the dominant industrial power of the world. As Williams points out, abolition was more than an attack on slavery. "It was an attack on monopoly . . . The reason for the attack was not only that the West Indian economic system was vicious but that it was so unprofitable that for this reason alone its destruction was inevitable" [1987: 135].

Abolitionist sentiments were reinforced by the fact that domestic demand expanded more quickly than the foreign market in the nineteenth century, especially after the war of 1812 as Britain lost its major market, North America. An end to slavery in the 1770s would have led to a loss of demand for English manufactures, but this was not the case in the 1820s onwards, as a far wider internal market existed [Solow and Engerman 1987: 14-15]. Other factors of importance included the Abolition movement and unrest on the part of the slaves themselves, most notably (but far from exclusively) in Saint Domingue in 1791.

Indentured Labour and Development in the Caribbean

After slavery was abolished in the Caribbean (officially in 1834, but followed by four more years of effective slavery under "apprenticeship"), a system of indentured labour was introduced. It was most common where the soil was most fertile – in particular in Trinidad and British Guiana. The system lasted until 1917 and was based on the importation of labour from various parts of the world, but in particular from India, and to a lesser extent China (for details of the Trinidad case see chapter two). Indentured labour was based on a system whereby people worked for a number of years for a particular employer (they were forced into this position through destitution), in return for free passage back to their country of origin or a plot of land in the country to which they migrated. Although the system was based on wage labour, in practice it was combined with noneconomic coercion where planters utilized a pass system which restricted the labourers' freedom of movement beyond the estate on which they worked. In the absence of adequate regulating mechanisms, planters could effectively treat the labourers as they wished and so they competed with other estate owners on the basis of low wages rather than rapid technological innovation.

This system of labour control once again left the Caribbean in an unfavourable trading position in the world economy. The planters were far from the "revolutionary bourgeoisie" described by Marx in the "Communist Manifesto"; instead of attempting to improve sugar production through constant technological development, they decided to try to maintain short-term profitability through either cheap, indentured labour, or unequal exchange with the peasantry. As Sebastien argues, "The fact that they could pay wages to indentured laborers way below the value of their labor power, and below that of other laborers, impeded the widescale use of machinery in the cultivation process, so that though in the short run it may have proved less costly, in the long run it was the downfall of many" [1979: 131–32]. This was reinforced by state encouragement of labour intensive methods of production (for instance in sugar and cocoa in Trinidad) outside of the indentureship system.

In Trinidad, the colonial government actively encouraged permanent labour settlement, and this process aided a process of proletarianization as independent production became more difficult.

Labour and Peripheral Capitalist Development

Peripheral Capitalism and Uneven Development

So far I have placed much emphasis on the relationship between different systems of labour control and particular patterns of development. In Trinidad from the 1930s, the capital-free wage labour relation was established as the main relation of production. However, this relationship was established far more unevenly than in advanced capitalist countries, and this again has important implications for the wider process of development. This point is crucial because it undermines both neoclassical and neo-Marxist theories of development, as well as the basic assumptions upon which government economic strategy in Trinidad has been based since 1956.

The Lewis model, neoclassical and some neo-Marxist theories all share the belief that capitalism has certain "equalizing tendencies". The late Bill Warren for instance utilized a Marxist approach to argue that imperialism was a progressive force in the "Third World" because it enabled backward countries to "catch up" with advanced capitalist countries [Warren 1988]. As I have showed, the Lewis model was based on a similar belief that Caribbean countries could exercise their comparative advantage in cheap, "unlimited" supplies of labour in order to attract foreign capital and thereby sustain rapid economic growth.

These theories have their roots in (a particular reading of) the work of Ricardo, and were most fully developed in the work of Eli Heckscher and Bertil Ohlin [Ohlin 1933]. They have also enjoyed a revival in development economics in the 1980s [see especially Bauer 1981; Lal 1983], as well as in the World Bank and the International Monetary Fund (see chapter six for details of the Trinidad case). As I have already stated, the basis of the theory is that each country or region in the world economy should specialize in producing those goods that it can make most cheaply, that is, those goods in which it has a comparative advantage. According to the Heckscher–Ohlin model, equilibrium in exchange is based on equally available factor endowments throughout the world [Ohlin 1933: 34-49]. Country A may have an initial comparative advantage and therefore produce, for example, corn and cloth more cheaply than country B. However, if country A produces cloth more cheaply than it produces corn, it should specialize solely in the former, because it could then produce more cloth which it can exchange with country B's corn. In this way world production of both cloth and corn is stimulated and both countries benefit from the trading relationship.

In the model, if corn is labour intensive relative to cloth, and if labour is relatively abundant in country B, then that country will specialize in corn production. As production continues, there is a tendency for wage rates (and other factor endowments) to be equalized; Heckscher and Ohlin argue that this is the case because as country B specializes in corn production, its production pattern becomes more labour intensive, thus reducing labour abundance and increasing marginal labour productivity and wages. Meanwhile, in country A, as cloth production increases, labour will become less scarce, and marginal labour productivity and wages will fall. What this means in monetary terms is that country A cannot indefinitely run a trade surplus with country B because the inflow of gold from country B to country A will lead to an increase in prices in country A and a decrease in country B's prices. Therefore, in the long run, equilibrium will be restored (for summaries see Edwards [1985:17–43]; Shaikh [1979]).

In practice, equalization of factor endowments across the globe (especially wage rates) has not occurred. I will attempt to explain why this is so below, but before doing so I provide some evidence to show that capital flows to the Caribbean have not been (nor are likely to be) sufficiently large enough to lead to an equalization of factor endowments between North America and Western Europe, on the one hand, and the Caribbean, on the other.

Successive postwar governments in the Caribbean adopted programmes designed to encourage foreign investment, such as tax holidays (see chapter four for more details). However, these policies did not have the desired effect of attracting a substantial inflow of foreign capital. For instance, while direct foreign investment in Trinidad rose from TT $48 million in 1956 to TT $100 million the following year, it had fallen to TT $42 million by 1966 [McIntyre and Watson 1970: 18]. Moreover, in only one year between 1957 and 1965 did direct foreign investment exceed investment outflows [1970: 19]. United States' direct foreign investment in Latin America and the Caribbean in 1945 constituted 37 percent of total US direct foreign investment; by 1981, the proportion of US direct foreign investment allocated to the region was down to 17 percent [Ramsaran 1985: 85]. These figures follow a pattern which is typical of the Third World as a whole: in the early 1980s, just over one-quarter of all direct foreign investment was in developing countries, and over half of this was concentrated in just eight such countries [Jenkins 1987: 13].

The underlying reason for the failure of all trade equilibrium models is that they lack an adequate account of the production process. As Brett argues "[t]he fundamental weakness of bourgeois theory is not that it ignores dynamic changes in production relations, but that it assumes that capitalist development will take a particular form – one characterized by even development throughout the system, reciprocal benefits to all of those engaged in its exchange relationships, and equilibrium solutions to the input-output equations generated by the international division of labour" [1983: 90]. By looking at the production process, and how this is integrated with exchange and distribution, one can see the relative advantages that accrue to "early developers" – generally those countries that were not colonized and subject to regimes of forced labour, or escaped them early enough to enjoy a competitive position in the world market.

Neoclassical theory's assumption that the world economy is made up of equally competitive individual units is a fallacy. In practice, some economies are far more powerful than others and are therefore in a far greater position to attract capital than others. Economies of scale ensure that increasing returns prevail when average costs are a decreasing function of output. The strongest countries secure economies of scale through factors such as the exploitation of mass production techniques (for instance – specialization of labour, machinery and management, the accumulation of knowledge), access to credit and to cheap inputs (such as wage goods and capital equipment), which in turn improve the prospects of substantial infrastructural facilities, and the organization of research and development facilities (around 98 percent of which – in the capitalist world, at least – is concentrated in the advanced capitalist countries [Griffin 1978: 15; also, Brett 1983: 90-93]. In monetary terms, the effects are very different from the expectations of the Hecksher-Ohlin model – the outflow of gold from country B will not automatically lead to a reduction in prices and the restoration of a trade equilibrium with country B, but will instead have the effect of decreasing the supply of credit, which will in turn decrease production and raise interest rates. In country A, gold flows will be absorbed by the expanded circulation requirements of increased cloth and corn production, increased luxury production and expanded bank reserves. This final factor will increase the availability of credit at low interest rates and therefore promote the continued expansion of production. Finance capital may be attracted by the high interest rates of country B but this does not lead to a new equilibrium because the credit still has to be paid back to country A with interest, which eventually leads to an ever greater flow of gold from country B to country A [Shaikh 1980: 38-39].

So, capitalism creates hierarchies at both the level of production and the level of the world market, the latter of which is based on a "tendency towards locational agglomeration, a tendency based on the search for the economy of time" [Murray 1972: 171]. At the level of the world market, productive activities tend to be gathered together into agglomerations, and most capital is invested in these areas. Capital will continue to be invested in those areas where "agglomeration tendencies" are relatively low for a number of reasons – exhausted markets in the advanced countries, or vital raw materials, cheap labour or protected markets in the Third World – but none of these (on their own) are sufficient to overcome the competitive advantage enjoyed by the advanced capitalist countries and so most capital remains there [Edwards 1985: 123-65]. Indeed, even more crucially, there is a net capital flow from Third World countries to the "advanced" world, as Third World capitalists seek to maximize their own profitable opportunities. Earlier I referred to capital outflow in Trinidad around the period of independence, but even during the boom years, from the mid 1970s to early 1980s, there was an endemic problem of capital outflow. It has been estimated that from 1976 to 1984, there was a capital outflow of more than US $1 billion. At the height of the boom (1976-80) capital outflows amounted to 63 percent of the growth in external public debt during the period [Bennett 1988: 64]. This export of capital, based on a particular conjuncture of production, exchange and distribution, has important consequences for class formation, as I discuss below.

Finally, the direct foreign investment which does go to the Third World is not as benevolent as is supposed in the neoclassical and Lewis models. Many labour organizations in Trinidad and elsewhere have been critical of foreign ownership of important parts of the economy, especially, as I show in my case study, the oil industry. They have argued that the "national interest" of small developing societies have been subordinated to the global concerns of large transnational corporations. (This is discussed in more detail with reference to the Trinidad oil industry in chapter six.) Although this argument is often couched in overly nationalist terms (which all too often fail to condemn local capitalists who are just as prone to export capital), its basic premise is useful. Neoclassical theory regards international economic relations as market transactions between national units. In practice, trade is increasingly dominated by large firms exchanging with their own subsidiaries. The result is that prices are "administered" and are not "arm's length" market prices; in other words, transnational companies transfer price. Transfer pricing refers to "the setting of prices on transactions between different parts of the same firm, as distinct from the setting of market prices on transactions between independent producers" [Murray 1981a: 1]. Transnational corporations may transfer price in order to reduce the tax burden in specific countries, to avoid limits on profit remittances, to take advantage of a more favourable exchange rate where a dual exchange rate mechanism exists, to avoid accusations of "imperialist exploitation" or to obtain greater flexibility as transfer prices can be used to generate a continuous flow of funds as imports or exports are made, whereas profit remittances usually have to wait until the end of the financial year [Jenkins 1987: 117–18].

Class Formation and Third World Labour Studies

The implications of my discussion of uneven development should be clear for any study of labour in the Third World. As I argued above, class formation is highly uneven and so an industrial relations model is not very useful. In Trinidad, the capital-labour relation is the main relation of production in that the direct producers are separated from the means of production, but the export of capital which is so common in peripheral capitalist economies ensures that the processes of class formation and development are highly uneven. The result is that the securely employed, unionized, usually male, wage worker of the industrial relations school represents at most a large minority of the labour force, and there is large-scale and constant unemployment and a large informal sector. In Trinidad, out of an estimated labour force of 369 600 in 1985, approximately 100 000 were unionized [Council of Progressive Trade Unions 1985c: 1]. Moreover, the labour force as a whole is stratified along the lines of race and gender, and these factors must be accounted for in any study of labour.

Labour Organizations and Labour Resistance

The case study outlined in chapters two to six focuses mainly on the organized labour movement, and in particular on political parties and trade unions. However, I argue that the character of these institutions must be seen in the context of wider uneven class, gender and ethnic relations. Before moving on to my case study, I will briefly discuss the general character of trade unions and political parties, and relate this to the specific conditions in peripheral capitalist economies.

The orthodox Marxist–Leninist view of trade unions is that they are not particularly effective institutions in advancing the cause of socialism. Lenin [1988] distinguished between economic trade union consciousness and the revolutionary socialist class consciousness embodied in the vanguard party. Perry Anderson has similarly "written off" trade unions as vehicles of socialist advance, arguing that they "do not challenge the existence of a society based on a division of classes, they merely express it. Thus trade unions can never be viable vehicles of advance towards socialism in themselves; by their nature they are tied to capitalism. They can bargain within the society, but not transform it" [Anderson 1978: 334]. A general strike is dismissed as "an abstention, not an assault on capitalism" [Anderson 1978: 336]. This view of trade unionism is contrasted with the political party, which is seen as "a rupture with the natural environment of civil society, a voluntarist contractual collectivity, which restructures social contours: the union adheres to them in a one-to-one relationship . . . Thus, the political party alone can incarnate a true negation of existing society and a project to overthrow it" [Anderson 1978: 335].

Such a sharp dichotomy between "economic" trade unionism and "political" parties is not dissimilar to the views of Kerr and his colleagues. In Trinidad, this view has informed both right and left wing politics in the labour movement. For instance, in the 1940s and 1950s advisers to the British Trades Union Congress (TUC) in colonial Trinidad advocated a complete separation of industrial and political demands (see chapter three), while in the 1970s many Marxists took a similar position in the United Labour Front (see chapter five). Two left-wing Trinidadian writers have even argued that "[t]he biggest barrier to further development of the workers' self organization and initiative is the trade union which emasculates and limits the scope of working class activity, channelling it in a particular direction as determined by the wage system and bourgeois democratic process" [Howe and Rennie 1982: 135].

Earlier I outlined the reasons why the "economic" demands of trade unions can never be wholly separated from politics. From a socialist perspective, it should be stressed that, for all its limitations, "trade union consciousness" is never wholly compatible with capitalism. For instance, the basic trade union demand of a "fair day's work for a fair day's pay" can develop into more radical objectives; as Hyman states, "[i]f workers were to define 'fairness' in terms of 'the full fruits of their labours', a demand which is superficially economic would have obvious revolutionary implications . . . In some contexts, any demands for improvements are unrealizable; and in any situation, there will be some point in excess of which demands are intolerable" [1978: 386]. Lenin himself took a far more subtle position than is often credited to him and he was fully aware of the "educational functions" of a strike. He wrote that "[a] strike . . . opens the eyes of the workers to the nature, not only of the capitalists, but of government and the laws as well . . . Strikes, therefore, teach the workers to unite . . . This is the reason that socialists call strikes 'a school of war', a school in which the workers learn to make war on their enemies for the liberation of the whole people, of all who labour . . ." [Hyman 1978: 387].

In Third World societies, trade unions often play a more explicitly political role than similar organizations in advanced capitalist countries. As stated earlier, the presence of a large reserve army of labour weakens the collective bargaining position of trade unions and so compels trade unions to take positions on wider political issues – one factor behind the phenomenon of "social movement unionism", discussed in chapter six. Moreover, as Hyman points out, "[f]or a ruling class pursuing rapid capital accumulation within the constraints of an imperialist world economy the options are clearly limited: a fact which does much to explain the lack of tolerance for independent and assertive labour organization by most post-colonial regimes" [Hyman 1979: 329]. So, given the unevenness of development in peripheral capitalist societies, Third World capitalist states often attempt to control organized labour. Thus in practice, many states take a far more realistic view of the political nature of trade unions and often pass legislation which attempts to curtail their power – as was the case in Trinidad and Tobago in 1965 (see chapter three).

Conclusion

The approach offered here is influenced by, but in some respects attempts to move beyond, Marxism. Neoclassical, modernization and cultural pluralist theory are all incomplete because they do not adequately conceptualize the link between labour and development. Dependency and world systems theories at least have the merit of focusing on the international economy, but they tend to have a one-sided view of systems of labour control as the functional outcome of the mechanisms of the world system. While numerous Marxist approaches are overly reductionist and stagist, this does not have to be the case. A theory of uneven development, combined with a "human action" approach to class, "race" and gender, provides the framework for analysing labour and different periods of development, such as slavery, indentureship and peripheral capitalism.

Analysing development in order to explain the context in which labour operates is necessary, but is still insufficient. Labour is not simply a factor in explaining development; it is the *key* factor, for the exploitation of one country by another is based on the exploitation of one class by another. Robert Brenner has argued that three conditions must be fulfilled if there is to be an unprecedented expansion of the productive forces. First, there must be a potentially mobile labour force (that is, one not tied to the land or a particular owner). Secondly, there must be the potential for developing labour productivity through the specialization of tasks. Thirdly, the potential must exist for enforcing continued pressure to increase labour productivity: "Only under conditions of free wage labour will the individual producing units (combining labour power and the means of production) be forced to sell in order to buy, to buy in order to sell and reproduce, and ultimately to expand and innovate in order to maintain this position in relation to other competing productive units" [Brenner 1977: 32]. In the Caribbean, such conditions have largely not existed and so its incorporation into the world market has historically been an unfavourable one.

Even in the period of postwar capitalist industrialization, the region has either had to compete with countries that have superior technology and therefore higher productivity, or it has been forced to produce low productivity, unfinished goods, where the "value added" is low and so potential for "modernization" is not high. In the case of the former, the region has therefore had to import technology which has led to balance of payments problems, and has failed to attract sufficient capital investment (due to capitalism's "agglomeration tendencies" within the world market) so that new employment opportunities could be created. In the case of the latter, the terms of trade are generally unfavourable. This is not due to the higher wages of workers in the metropolitan countries, as Prebisch argues, but is instead caused by different rates of labour productivity (of which wages are a reflection).

The politics of labour should therefore be analysed in the context of uneven capitalist development in the periphery. "Political" trade unionism should not be seen as a sign of the "political immaturity" of a labour movement but should be regarded as a rational response to the conditions of capital accumulation in the Third World. The political potential of less organized groups such as those working in the petty commodity sector should also come under scrutiny. In the case study outlined in chapters two to six, I reject both standard industrial relations and fundamentalist Marxist approaches and instead present a labour history of Trinidad and Tobago which focuses on how the processes of colonialism, imperialism and different stages of development have divided the labour force. The study concentrates on gender, ethnicity, the fluid class structure and politics as the main lines of division. In chapter two I try to show how ethnic and gender divisions are rooted in the periods of slavery and indentureship. Chapter three focuses on political divisions, especially within the organized labour movement. The fourth chapter, in looking at the Black Power revolt of 1970, concentrates on the interaction of "race" and class, the fluidity of the class structure and the political potential of the so-called informal sector. Chapter five presents a specific case study of the one major labour party in Trinidad's history and analyses how it failed to come to terms with the long-term divisions within the working classes. Finally, in chapter six I examine how the recession of the 1980s has exacerbated these divisions, but at the same time I argue that, with the growth of social movement unionism, there may be some cause for optimism for the future of labour in Trinidad and Tobago.

2

Class Formation

and

Labour History

As I showed in chapter one, the Caribbean's integration into the world economy was an unfavourable one, a situation strongly influenced by processes of class formation in the area. While Trinidad suffered a similar fate to the rest of the region, the actual process of class formation was significantly different (with the partial exception of British Guiana) from the rest of the West Indies. My purpose in this chapter is to examine the particular way that classes developed from the late eighteenth century to the late 1930s, and in doing so show how these patterns helped to shape labour resistance. In particular, I am concerned with how uneven development interacted with ideology to create a fluid class structure divided by race and gender.

To clarify the events of this period, the chapter is divided into three sections. First, I look at the period of slavery, from its comparatively late establishment in the 1770s to its abolition in 1834. The second section investigates the period from 1838 to 1917, and in particular the system of indentured labour, the development of "reconstituted" peasantries [Mintz 1984: 132] and the unification of Trinidad with Tobago. Finally, the period from the 1890s to the 1930s is examined, a period characterized by intensified proletarianization and the beginnings of organized labour, the development of the oil industry and the emergence of "modern" trade unionism.

The Period of Slavery

Introduction: Trinidad as a "Colonial Slum" – 1498 to the 1770s

Columbus is alleged to have discovered Trinidad on 31 July 1498. In fact this "discovery" was the beginning of the island's contact with the developing European commercial network, led at this stage by Spain and Portugal. The actual discovery of Trinidad was made by the Arawak and Carib Indians who inhabited the island for hundreds of years before Columbus' arrival, and had established an agrarian society based on soil cultivation, hunting animals and gathering shellfish [Williams 1964: 1].

The Spanish colonization process was markedly slow in Trinidad, and the first permanent Spanish settlers probably did not arrive until 1592. Even after this, Trinidad remained undeveloped compared to the rest of the Iberian Empire. It was basically an "outpost of Spanish colonialism" [Brereton 1981: 2], where a few Spaniards and Spanish-Americans (mestizos) cultivated a little tobacco and cocoa for export, but most production was for direct subsistence. The plantation form of production did not yet exist, but attempts were made to develop it in the seventeenth century.

Up to the 1780s, the Arawaks and the Caribs provided much of the labour for the developing estates. Production was based on the encomienda system, whereby the Spanish encomendero was granted a parcel of land, and had the right to extract tribute (in the form of labour and/or crops) from the Indians living on the land. This system of production was typical of the Spanish Empire in the sixteenth century but was limited in Trinidad to just four encomiendas, and in 1712 only about 600 Indians lived in them [Brereton 1981: 5]. Most Indians still lived in the forest, in independent settlements.

There were further attempts to control the labour of, and to "Christianize", the Indians. These included the mission villages established between 1687 and 1708. Each mission was ultimately controlled by the Capuchin missionaries, and Indians were required to work for several days a week on the settlement. These efforts to increase labour control met with only limited success and they were abolished in 1708. Nine years previously, the Indians at the mission of San Francisco de los Arenales rose up against the Capuchins and killed them [Brereton 1981: 6].

Various half-hearted attempts to establish forced labour systems continued, but until the late eighteenth century, slavery was not utilized. Up to this period, Trinidad remained "a colonial slum of the Spanish Empire", in which "[n]o serious attempt was ever made to develop its resources . . ." [Millette 1985: 1].

The "Modernization" of Trinidad, 1773–1797

It was clear by the 1770s that if Spain wanted to maintain its Empire, it must develop its colonies. This view was reinforced by the fact that Britain was increasingly dominant in the region. From 1761, Spain and France were allies, and by 1776 the Spanish recognized that immigration was necessary to develop Trinidad. The following year Trinidad's Spanish governor, Manuel Falquez, received a visit from the French–Grenadian planter, Roume de St Laurent. The latter became the semi-official spokesperson for a group of French planters who suffered discrimination at the hands of the British after the latter had taken Grenada in 1763. Under St Laurent, these planters were encouraged to move to Trinidad.

Almost immediately, foreign immigration commenced and this procedure was given official recognition in the 1783 Cedula of Population. This decree offered incentives to prospective new planters, such as a free grant of land to every settler who came to Trinidad with his slaves. The size of the land depended on the number of slaves owned by the planter; therefore the larger the number of slaves owned, the larger the amount of land awarded. A free coloured, property-owning class was also encouraged to settle, as they too were awarded land (albeit half as much as their white counterparts), often as slave owners. Also, provisions were made for the granting of full Spanish citizenship for all free settlers, including coloureds, after five years' residence, provided that they adhered to Roman Catholicism.

The effect of the Cedula was quite clear. In 1784, there was a population of almost 6000, of whom 2627 were slaves (there were a further 1495 Caribbean Indians). This section of the population was in decline due to overwork, food shortages, contact with European diseases and murder); by 1797, the population had increased to 17 643, over 10 000 of whom were slaves [Brereton 1981: 14-15; Williams 1964: 47].

Unlike many of the other islands, Trinidad's economy was not based solely on one crop and the production of sugar was (at least initially) accompanied by that of cotton, cocoa and coffee. Nevertheless, by the 1790s, the economy shared most of the features of slave society outlined in chapter one and it was centred on the production of sugar for export.

Trinidad as a British Slave Colony, 1797–1838

Spain's attempts to prevent further British expansion were in vain and the latter conquered Trinidad in 1797. This takeover reflected the increasing dominance of the British in the region. It was tolerated by the planters because they feared that the revolutionary events in France and Saint Domingue would spread to Trinidad if it continued under weak Spanish rule.

The conquest was led by Sir Ralph Abercromby, but he left the island after a few days and left one of his officers, Sir Thomas Picton, as military governor and commander-in-chief. From 1799 to 1802, Picton ruled Trinidad as an effective tyrant. Harsh treatment such as flogging and execution was inflicted on people of all classes and colours, but the most severe was usually reserved for the coloureds and blacks and, although Picton was eventually disgraced, successive governors were only marginally more humane.

The slave owner had absolute power over the slave; the slave was the master's legal property. There were laws which supposedly protected slaves from the worst kind of abuse by their masters, but in practice murder or rape often went unpunished [Patterson 1975: 82]. Work on the plantations was very hard, particularly in the sugar crop season. Slaves were also subject to ill treatment on the estates by overseers, and received little effective protection.

There was no sexual division of labour under slavery. Female slaves were expected to work on the estates from an early age and, on at least one island, Jamaica, there were more women field slaves than men [Reddock 1985: 64-65]. As Patterson argues, "Slavery abolished any real social distribution between males and females. The woman was expected to work just as hard, she was as indecently exposed and was punished just as severely. In the eyes of the master she was equal to the man as long as her strength was the same as his" [Patterson 1975: 67]. The family was generally treated with contempt by slaves, and women were not keen to bear children, probably because of their demanding tasks on the estates. Abortion and infanticide were widely practised [Patterson 1975: 106-7]. This suited the planters' interests, as it was usually cheaper for them to buy new slaves, rather than pay the social reproduction costs of children.

Slave resistance was a common occurrence, belying the myth of the "passive, happy, negro". At times, this resistance took the form of open rebellion (for example in Jamaica in 1798 and 1831), or even revolution (Saint Domingue in 1791), but more commonly it involved everyday, "hidden" forms of protest such as laziness, satirizing their master's prejudices (the Quashee person- ality), running away, and poisoning their masters [Patterson 1975: 261; Heuman 1986; Bauer and Bauer 1942]. In Trinidad, resistance tended to take the form of more covert protest, but even in the most "passive" of slave colonies there were planned open rebellions. In 1805, martial law was declared by Governor Hislop in response to the fear of an imminent slave revolt. As a result of this planned uprising, four slaves were executed, five were deported after their ears had been cut off, and many others were flogged [Craton 1982: 236]. There was no other known planned rebellion in Trinidad before Emancipation, but resistance in its everyday form persisted. Open rebellions were the exception rather than the rule and they usually affected only a small minor- ity of slaves. However, this had less to do with the so-called "happy, contented Negro" than with the fact that the slaves "had to accept the institution of slavery and make their adjustments to their institution" [Bauer and Bauer 1942: 390]. The monopoly of the means of coercion by the planters was such that everyday resistance could only realistically take covert forms.

Slavery was abolished in 1834 although an apprenticeship period of six years (reduced to four) was inaugurated, under which former slaves had to work for their master for three quarters of the week without a wage, while they were free to seek paid work for the rest of the week. The planters were also paid £20 million compen- sation. The announcement of the apprenticeship period led to spasmodic resistance by the former slaves, some of whom protested outside Government House in Port of Spain. These protests eventu- ally died out, a reaction reinforced by the conduct of Governor Hill, who ordered the arrest and flogging of the protesters.

The Period 1838–1917: Indentured Labour, "Reconstituted Peasantries" and the Unification of Trinidad and Tobago

Trinidad after Emancipation

The end of the apprenticeship period in 1838 opened up a new period in the history of the Caribbean, and the newly emancipated societies followed divergent paths of development. In Barbados, for example, the plantation system was easily maintained as there was a limited availability of land to which the former slaves could move. In Trinidad, on the other hand, a period of covert, yet intensified, class struggle took place in which the planters attempted to maintain a labour supply for the plantation, but the former slaves tried to secure a degree of freedom beyond that of "free" wage labour. The former slaves wanted to leave the plantation and become independent peasant proprietors; they "demanded control over their own labour and access to their own lands to use for the production of food and other crops" [Klein and Engerman 1987].

This struggle was initially balanced in favour of the former slaves. In 1838, only 20 656 former slaves inhabited the island, a high proportion of whom were domestics. At the same time, only 43 000 out of a total of 1.25 million acres of land were cultivated [Brereton 1981: 77]. This abundance of land relative to population aided a movement by the ex-slaves off the estates on to land that was previously uncultivated. By 1861, there were 5833 freeholders owning land of between one to ten acres. One should not conclude from this, however, that population was the decisive factor because "natural" factors exist in an historically determined, social environment. A situation of widespread land availability, or "open resources" [Nieboer 1971: 384–85], can only aid social phenomena, they cannot determine them. In post-Emancipation Belize, for instance, former masters maintained their mahogany-producing labour force, in a situation of "open resources", through a system of debt peonage [Bolland 1981: 608].

In Trinidad, the planters carried out a variety of measures in an attempt to maintain a constant labour supply. These included relatively high wages (which were also in part forced on them as the demand for labour exceeded the supply), and accommodation and food for labourers. Wages increased from 15d. in 1838 to 25.5d. in 1839 [Sebastien 1979: 53], and payment was also made by "task". Under this system a specific piece of work was given to the labourer and a fixed payment was made, so high wages could be made by those who completed a number of tasks in one day. The planters also used their dominance in the Legislative Council and passed a Territorial Ordinance which prohibited the purchase of land below one hundred acres.

None of these measures were particularly successful and the ex-slaves responded to the Territorial Ordinance by squatting on Crown land or abandoned estates. There were 11 000 field slaves in 1834; only 4000 of these had remained on the estates by 1859 [Brereton 1981: 79]. The former slaves became independent producers of cocoa and coffee, or petty traders, while the prosperous few became shopkeepers. Many combined "independent" work with occasional work on the plantations. These independent producers were by no means wealthy and they led a materially precarious existence, but they at least had freedom from direct control by the plantation owners.

Attempts to remove squatters were largely ineffective. Communications and policing were poor, and some of the smaller planters were happy with a system of occasional and/or seasonal labour because it meant that wages did not have to be paid all the year round. The larger planters, such as W.H. Burnley, who could afford to pay wages all the year round, were the real opponents of squatting. A proclamation of 30 March 1839 empowered Stipendiary Magistrates to evict squatters of less than one year's standing. However, many of the smaller estate owners "were unwilling to lay information before the Magistrates about those squatters who were a source of labour for their own estates" [Wood 1968: 51].

The larger plantation owners therefore began to look to external sources for a supply of labour. The first source was the Eastern Caribbean, and from 1839 to 1849 over 10 000 immigrants arrived from Grenada, Nevis and Montserrat. A steady inflow continued throughout the nineteenth century, particularly from Barbados, but few stayed on the plantations and instead went to the towns or settled as independent cultivators. Alternative sources from China, Sierra Leone, St Helena, Madeira, and even France and Germany suffered a number of setbacks such as the high mortality rates of the settlers, expense of importation (in the case of China) and insufficient numbers to fill the gaps in labour supply. However, an alternative supply was found and the *Fatel Rozack* arrived in Trinidad on 3 May 1845, complete with the first "load" of labourers from India.

The Indentured Labour System and the Recovery of Sugar

The sugar planters' need for a steady labour force was highlighted by the crisis that hit West Indian sugar immediately after Emancipation. Sugar production declined from 14 312 tons (1838) to 12 228 tons in 1840 [Brereton 1981: 82]. The arrival of the first shipload of labourers from India in 1845 was therefore directly linked to the crisis of the sugar industry. In the first wave of immigration, from 1845 to 1848, 5167 Indians arrived in Trinidad [Wood 1968: 114]. At this time, it was widely believed that the appearance of Indian labour would be a temporary phenomenon, and part of their labour contract included provision for a return passage (see below). However, in 1846 the Sugar Duties Act was passed by the British government, which made provisions for the equalization of duties on foreign and British colonial sugar. One consequence of this Act was that Trinidad (and the rest of the English Caribbean) would have to compete with cheaper sugar, including that produced by slave labour in Cuba and Brazil.

This prospect convinced planters of the need to reopen the link with India and in 1851, the second wave began, which lasted until 1917. Altogether, from 1845 to 1917, Trinidad imported 143 939 Indians, and it was their labour which restimulated the sugar industry [Sebastien 1979: 223]. In the 1850s, production consistently expanded, and by 1866 had reached 40 000 tons per annum [Brereton 1981: 84].

The labour system utilized by the planters was not one based on free wage labour. Instead, a system of indentured labour was used. Changes were made to the immigration rules over time and were embodied in the 1854 Consolidating Ordinance. Indians who had entered Trinidad before 1854 were entitled to a free return passage after five years, while others had to spend ten years in the colony. Both groups had to serve as labourers for a period of three years, and could then reindenture themselves for a further two years or buy out their remaining time by paying a certain sum to the colonial government. These conditions were subject to continual amendment throughout the century; for example, under Governor Gordon (1866-70), the Indians were awarded a plot of land at the end of their period of indentureship, and by the 1890s, Indians wishing to return home were expected to pay a substantial proportion of the package themselves.

As well as conditions concerning duration and termination, the contract contained a number of additional stipulations. The labourer was guaranteed medical attention, housing and a wage under the contract. However, although a wage was paid the labourers were not "free" wage labourers. This was because regulations were introduced (initially in 1846, but they were also incorporated into the 1854 Ordinance) that made it illegal for Indians to move off the estates without a pass granted to them by their employers, and which disallowed them from giving up work with one employer without a certificate of discharge. Moreover, negligence and absence from work were defined as criminal offences.

This degree of control over the labourers enabled planters to pay low wages. The Immigration Ordinance of 1870 stated that indentured labourers should not receive less than the average wage, but planters could easily ignore these regulations. When the labourers broke the rules of the pass system, and illegally left the estates, they were not always guaranteed a sympathetic hearing. In giving evidence to the 1909 Sanderson Committee on indentured labour in the Empire, W.H. Coombs, Trinidad's Protector of Immigrants described his usual response to Indian complainants: "I take down their complaint and I tell them plainly that I do not believe them . . . If the man comes to me and makes what I consider a frivolous complaint . . . then I give the manager a certificate to that effect so that I can prosecute him" [Tinker 1974: 432]. Six years previously, Coombs did precisely this in response to a strike at the Harmony Hall estate, after sixty-seven labourers marched off the estate, complaining about conditions and wages. The strikers refused to return to the estate after Coombs dismissed their grievances, and sixty-four of them were given seven days' imprisonment. The strike leader, Daulat Singh, was repatriated to India [Tinker 1974: 228-29]. It was hardly surprising, then, as Coombs himself noted (though apparently oblivious to the reason why), that complaints "got less and less every year . . . there are scarcely any" [Tinker 1974: 309].

Although wages were fixed, this did not help the Indians, even in times of economic recession. During the sugar crisis of the mid 1880s, employers still had to pay the statutory minimum wage of 25c per task; their response was simply to increase the size of the task, which had the same effect as reducing wages.

The wages of indentured labourers may have fallen by as much as an average 60c per day to 35c in the 1880s [Tinker 1974: 186].

Wages for Creoles were consistently higher, and they monopolized the supervisory positions on the plantation. As Sebastien notes, "The very principles on which the indentureship system was founded divided labour within itself. Especially during the early period of the system, the creole was virtually the coolie's policeman" [1979: 249]. Numerous ordinances empowered Creole servants to arrest a "coolie" who had fled the estate. In the district of Tacarigua, a bounty system was introduced in 1862, awarding servants a bounty of six pence for every mile away from the estate for capturing escaped "coolies".

Social conditions on the estates were very bad. Although the labour contract guaranteed housing and medical treatment, the actual quality of these services was very poor. The 1897 Royal Commission on the West Indies described hospitals as "pig sties . . . unfit for human habitation" [Sebastien 1979: 273]. A Creole witness told the Sanderson Committee that the Indians were housed in "something like a mule pen, about 150 feet long, and about eight to ten feet square; and sometimes two or three are housed in each room" [Tinker 1974: 208]. Alcoholism was common among the Indians, and the practice of the truck system often went so far that a monetary transaction did not take place and the labourer received payment in rum in its place.

The degrading conditions that the Indians lived under, and the superior economic and social position of the Creole led to a "process of voluntary segregation" [Oxaal 1968: 44], reinforced by the compulsory pass system, on the part of the Indian population. Mutual suspicion and racial stereotyping became common, and Indian men were regarded as wife-murderers, perjurers and misers. Ill feeling was also increased by the fact that the abundance of labour that indentureship engendered led to a decline in the bargaining position of the whole of the labour force. This was especially the case during the sugar crisis of the 1880s. These factors led the Indians to resist assimilation into the European or Creole cultures, and Hinduism remained their major religion.

It was, however, the minority Muslims who successfully established a festival that rivalled the Carnival of lower class Creoles. The Muharram festival of the minority Shi'ite Muslims commemorated the deaths of Mohammed's grandsons, Hassan and Hussain. Although the festival's religious significance was restricted to a tiny section of the population, by the 1880s it had genuine mass appeal and some Creoles, as well as Sunni Muslims and Hindus, took part. In the economic crisis of the 1880s (see below), the colonial authorities became increasingly intolerant of the festival, and prohibited the 1884 festival from entering any towns. The procession attempted to enter the town of San Fernando, only to be shot at by the colonial police and British soldiers. Sixteen people were killed as a result and over a hundred were wounded [Singh 1987: 1-41].

The division between "African" and "Indian" was therefore "racialized" at this time. A process of racialization occurs in instances "where social relations have been structured by the signification of human biological characteristics in such a way as to define and construct differentiated social collectivities" [Miles 1989: 75]. The ideology of racism is not therefore a capitalist or a colonial conspiracy, or simply a function of capitalist exploitation, as some writers have implied [Cox 1959]. Racism is a way of "making sense", albeit wrongly, of the way in which the world operates [Miles 1989: 80-81; Hall 1978: 26]. In Trinidad, the newly freed slaves of African descent, saw that their bargaining position with the planters was undermined by the arrival of indentured labourers from India. Their response was to "blame the victims", the East Indians, rather than the perpetrators, the plantation owners. The impact of these developments on what is now called "race relations" in Trinidad is particularly significant, because it shaped the pattern of labour resistance that persists, in a modified form, to this day. The roots and nature of racism may have changed, but its origins lie in this period. The significance of the impact of racism on dividing the labour force should not be underestimated, as most labour histories have done [Rennie 1974; Ramdin 1982], but at the same time the historical roots of racism must be explained, rather than described (as is the case in the plural society model), in terms of a timeless cultural group conflict. East Indians, like Africans before them, were taken to Trinidad to perform a specific task, as labourers, and as labour control and social life became segregated, so too did labour resistance.

The Development of Other Classes

Cocoa Farmers

As I have shown, after Emancipation a new peasantry emerged, but they owed their existence largely to the lack of enforcement

measures against squatting. Under the governorship of A.H.
Gordon (1866-70), a new policy was carried out which encouraged the development of a small, legally recognized, peasant
class. The price of land was reduced to £1 per acre and the minimum requirement for purchase was reduced to just five acres.
The result was an increase in the sale of land, along with a simultaneous move against squatting (a policy reinforced by programmes to develop communications and transportation). Most
people bought their land and forests were cleared to accommodate
the increase in land ownership.

Most of the new landowners cultivated their land in cocoa and
this became very lucrative, at least for the larger planters, from
the 1860s onwards. By the 1890s, cocoa had emerged as
Trinidad's largest export earner. As sugar production became
increasingly concentrated in fewer, mainly British hands, so
cocoa became dominated by planters of French-Creole origin.
Technological advances in the processing of cocoa in Europe
turned cocoa and chocolate into goods of mass consumption,
which in turn led to an increase in the demand for unprocessed
cocoa (cacao).

The development of cocoa in Trinidad was largely built up
through two similar means. First, a peasant would buy a portion
of Crown land, clear it, and plant cocoa trees. After the trees
began to develop, the peasant would sell the plot to a cocoa
planter and buy new land, and repeat the process. Secondly,
there was the contract system, under which a planter would buy a
large amount of land and fell the forest. He would then contract
out the land to a peasant on the condition that the latter would
plant cocoa trees. When the trees developed the owner took over
the land, paying agreed sums for each tree. During their period of
occupation of land, the contractor/peasant was allowed to grow
food on the land. The major contractors were initially the peons,
who were of Spanish-Indian origin, but the other ethnic groups
(including in the 1870s, the Indians) followed.

While many of the cocoa peasants may have regarded access to
land as a means of independence from the plantation, the contract system actually increased the growing hegemony of capital.
Temporary land tenure was often insufficient in terms of food provision and so peasants were often forced, by economic necessity,
to try to find work on the cocoa estates. Secondly, the actual contract system was, from the point of view of the planter, a cheap
way of developing cocoa, as they "bought cheap and sold dear".
As Sebastien states, "Cocoa contractors were in truth and in fact

hired underpaid laborers of the big cocoa planters" [1979: 403].

Sugar Cane Farmers

The development of cocoa was reinforced by the crisis of the sugar industry of the mid 1880s, caused by competition from subsidized European beet sugar, and overproduction on the world market. The response of the sugar planters was to encourage the development of "independent" sugar cane farming. This had existed before the 1880s, but it was in spite of the large planters, rather than because of them. The planters now became more willing to foster the development of an independent peasantry because they bought the crushed sugar cane relatively cheaply, and after grinding, it was sold at a more expensive price. By 1899, cane farmers produced 20 percent of all the cane that was crushed; by 1919, it had increased to 49.5 percent [Sebastien 1979: 408].

Although cane farming was initially taken up by the Creoles, it was the Indians who became increasingly dominant in this sector. From 1869, under Governor Gordon, a new policy was introduced whereby Indians could be awarded a plot of land at the end of their period of indentureship, in return for relinquishing the right to a passage back to India. Most Indian cane farmers simply purchased their land, however. From 1891 to 1895, 34 percent of the sales of Crown lands was to Indians and, although some was utilized for rice and cocoa production, the majority was for the purpose of sugar [Sebastien 1979: 408].

These developments led to the restoration of Indian women to a position of subservience to Indian men. Women were always a minority of the indentured labourers, and those that entered Trinidad were often single, or separated from their husbands [Reddock 1986: 35]. A major reason for their leaving was to escape the patriarchal relations that existed in India, and their work on the estates gave them some independence from Indian men (although not from male planters or their overseers). The increase in sugar cane farming resulted in a reduction in the demand for female labour on the estate and provided the basis for a reconstitution of the traditional Indian patriarchal family [Reddock 1986: 35]. The challenge to women's independence manifested itself in a number of ways, including a high rate of wife murder among the Indian population [Wood 1968: 154], which in turn increased the incidence of racial stereotyping amongst the African population. By 1891, 54.7 percent of Indo-Trinidadians was resident outside of the plantation system [Poynting 1987: 233], and the traditional Indian village, and patriarchal relations, were revived. Some women were forced to work unpaid on Indian land, and with the continued scarcity of women, child marriage became the norm. So, by the late nineteenth century, a complex pattern of class, race and gender stratification had emerged.

The Development of an Urban Indian and Chinese Middle Class

An urban middle class was also established among the Indian population. A significant number became shopkeepers, merchants, and even estate owners. According to the Royal Protector of Immigrants, in 1874 all the wealthy Indians were of high caste origin [Sebastien 1979: 279-81]. Wage labour alone was not sufficient to provide the means for movement to the middle class. Instead, "[i]t was wage labour above the average, in the form of the headman (sirdar) and men of upper caste, many of whom were also sirdars and who readily won status on the plantation both among management and workers, that advanced their social position above the average worker by using above average means" [Sebastien 1979: 84]. On the estates, the sirdars acted as overseers for the planter and they used this position to accumulate wealth at the expense of the field labourer. For instance they often made the "coolie" pay a percentage of their wage to them. Once a certain amount of wealth was accumulated, the sirdars would buy shops near the estate, or alternatively they may have controlled the shop owned by the planter. These shops were generally run along the lines of the truck system and the credit given to labourers was often repayable at extortionate rates of interest. Sirdars also loaned money to indentured labourers in order that the latter could purchase their freedom. However, this led to a new system of bondage to the sirdar – debt peonage. Interest rates were again extremely high, and generally varied from 60 to 120 percent, but far higher rates were also recorded [Sebastien 1979: 288-9]. On the whole, the Indian population continued its isolation from the rest of the population, and tended to confine itself to the rural areas.

The smaller Chinese population was more easily accepted by the rest of the population than the Indians, but they too suffered harsh treatment. A great number of the Chinese indentured labourers were denied the chance of social advancement because of maltreatment, on both the journey to Trinidad and the plantation, which led to a very high mortality rate among them. A large proportion of those that survived did prosper and became artisans, market gardeners, butchers and shopkeepers. By 1895, there were Chinese rum and grocery shops throughout the island, some owned by the Lee Lum family, who later developed their business interests and formed an influential part of the national bourgeoisie.

Class Development among the Creole Population

The period after Emancipation also saw the development and consolidation of a black and coloured middle class. This sector of society originally emerged before Emancipation, from the coloured and black population freed from slavery. With the concentration in sugar ownership after Emancipation, this small group was forced into new occupational groupings including small business operations, such as pharmacies and printers. Others were lawyers, doctors and newspaper editors. Some members of this group were "self-made" and basically owed their position to the education system. Education expanded after Lord Harris founded fifty-four primary schools in 1846, but its development was held back by religious differences, poor attendance and bad administration. Nevertheless, the system still provided one of the few means of escape from a life of poverty and drudgery. Mobility did not, however, always involve entry to a higher class; it also led to the development of an "upper working class", composed of teachers, and low ranking civil servants and clerks.

Some members of this new class attempted to shed their cultural roots, and disassociated themselves from the black masses. On the other hand, a significant number, particularly those in white collar work such as teaching, championed the cause of "black pride". One of the outstanding black figures was J.J. Thomas, who in 1889 wrote a perceptive reply to a racist diatribe by James Anthony Froude, in which he outlined how the black population was subject to racial discrimination and social and economic exploitation [J.J. Thomas 1969; Froude 1888]. Thomas was himself a victim, and was continually passed over for the job of Inspector of Schools, despite his superior qualifications for the job. Other leading black teachers included H.A. Nurse and Henry

Sylvester Williams, who later founded the Pan-African Conference in the USA in 1900. Nurse had a son called Malcolm who, under the pseudonym George Padmore, became an influential Communist and later led the Pan-Africanist movement.

The urban working class, which was still primarily of African descent, increased dramatically from the 1870s, mainly because of internal immigration from the rural areas and external immigration. The net immigration into Trinidad between 1871and 1911 has been estimated at around 65 000 [Brereton 1979: 110]. These immigrants entered occupations such as domestic service, petty trading, shopkeeping, cab driving, dock work and shop work. Some light industry also developed, involving the establishment of a brewery, some bakeries and a match factory. Most of the working class lived in barrack ranges, situated behind the front of each city street (with their respectable shops), hidden from the passer-by. The barrack ranges were long sheds built along a back wall, each one divided into a number of small rooms. Water supply was communal and shared among a large number of people. Overcrowding was common and made worse by urban growth. A building ordinance of 1868 prohibited the erection of new wooden buildings, thus worsening the situation. Disease was common, and the inadequate health system was run on the basis of curative rather than preventive medicine, an arrangement conducive to the interests of the wealthier classes, but one that did not benefit the urban poor in their overcrowded conditions. The infant mortality rate was high: in 1891, 18.4 percent of children under the age of one year died, and children under the age of five accounted for 44.6 percent of all deaths [Brereton 1979: 120].

An urban working class culture began to develop, especially during the 1880s, when the sugar depression led to increased unemployment. This did not yet take the form of organized labour resistance, because there was no major concentration of the labour force in any one industry; although sugar was a partial exception, even in this sector, labour was dispersed and isolated through the growth of cane farming. There was also the factor of the urban masses' cultural diversity, as the population had cultural roots in St Helena, Sierra Leone, North America, the East Caribbean, and pre-Columbus Trinidad. Nevertheless, a common black culture, one which excluded Indians, began to develop on the basis of a response to exclusion from political life, racist discrimination and a low socioeconomic position. Of particular importance were the gangs of unemployed, the jamettes, who dominated the Carnival in the 1860s. Many of these gangs were involved in petty crime and there was a great deal of tension between the colonial government and the jamettes at Carnival, culminating in riots in 1881.

"Race Relations"

"Race relations" in this period were extremely complex because Creole-Indian tensions tended to conceal the fact that European culture was still predominant. As I have shown, middle class and white-collar blacks and coloureds were the victims of discrimination. The *Trinidad Telegraph* reported in 1872 that a Secretary of State had told a West Indian Governor "that on no account whatever was the 'subject race' to be employed in any office . . . of trust and responsibility" [Brereton 1979: 100]. Such a view was reflected in the crude racist tracts of the time, most notably Thomas Carlyle's *Discourse on the Nigger Question* and Anthony Trollope's *The West Indies and the Spanish Main* [Trollope 1968]. It was also developed by pseudoscientific theories of "social Darwinism", which regarded black people as lower down the evolutionary scale, and therefore biologically inferior.

Such views "justified" social discrimination against blacks and Indians throughout the Empire. In Trinidad, the government often "promoted" the most capable of the middle class to positions in remote areas, thus making sure that they were safely out of the way; this was the fate of the aforementioned J.J. Thomas, who was "promoted" to the Clerkship of the Peace for Cedros, in southeast Trinidad, in 1871-72. Nevertheless, it was the lower class Creoles and Indians, who were the chief victims of racial discrimination. As well as socioeconomic exploitation (that is, low wages and poor living conditions), attempts were made to deprive the workers and peasants of their "inferior" cultural roots. The practice of obeah, a form of magic that had its origins in Africa, was subject to criminal punishment. This failed to curtail its practice, however, and the Creoles, as well as the Indians, were generally successful in maintaining some of their values and traditions (best reflected in Carnival, which was still potentially subversive at this time). These traditions were important because they were "a source of strength and comfort to people whose material living conditions were usually wretched, just as religion and traditional cultural forms performed the same function for the Indian population" [Brereton 1981: 135].

Social Structure and Underdevelopment

This was the shape of Trinidad's basic social structure from 1845 until the early twentieth century, when oil production became significant. In chapter one I outlined the link between forms of labour control and development and argued that the system of indentureship left Trinidad in a disadvantageous position against the economies of western Europe. This can be demonstrated by looking at the international sugar industry at the time.

Over the period 1840 to 1890, the share of beet production for the world sugar market increased from 4 percent to 60 percent [Sebastien 1979: 480]. The total sugar cane production of all the Caribbean territories together was still less than Germany's quantities of sugar beet output. As Williams points out, "The European beet sugar industry represented the triumph of science and technology. Beet was the great school of scientific agriculture. Where the Caribbean planter remained dependent on the man with the hoe, the beet cultivator introduced deep ploughing . . ." [1964: 154].

Trinidad's sugar economy was the most advanced in the British Caribbean, but its development was "held back" by its comparative lack of technological advance. A contemporary observer commented that "The planters of this island are not very advanced in the science of agriculture, if we measure their skill by the product of their estates . . ." [Sewell 1862: 102]. This was measured at 1 to 1.5 hogsheads of sugar to the acre. At this time, 165 mills were worked with steam, around 100 with cattle, and a few with water power [Sewell 1862: 102]. Planters were reluctant to improve sugar cultivation methods and were content to make profits through cheap labour. This was because there was little incentive to innovate as commodity production was not generalized: that is, the direct producers still had direct access to land (see chapter one).

However, while science could narrow the gap between beet and cane, it could not overcome it. This was because sugar cane had a superior sucrose content. According to the 1897 Royal Commission on the West Indies, the yield per acre in Trinidad was 18 tons, compared with 10.7 tons of beet in France and 12.85 in Germany [Williams 1964: 156]. While superior technology almost overcame these differences (the rate of extraction was 12.5 percent in Germany, compared with only 9.5 percent in Trinidad [Williams 1964: 156]), production costs remained slightly cheaper in Trinidad compared with Germany. The crisis in sugar was actually brought to a head by the European practice of subsidizing beet production (the bounty system) and flooding the European market with cheap sugar. This led to West Indian sugar losing a substantial proportion of the British market, and to the collapse of some of the most backward sugar producers (including those in Tobago, as I shall show).

The use of outdated methods was more common in the rest of the British West Indies, British Guiana apart, than it was in Trinidad. While many of the islands concentrated on producing low grade, muscovado sugar, almost one-third of Trinidad's sugar (in 1891-92) was produced by the more advanced vacuum pan method [Sebastien 1979: 128]. The result was that the crisis affected those manufacturers that employed the most outdated methods. This in turn led to a concentration of capital in the sugar industry. In 1878, there were 130 estates; by 1917, the number had been reduced to just 49, with only 13 owners [Sebastien 1979: 113].

With the crisis of the sugar industry in the 1880s, cocoa emerged as the nation's leading export, and remained so until the 1920s (when the crop was devastated by witchbroom disease). Although production methods were similarly "backward" in this industry, it did not matter so much because there was little foreign competition. Trinidad was in fact one of only three producers (the others were Ecuador and Venezuela) of fine cocoa in the world at this time. However, archaic methods of production meant that decline eventually occurred and Trinidad's proportion of world production was reduced from 14 percent in 1895 to 5 percent by the late 1920s [Sebastien 1979: 506-8].

Tobago

Tobago was also "discovered" in 1498 by Columbus and, like Trinidad, developed very slowly. It was subject to the rivalries of competing powers and control of the island changed hands many times. It was annexed to Britain in 1763, (although it was briefly recaptured by the French in 1781, who controlled the island until the British reestablished control in 1793) and the production of sugar by slave labour was rapidly generalized. Slave rebellions were common, including two particularly bloody revolts in 1771 and 1774 which were brutally suppressed by the British. In the case of the latter, six rebels were burnt to death after their hands had been chopped off [Craton 1982: 156].

Production on the estates was probably the most inefficient in the Caribbean. On his arrival in Tobago in 1807, Governor Young commented on the "distressed condition of the Colony" [Craig 1988: 3]. The situation was aggravated after Emancipation by Britain's free trade policy and a hurricane in 1847, which destroyed twenty-six sugar works and damaged a further thirty-three. The major problem, particularly in the long term, was Trinidad's social structure and the effect that this had on living and working conditions, and on Tobago's international competitiveness.

Tobago's social structure after Emancipation, and particularly from the 1850s, was based on the métayage system, under which the métayer worked on his or her own plot of land, but also worked on the plantation. This represented "a 'halfway house', in which planters could secure labour, and labourers, land, since under the economic and political conditions of the island neither class could fully achieve its goals" [Craig 1988: 7]. The social structure was such that there was little incentive to innovate and planters relied on the system as a provider of cheap labour and profitability. The métayers therefore had a number of grievances, including low wages, the truck system, and debt peonage, and these were the chief factors behind the "Belmanna Riots" on the Roxborough estate in 1876 [Brereton 1984: 113]. It was largely as a result of these riots that "representative government" (representative, that is, of a few planters) was abolished and Crown Colony government introduced the following year.

While Trinidad's sugar industry was backward vis-à-vis European production, Tobago was backward vis-à-vis the rest of the Caribbean. The inefficiency of the system of production was exposed by the virtual collapse of the sugar industry in Tobago in 1884-85. Unlike Trinidad, the sugar produced in Tobago was almost totally the low grade muscovado variety, which European-subsidized beet could easily undersell. The British no longer regarded Tobago as an island with a viable separate economy and polity, and it was united with Trinidad in January 1889. Originally Tobago retained its own separate treasury and financial board, but in October 1898 these last vestiges of independence from Trinidad were removed, and Tobago was declared a "Ward of the Colony of Trinidad and Tobago".

Proletarianization, Resistance Movements, the Oil Industry and the Development of Trade Unionism

Proletarianization

In the period from 1898 to 1938, wage labour became more gener-alized, and some light manufacturing and the petroleum industry developed. This was reinforced by the aforementioned policy (see chapter one) of encouraging Indian settlement within Trinidad, which made independent peasant production more difficult.

It was also in this period that the role of women as independent labourers was further undermined, especially amongst the Creole population. The European concept of the family wage was imported, and where women remained employed, it was usually in a subordinate role to that of men [Reddock 1984a: 274–306]. The percentage of women employed in the labour market declined from 73.9 percent in 1891 to 26.1 percent in 1946 [Reddock 1987: 13]. However, the withdrawal of many women from the formal labour force did not always lead to them working as house-wives, and many continued to work as peasants or petty traders.

Early Resistance Movements

In the late nineteenth century, sections of the coloured middle class began to question the justice of colonial government. They resented the domination of sugar interests, the racial discrimina-tion that held back their life chances, and their lack of political representation. A petition in 1887, containing about 5000 signa-tures, called for elections to the Legislative Council. Demands for representative government continued in the 1890s, but the British response was unsympathetic. In 1898, the Unofficial majority on the Legislative Council was removed by the Colonial Secretary, Joseph Chamberlain, and the following year, the Port of Spain Borough Council was abolished. These measures were regarded as further examples of authoritarian colonial rule, especially so in the case of the latter, because it was the one institution that allowed for some autonomy from the colonial government.

A number of short-lived resistance organizations were formed at this time, partly as a response to such measures, including the Pan-African Association. By 1902, many of its members had defected and had joined the Ratepayers Association, an organization that was designed to safeguard their interests in the absence of the Borough Council. Protest became centred around government plans to cut off water supplies to homes where taps leaked and to introduce a meter system. This issue seemed unlikely to attract working class support, because most workers did not have their own water supply. Nevertheless, it did attract widespread support, possibly because of a threat to communal water supplies, and because workers may have regarded it as an issue of wider significance, indicative of authoritarian colonial government. A mass protest against the government's planned measures, known as the "Water Riot" of 1903, led to police killing sixteen people and wounding many others. In a Colonial Office inquiry into the causes of the riot, it was argued that the matter was simply a dispute between ratepayers and the promoters of the planned Water Bill. However, Chamberlain told Governor Moloney to pay more attention to the wishes of the Unofficials in the Legislative Council, and in 1914, the Borough Council was revived (albeit, once again, on a limited franchise).

Working class opposition was also developing at this time, although this was at a comparatively slower rate. In the late 1890s the Working Men's Reform Club and the Trinidad Working Men's Association (TWA) were founded. Although the former rapidly declined, the latter, formed by Walter Mills in 1897, eventually emerged as an important political force. In its early days, it was basically a friendly society, although it also had a number of policies on political and social matters. Under the leadership of Alfred Richards (1906–14), links were established with the British Labour Party, and in particular two MPs, William Summerbell and Joseph Pointer. However, the weakness of the TWA's (and Pointer's) essentially urban, Creole-centred, approach to politics is shown by its attitude toward indentured labour. The Indian population was basically regarded as passive and uninterested in politics. On a visit to Trinidad, Pointer failed to denounce the harsh conditions faced by the Indians on the estates, and instead stated that "creole labour was paid less than it would be if there were no Indians" [Charles 1978: 5]. In its submission to the Sanderson Commission, the TWA expressed regret that indentureship had not been abolished, not on the grounds of opposition to forced labour, but rather because of who the forced labourers were. The Indian population responded by forming their own organizations, such as the East Indian National

Association, which refused to work with the TWA as it believed that "opposition to indentured immigration was actually opposition to their presence per se" [Charles 1978: 5].

Sporadic resistance continued up to 1914 but trade unions, regarded as "criminal conspiracies" under common law, did not yet exist. The colonial authorities had not yet considered the introduction of widespread labour legislation, and they would only be forced to do so by the events of 1919.

The Post-1918 Labour Revolt and its Aftermath

Indentureship was abolished in 1917, after the First World War, while the oil industry continued to benefit from an increase in the demand for its product. The abolition of the indentured labour system was largely a result of pressure within India, particularly from G.K. Gokhale's Indian National Congress, rather than opposition from the indentured labourers themselves. The development of the oil industry was particularly marked in the war years, although its labour force only became a significant actor in the rebellion of the 1930s. Nevertheless, its development was important because although the majority of its labour force was Creole, there was (and still is) a significant Indian minority, far larger than is generally assumed [Ramsaran 1989: 55-56]. Although this desegregation of the labour force did not alleviate mutual suspicions, it did manage to break down some barriers and there were a number of strikes in the oilfields as early as 1917.

Of most immediate importance, however, was the impact of the First World War. This was fought by Britain on the alleged basis of a war for democracy against tyranny, and this rallying cry had an impact in the British West Indies. The British West Indies Regiment was formed to "join the fight for democracy", but these soldiers instead suffered racial discrimination (for example, through lower wage rates and racial abuse by officers), and so they began to question the legitimacy of British rule. In Italy in 1918, the Caribbean League was formed by some of these soldiers, and plans were made to improve the grievances of West Indians at home. Feelings of injustice were increased by news of racist attacks on blacks, including West Indian sailors, at Liverpool and Cardiff. On their return to the West Indies, the soldiers and sailors recounted their experiences, and this in turn influenced the growing consciousness of the working classes, particularly among the Creole sectors. This was reinforced by the importation of black nationalist literature (despite official hostility), especially the Garveyite movement's (officially banned) *Negro World*.

It was clear, then, that employers and the government faced a different situation to that existing prior to 1914, when resistance was spontaneous and individualized. However, they did not at first appreciate this change and in 1918 the Habitual Idlers' Ordinance was passed. This particularly repressive piece of legislation stated that any male worker lacking means of subsistence should be made to work; if he failed to do so he could be confined to a government run agricultural settlement to be taught the "habits of industry" and then handed over to private industry where he would be paid a low wage. The bill eventually became law in 1920, after some doubts by the Colonial Office, but it was never effectively implemented and the "agricultural settlements" were not constructed. The legislation was of more immediate significance because of the ill feeling that it bred. Workers regarded it as a replacement for indentureship and a means of maintaining low wages. By the end of 1919, the cost of living had increased by 148 percent since 1914, while wages had increased by 36 percent for men and 28 percent for women [Basdeo 1983: 26].

It was against this background that the labour unrest of 1919 took place. The first major strike in May 1919, involved asphalt workers, who employed the services of a rejuvenated TWA to demand a wage increase, a reduced working day, and better overtime rates. In November 1919 the waterfront workers struck for higher wages and better working conditions. The strike actually reflected wider issues such as repressive management, the lack of any institutional bargaining mechanisms, and the heightened consciousness of the developing working class [Rennie 1974: 25]. Strike breakers were used to ensure minimum operations, but on 1 December the strikers chased them off the waterfront, and then proceeded to march to Port of Spain. This led to an increase in strike activity, as workers in other sectors, including sugar, oil, construction and council employees, made similar demands to those of the dockers. Two days later a compromise was reached and the dockers were awarded a 25 percent wage increase. This agreement did not lead to moderation on the part of the workers and instead encouraged others to strike for higher wages. Riots also continued, most notably in Tobago, where an attack on a government wireless station was suppressed by troops from HMS *Calcutta*. The events of 1919 were the first time that Creole and

Indian had cooperated on any significant scale: the 1919 strikes "seem to indicate that there was a growing class consciousness after the war and this transcended racial feelings at times" [Samaroo 1972: 218].

The significance of the events of 1919 cannot be underestimated and were in many ways the forerunner of 1937 and 1970 [Samaroo 1987: 21; Elkins 1969: 75]. Their importance was not lost on the employers at the time, but rather than respond with widespread reform, as in Jamaica and British Guiana, where limited trade union laws were passed in 1919 and 1921 respectively, the government introduced new repressive measures. A number of arrests and/or deportations were made, including TWA leaders active in the strikes. The Dispute Settlement and the Industrial Court Ordinances passed in 1920 together had the effect of prohibiting strikes and making arbitration compulsory. The dilatory attitude towards labour reform at this time is demonstrated by the fact that the proposed Industrial Court was never actually set up and so the law remained a dead letter. A Sedition Ordinance, also passed in 1920, made provisions for strong penalties for seditious libel and the circulation of seditious publications.

Some reforms were made, however, including the Truck Ordinance 1919 which required, with some exceptions, that wages be paid in money, and the Labour Bureau Ordinance, which attempted to improve recruitment practices through the provision of information to employers. In 1921, the Wood Commission of Inquiry was set up to investigate the social and political climate in Trinidad and Tobago and, after extensive consultation with a number of informants, including the TWA, made its recommendations the following year. As a result of this report, it was decided that the first ever elections to the Legislative Council would be held in 1925, albeit with a very limited franchise.

The TWA and Colonial Labour Policy in 1920–1931

The events of 1919 showed that there was still not a consistent labour policy on the part of the British government. The haphazard reforms which followed were clearly inadequate, and pressure for more far-reaching reforms was made by various institutions, including the British Labour Party and the TUC, and the newly established International Labour Organization. In 1920, the Labour Party set up a Colonial Affairs Committee, followed two years later by a Labour Committee, whose task was to examine colonial labour problems. Links were reestablished between the TWA and the Labour Party in 1921 when the former sent J. Howard Bishop to London to discuss social and economic questions.

Within Trinidad and Tobago, the TWA reached new heights of popularity and, despite a limited franchise, returned three deputies to the Legislative Council in the 1925 elections. One of these was A.A. "Captain" Cipriani, who had fought in the war, and on his return had emerged as the champion of the labouring masses (colloquially known as the "bare-footed man"). He was chosen as leader of the TWA in the hope that a "neutral, white man" could unite the Creole and Indian working classes. His success in this regard was limited, and the TWA remained a primarily Creole supported movement. Support for Indian petty bourgeois organizations such as the East Indian National Association remained strong among (largely male) East Indian workers and peasants.

Nevertheless, under Cipriani's leadership the TWA became a popular organization and campaigned on a wide variety of issues, including the abolition of child labour (an Ordinance was passed to this effect in 1925), the need for trade union legislation, and the introduction of an eight-hour working day. Cipriani was not a radical however; his campaigns were not fought through popular demonstrations or strikes, but were instead limited to pleas to the Colonial Office and debates in the Legislative Council. Furthermore, he placed great faith in the ability and will of the Labour Party to carry out reform in the colonies. In 1925, Cipriani visited England and met with Sir Samuel Wilson, Permanent Under Secretary at the Colonial Office, and attended the Labour Commonwealth Conference. The following year, the Labour MP Frederick Roberts visited Trinidad and British Guiana. Cipriani joined him in British Guiana, where they attended the Conference of the British Guiana Labour Union.

These links reinforced Cipriani's commitment to the belief that a Labour government would introduce labour reform in Trinidad and Tobago. He therefore placed much faith in the imminence of change when the second Labour government was elected in 1929. A Royal Commission on West Indian sugar was set up and chaired by the Caribbean specialist Lord Olivier, and recommended continued imperial preference for Empire sugar and some loans to producers. These measures were carried out but it was trade union legislation that most concerned Cipriani. In 1930, the

Colonial Secretary Lord Passfield chaired a Colonial Conference which discussed the need for labour legislation in the colonies. Two months after the conference (in September), the "Passfield Memorandum" was issued, which requested of the colonies that workers' compensation and trade union legislation be introduced as soon as possible.

However, in Labour's period in office (1929-31), no significant labour reforms were carried out in Trinidad and Tobago. The basic excuse used by the Trinidad government was that economic depression (see below) made labour reform impossible. For instance, in response to the request that Masters and Servants Ordinances be repealed, the Trinidad government said that this would be done "when a suitable opportunity presents itself" [Basdeo 1983: 92]. The Labour government in Britain appeared to accept this explanation. There was widespread disappointment with the performance of the Labour government in office, and by implication (because of his heavy reliance on the Labour Party), with Cipriani himself. This disillusionment was to increase in the period of unrest in the 1930s.

The 1930s: From Labour Rebellion to Trade Unionism

The labour rebellions in the 1930s were of great significance because they paved the way for the emergence of an organized labour movement in the Caribbean. Their importance is in fact deeper than this because the riots also led to the adoption of universal suffrage, which operated first in Jamaica in 1944, and in Trinidad two years later. The rebellion also expressed, albeit in an incomplete way, growing (and, more importantly, organized) anti-colonial feeling in the region. In this section, I examine the background, the main events and leading figures, and the consequences of the disturbances in Trinidad and Tobago.

Economic and Political Background

Trinidad and Tobago's economy was still comparatively underdeveloped in the 1930s. Although "free" wage labour was more widespread than it was under indentureship, it was now difficult to industrialize in the same way that Britain had because the "rules of the game" had changed. Underdeveloped countries had to rely on the import of machinery from, and more profitable opportunities in the "advanced" countries. As a result, despite the increased existence of free wage labour, Trinidad and Tobago's economy remained particularly vulnerable to changes at the international level such as those which occurred in the depression of the 1930s.

Sugar recovered from the crisis of the 1880s, and the industry enjoyed a boom period both during and immediately after the First World War. Although prices fell in the early 1920s, production steadily grew and sugar once again became the major export. However, this was at the cost of large state subsidies and low wages paid to agricultural workers. The sugar cane farmers were particularly vulnerable to "market forces", as the sugar companies often prohibited them from selling alternative crops. The economic recession of the 1930s significantly worsened the situation as world demand for sugar contracted and as a result, wages declined, peasants could not sell their crop, and unemployment increased. By the mid 1930s, the dispossessed organized hunger marches to the capital, protesting against bad working conditions, poor wages (in the case of those who had work) and squalid living conditions.

Cocoa's boom period ended in the 1920s as increased production elsewhere, and the decline in importance of fine cocoa, led to a collapse in the world market price for Trinidad's produce. Problems were reinforced by the spread of witch broom disease in the late 1920s, so that by the recession of the 1930s, it was only low wages and subsidies to planters (such as the Agricultural Relief Ordinance 1921) that kept production going.

Even more critical, however, was the development of the oil industry. The existence of oil in the south of Trinidad was well known, but it was only with the development of the internal combustion engine that ongoing attempts were made to develop it. This was reinforced by the conversion of British ships to oil power (from the first decade of the twentieth century), which led to British investment of capital in the sector. Higher wages, unemployment, the importation of labour and the problems in the sugar and cocoa sectors meant that a labour force for the industry was guaranteed. By 1913, there were two major oil companies, United British Oilfields of Trinidad, a subsidiary of Shell, and Trinidad Leaseholds Limited. The industry enjoyed a sustained boom period during and after the First World War, and, except for a brief recession in the early 1930s, it largely escaped the problems that beset sugar and cocoa at this time.

Nevertheless, there were a number of long-term grievances, including debates about foreign ownership, and the small amount of taxation incurred by the industry. The workers also suffered racial discrimination, low wages (these were higher than in other sectors, but low in comparison to productivity levels), poor working conditions and the infamous "Red Book". Under this system, any worker wishing to change her or his job had to show a book describing her or his employment record to any prospective employer. However, it was not the grievances per se that were of most significance, but the changing context in which they operated. The development of the industry had entailed the creation of a highly concentrated and potentially powerful labour force which numbered about 14 000 people.

The changing economic, political and social circumstances also aided the demise of Cipriani's leadership over the Creole working class. Constitutional methods and reliance on the Labour Party were insufficient in the context of depressed living standards. This had been demonstrated as early as 1927 when he introduced the Workers' Compensation Bill, which planned to compensate labourers injured at the workplace. This was passed but it applied only to a small number of workers, and not to domestic servants or field labourers. Cipriani's position was further undermined by the aforementioned disappointments of the second Labour government, and by his failure to support the liberalization of laws on divorce, which divided the TWA and led to the mobilization of prominent women against him. (Of these, Audrey Jeffers, the first woman to be elected to the City Council, was the most famous.) Finally, Cipriani failed to give unequivocal support to hunger marchers from Caroni in 1935.

There was one further piece of legislation which simultaneously hastened Cipriani's decline and demonstrated the necessity for extra-parliamentary activity: this was the Trade Union Ordinance of 1932. The passing of this piece of legislation was a response to the Passfield Memorandum, but it did in fact constitute a reform of limited value. Although trade unions were now accorded legal status, the Ordinance did not include provisions for peaceful picketing or immunity from civil actions by employers for restraint of trade (which effectively deprived trade unions of the right to strike). The Ordinance also called for the compulsory registration of trade unions, and the strict audit of funds (which could not be used for political purposes, for example). After two years of discussion with the British TUC, Cipriani decided not to register the

TWA as a trade union and instead re-formed it as a political party under the new name of the Trinidad Labour Party (TLP).

Labour Unrest and the Rise of New Leaders

With the decline in Cipriani's leadership of the Creole working classes, new organizations and leaders emerged to fill the void. These included the Marxist and protofeminist Negro Welfare Cultural and Social Association (NWA), which was founded in 1934 and led by Elma François, Jim Barrette and Christina King. The NWA was very effective in mobilizing the urban Creole working classes in protest against the Italian invasion of Ethiopia in October 1935, and in particular against Britain's conciliatory approach to Mussolini. This issue was instrumental in raising the consciousness of blacks in the world, and it played a significant part in increasing tension in the West Indies. A contemporary observer noted that "West Indians felt that in that issue the British government betrayed a nation because it was black, and this has tended to destroy their faith in white government, and to make them more willing to take their fate into their own hands" [Lewis 1977: 19].

The NWA was, however, largely confined to Port of Spain, and the real "centre of gravity" had shifted to the oilfields and the sugar belt in south and central Trinidad. This was clearly demonstrated by the strike at the Apex Oilfield in March 1935. Although the strikers settled for a small wage increase, its real importance was the emergence of Tubal Uriah Butler as a working class leader. During the strike Butler led a march to Port of Spain which was intercepted by Cipriani, who was mayor at the time. Cipriani promised to take up the strikers' grievances, but once again his constitutional methods were a failure. It was this lack of action that led to a final rupture between the radicalizing working class and the conservative Cipriani.

Butler was among those who had previously sympathized with Cipriani (he was a member of the TLP) but in August 1936 he formed the British Empire Workers' and Citizens' Home Rule Party. The name of the party reflected Butler's belief in the legitimacy of the Empire, despite frequent outbursts condemning it. His attitude to the Empire was expressed at the Party's foundation when he stated that "We are British . . . I am proud to be British" [Rennie 1974: 79]. In an open letter dated 10 June 1937, Butler wrote that "[w]e who have sworn to lead you on to victory or die in the attempt, order you to prepare if necessary to shed your loyal Black British Blood so that Black British Trinidad might enjoy the principles of British freedom and Justice on equal terms with all others in our Trinidad" [Oilfields Workers' Trade Union n.d.]. As well as a conciliatory approach to the Empire and a naive view of British justice, Butler's party lacked a consistent political approach and was poorly organized.

Nevertheless, Butler remains one of the most significant figures in the labour history of Trinidad and Tobago. His importance lies in his role as a "catalyst", whose historical role was "to crystallize and articulate the grievances that people had long nursed, and to offer them an 'acceptable' outlet for aggressive dispositions which Cipriani had held in check" [Ryan 1974: 56]. His emergence as a labour leader reflected the consciousness of the working class in the 1930s. He was a physically disabled oil worker who had left his native island of Grenada in search of work in Trinidad. Unlike Cipriani then, he was a "man of the people", sharing a similar underprivileged background and similar economic and social grievances. He therefore found a willing audience among workers and peasants of both African and Indian origin, playing the role of "an agitator, with the gift and energy for prolific emotional word spouting, that sometimes meant very little when analysed but . . . nevertheless, at that time, touched the depths of working class feelings which proved to be enough" [Rennie 1974: 64]. Butler was also unique in Trinidadian labour history in that he managed to achieve a significant degree of unity between Creoles and East Indians.

In Tobago, on the other hand, the TLP remained dominant among the more radical sections of society. There was not yet a sector in which a concentrated working class existed. The TLP enjoyed a strong base in the more populous Leeward district where there were some wage labourers, but they did not generally share the more radical politics of the strategic sectors of Trinidad's economy.

The Events of 1937 and their Aftermath

The general climate of Butler-inspired unrest continued and hunger marches and strikes persisted, and police leaders in the south of Trinidad were keen "to deal with him as an undesirable person" [Oilfields Workers' Trade Union n.d.]. In June and July of 1937, the unrest reached a climax. The rebellion started with a sit-down strike at the Forest Reserve Oilfield on 19 June, which turned into a bloody riot after the police attempted to arrest Butler. He was forced into hiding, but the absence of the workers' main agitator did not stop the momentum of the strike. The following day, workers in other oilfields joined the strike, and by 21 June, it had spread to other sectors, including sugar. Within a week, most of the economy in Trinidad (but not Tobago) was at a standstill.

In Butler's absence, leadership had passed to his assistant, the East Indian, Adrian Cola Rienzi. He realized that the spontaneous nature of the rebellion meant that it would only last for a short while, a view reinforced by the arrival of HMS *Ajax* and HMS *Exeter* three days after the start of the strike. This view was confirmed and by 6 July, the rebellion was over.

In the meantime, Rienzi set about winning concessions from the relatively liberal governor, Murchison Fletcher. A Mediation Committee was set up to investigate the causes of the rebellion, but this was suspended (through employer pressure) pending the arrival of a Commission of Inquiry from London. This inquiry, chaired by John Forster, made no specific recommendations concerning wages and working conditions, but did advise the establishment of the machinery for collective bargaining, and of Labour Departments to assist in this process and withhold recognition in "unsatisfactory" circumstances [Forster Commission 1938: 81, 86-87].

This recommendation had already been forced on the Colonial Office and the more sympathetic Trinidad and Tobago government and by the end of 1937 several trade unions had obtained government recognition. These included the Oilfields Workers' Trade Union (OWTU), the All-Trinidad Sugar Estates and Factory Workers' Trade Union (ATSEFWTU), the Federated Workers' Trade Union (FWTU), the Amalgamated Building and Wood Workers' Union (ABWWU), the Public Workers' Trade Union (PWTU), and the Seamen and Waterfront Workers Trade Union (SWWTU). In 1938, on the advice of the British TUC General Secretary, Walter Citrine, the Trinidad and Tobago Trades Union Council (TUCo) was founded. The Trade Disputes (Arbitration and Inquiry) Ordinance 1938 laid down the conditions for a tripartite system of collective bargaining, although peaceful picketing and immunity from civil actions were not introduced until 1943, when the Trade Disputes and Protection of Property Ordinance was passed.

The unions still faced many problems such as the continuation of low wages and poor working conditions, high unemployment, and employer recognition, so the context in which collective bargaining was to operate was automatically unfavourable towards the working class. There was also the problem of the diffuse nature of the working classes, as capitalist development was very uneven. In the oil industry, where there was a large concentration of workers, union membership was high. In sugar, on the other hand, where a high proportion of production was still carried out by cane farmers, union membership was low. These problems were to be reinforced in later years as rival unions competed for the right to represent workers. Any prospective labour party that would arise out of the trade union movement would also have to deal with the question of uniting a labour force divided by race and gender.

Notwithstanding these difficulties, the development of trade unions was an important step forward for the working class. A further stride was taken when the Moyne Commission recommended universal suffrage for the English-speaking Caribbean in response to the labour rebellions that took place throughout the West Indies in the 1930s [West India Royal Commission Report 1945: 379-80]. In the postwar period, the British government played a more active role in the colonies, including in the field of labour relations, as they prepared for gradual "constitutional decolonization" [Munroe 1983]. Trinidad's postwar labour history will be discussed in chapter three.

Summary and Conclusion

The labour history of Trinidad and Tobago cannot be described as one notable for the "liberty" or the "well being of its inhabitants". British colonial rule in Trinidad and Tobago was actually quite mild compared to Ireland, India and parts of Africa, but it still had the classic hallmarks: repression, racism, exploitation and uneven development, and neglect when economic and political interests turned to other parts of the world. Intellectuals therefore had to invent justifications for colonialism, and it was on this basis that (judging by the view cited at the start of this chapter) still powerful falsehoods emerged. The actual history was one in which economic growth benefited a tiny minority and social and political factors, including labour relations, were largely neglected.

At the risk of over-simplification, the history of Trinidad and Tobago from 1776 to 1937 can be divided into five major periods.

(i) 1776–1838
In this period, slavery became the dominant form of production, and Britain established its rule in both Trinidad and Tobago. Sugar became the major crop in both islands. Slavery was abolished in 1834, although this was followed by a four-year "apprenticeship period".

(ii) 1838–1865
The period following Emancipation saw a struggle in both islands between the planters and the newly freed slaves. In Tobago, a compromise was reached and former slaves won access to land and the métayage system became the dominant form of production. In Trinidad, planters used the state apparatus and legislation to secure new supplies of labour, in particular from India. Although these labourers were paid a wage, they were still not really free because they were subject to a number of restrictions, including a pass system which limited freedom of movement. It was in this period that race and ethnicity became powerful political factors as the major "racial" groups became divided, both as producers and in the wider social sphere.

(iii) 1866–1889
New peasant classes emerged after 1866, as it became easier to purchase land. The production of both cocoa and, from the 1880s, sugar, was carried out by many "independent" farmers. This can be regarded as a partial victory for the lower classes (at least in the case of cocoa) as they successfully resisted direct subordination to the employer (or his or her agents) at the workplace, but they were still indirectly controlled by capital because of the latter's stronger market position; indeed, in the case of sugar, planters actually led the way in encouraging the growth of small farmers. Planters benefited from these arrangements by paying low prices for peasant produce, a process facilitated by their control of the later, more lucrative, stages of production. It also meant that planters could pay low wages to those casual labourers who worked directly for them.

In this period a growing sexual division of labour emerged, in which women were forced into the home or into certain occupations such as domestic service that were considered to be consistent with their "domestic role". This process was intensified during the period of proletarianization from the 1890s.

The other major event of this period was the union of Trinidad and Tobago in 1889. This was forced on Tobago as the island was practically bankrupt, due to the crisis in West Indian sugar from 1884. The métayage system was too inefficient to effectively compete with the technologically superior methods of production employed in Europe.

(iv) 1890–1918

In Trinidad, this period saw a wider, but still highly uneven, process of proletarianization, and the beginnings of organized resistance to the worst excesses of colonial rule. A number of middle class organizations developed, such as the Ratepayers' Association and the East Indian National Association, but there were also organizations that attracted some working class support, of which the Trinidad Working Men's Association was most important. In Tobago, on the other hand, there was still little organized resistance and in this period the peasantry flourished.

(v) 1919–1937

Resistance reached higher levels in Trinidad, as workers became concentrated in certain sectors, particularly in oil and at the waterfront. Labour unrest and widespread strikes, especially in 1937, forced the colonial government to make some concessions to labour. As Lewis observed at the time, ". . . the general strike and the riot have been the worker's only weapon for calling attention to his conditions" [Lewis 1977: 19].

The events of 1937 are important because they (albeit momentarily) united the working classes across the lines of gender, race and politics. Despite the long-term process of "domestication", women played a key role in the rebellion, in both the Butlerite movement and the NWA. Butler was also successful in uniting both major ethnic groups behind his political programme. This unity was to prove short-lived, however.

In terms of the development of the labour force in Trinidad (less so in Tobago), the period 1797-1937 saw a transition from forced labour regimes to the development of a proletariat. Given the uneven character of this process (see chapter one for an explanation of such unevenness), class formation was extremely complex and diverse. The working classes were made up of the proletariat (both urban and rural), the peasantry (which was itself highly stratified), "informal" petty traders and producers (again present in both town and countryside), the unemployed and lumpen elements such as vagrants (more common at this time in rural areas). These divisions were further reinforced by racial and sexual divisions of labour and ideologies of racism and sexism, which were not simply products of colonialism or capitalism. Women were increasingly assigned domestic and related tasks, especially (but far from exclusively) among the Indian population, which left them in a subordinate position, both in the developing labour market and in society more generally. Indians arrived in Trinidad as indentured labourers and were initially the poorest ethnic group among the working classes. An Indian petty bourgeoisie emerged in the 1870s and 1880s, but the majority of Indians remained part of the working classes. These differences shaped the politics of the emerging labour movement in the period after 1937.

3

Labour Parties
and Trade Unions
in the
Independence Period

The period 1939-65 saw a number of political conflicts among workers and (to a lesser extent) the peasantry, which were expressed through political parties and different conceptions of trade unionism. No single political party managed to establish hegemony over a working class divided by ideological and ethnic boundaries. These divisions enabled a party dominated by the black middle class, the People's National Movement (PNM), to establish its leadership of the black majority and pave the way for independence in 1962.

This chapter documents and analyses the processes whereby the nascent "labour movement" lost the initiative it had established in 1937 to an organization led by the black middle class. This question is considered in four sections: first, I briefly return to a discussion of the relationship between trade unions and politics (see also chapter one), concentrating on Third World societies in the era of decolonization. I argue in this section that it is essential to grasp the political role of labour in order to understand events in Trinidad and Tobago (and elsewhere) before and after independence. This leads on to the second part which describes the political conflicts among trade unions and political parties from 1939 to 1956. The third section covers the period from the first election victory of the PNM (1956) to independence in 1962. Finally, I examine the conflicts between the PNM and a militant section of the trade union movement after independence.

Trade Unions and Politics in the Independence Period – A Critical Analysis of the "Berg–Butler" Thesis

Before documenting the "politics of labour" in Trinidad and Tobago from 1939 to 1965, I will first return briefly to a discussion of the relationship between trade unions and politics, this time confining the argument to colonies in the period immediately before and after independence. More specifically, I will discuss the work of Elliot Berg and Jeffrey Butler. In an influential article on trade unions in Africa, they ask three questions concerning the relationship between trade unions and politics in the independence period. First, what were the structural relations between trade unions and political parties? Secondly, what political activities did trade unions engage in, and how successful were they? And thirdly, how significant were unions after independence? [Berg and Butler 1964: 341]. They argue that "[i]n the period before independence, African trade unions were rarely the instrument of political parties. To the extent that they entered the political arena their role was usually negligible. After independence they were quickly subdued by governing parties . . ." [1964: 341].

Their basic argument, then, is that trade unions in Africa generally limited themselves to industrial, rather than political demands. Although their analysis is confined to Africa, Berg and Butler's thesis could equally "fit" the case of Trinidad and Tobago. The trade union movement failed to establish a political party that led the movement for independence, and it failed to win substantial concessions from the PNM for labour representation during, and after, 1956. If one takes Berg and Butler's arguments as a starting point, then one can easily conclude that trade unions were irrelevant to the political struggle for independence.

There are, however, valid reasons for rejecting the thesis as a starting point, because it is based on certain untenable assumptions. I argued in chapter one that the separation of the industrial and political spheres is purely arbitrary; as Alan Fox has stated, "[i]ssues have no intrinsic quality which lead us to put some in one category and some in the other. The difference simply lies in the methods by which we try to provide for their resolution" [1985: 162].

This arbitrary separation leads to two basic weaknesses in the argument. First, Berg and Butler show an "almost obsessive concern with trade union/nationalist party relationships . . ." [Sandbrook and Cohen 1975: 18]; a separation of a nationalist political party and a trade union does not necessarily imply that the latter is apolitical in nature. In the case of Africa "[m]any unionists were . . . conscious of the need to preserve a power base independent of the nationalist party even where they were in accord with common anti-colonialist objectives" [Cohen 1974: 243-44]. Secondly, strikes "have frequently had both an immediate and long term political impact unintended by the strikers" [C.H. Allen 1975: 118]. In the African case this has, for example, led to government changes in economic policy and undermined the security of governments.

Berg and Butler's attempts to marginalize the political role of labour in the independence period is therefore not a very useful starting point. Rather than assume that trade unions did not play a political role in this period, it is more fruitful to analyse the conflicting political tendencies among would-be representatives of the working class and peasantry. The basic idea of the Berg-Butler thesis, the rejection of political unionism and trade union confinement to industrial demands, can then be analysed as one particular political project among others. In the section below, I show that such thinking was behind the British TUC's policies for developing "responsible" trade unions in the colonies.

Trade Union and Party Conflicts, 1939–1956

In this section, I document the divisions in trade unions and political parties up to the first election victory of the PNM. The history of the trade unions and labour parties is analysed in three parts, in chronological order.

The Impact of the 1937 Rebellion and the Second World War

I showed in the last chapter that trade union organization accelerated after 1937, and that the Colonial Office began to take a
more active interest in the labour affairs of the colonies. The new
unions still faced the problem of small membership, as well as
the problem of organizing in what was still a predominantly rural
society. There was also the problem of what political direction the
unions would take. Would they, for instance, simply organize as
defensive institutions at the workplace, and rely on the Colonial
Office to introduce reforms culminating in a gradual process of
constitutional decolonization? Or would they organize outside of
the workplace, through a political party, in order to promote
their demands? And would the racial unity that had begun to
develop during the July events continue, or would the old divisions re-emerge? These basic questions of trade union strategy
were to dominate the nascent labour movement after 1937.

   Contrary to the intentions of the Colonial Office, the formation
of trade unions did not initially lead to a moderation of the
demands made by labour. This was reflected in struggles for
employer recognition of unions and for higher wages. The
Colonial Office therefore adopted, in addition to its reformist
approach, a strategy of repression. A number of labour leaders
were tried for sedition, including Butler, and NWA leaders Elma
François and Jim Barrette. Although François was found not
guilty, Barrette and Butler were both sentenced to imprisonment.
Butler successfully appealed to the Privy Council, but by the time
this appeal had been upheld, he had already been released after
serving twenty-one months of his prison sentence.

   On his release, he was welcomed by the Oilfields Workers' Trade
Union, but relations quickly turned sour, and he was expelled in
August 1939. Butler formed a rival union, the British Empire
Workers', Peasants' and Ratepayers' Union and resumed his strategy of widespread protest, which rejected the separation of "political" and "industrial" demands. As was shown in the previous
chapter, the colonial authorities in Trinidad were particularly
concerned about Butler because his agitation had brought the oil
and sugar workers together, and these two sectors were the most
important (in terms of foreign exchange earnings and employment) in the economy [Forster Commission 1938: 12]. Almost

immediately after his release, Butler was put under police surveillance, and there was a general feeling in official circles (in both Port of Spain and London) that, with war approaching, Butler's agitation must be curtailed. The Colonial Office in London regarded it as especially important to curb unrest in Trinidad because it was one of the largest suppliers of refined oil in the empire in the 1930s (and this supply became even more significant during the war years). In November 1939, Butler was detained for an "indefinite period", which in practice meant that he was imprisoned for the duration of the war. The Colonial Office was also concerned about the activities of other labour leaders, including Adrian Cola Rienzi, but differences were settled in July 1940 when the Trades Union Council (of which Rienzi was President) passed a resolution supporting the defeat of fascism.

During the war years, the economy recovered from the recession of the 1930s. The most important reason for this was the signing of the leasing agreement in March 1941 under which the British government gave land and military bases to the United States in return for a number of old US warships. Construction work at Chaguaramas, the site of the main military base, led to the employment of a large number of workers – at one stage, 28 000 men [Cross 1988: 294]. Labour was imported from Barbados, but the main source was indigenous labour attracted by relatively high wage rates. The oil industry also boomed in the war years and by 1943 it employed 15 000 workers and was responsible for 80 percent of Trinidad's exports [Brereton 1981: 211]. People abandoned traditional agricultural exports and as a result output declined in these sectors during the war years.

Despite the increased concentration of the workforce, labour made little advance in the war years. Labour parties were formed, but their development was hindered by personal and political rivalries and "ready made alternative symbols to those of class . . ." [Cross 1988: 296], factors that retained and indeed increased their significance after the war when universal suffrage operated, and industrial unrest revived. The most important of these "alternative symbols" was ethnicity. My analysis in chapter two showed how tensions emerged between African and Indian during the indentureship period as the former were given supervisory positions on the sugar estates and blamed the latter for effective wage decreases. The Indians similarly distrusted the Africans and generally regarded them as inferior. The events in 1937 were the first time that real ethnic unity had been achieved (with the possible exception of 1919 – see chapter two), but the long-term mutual suspicions quickly returned as the labour struggle began to wither. This process was reinforced when a major symbol of ethnic unity in 1937, Adrian Cola Rienzi, resigned from the trade union movement in 1943, and accepted a government post the following year.

Political rivalry for the labour vote after 1937 also became apparent in this period. In 1942 the West Indian National Party (WINP) was formed, and included David Pitt, Patrick Solomon and Roy Joseph among its leading members. Despite the party's pro-labour programme, it failed to attract the support of unions beyond the Federated Workers' Trades Union (FWTU). The Trades Union Council (TUCo) was already divided and it had formed its own party, the Socialist Party of Trinidad and Tobago, in 1941. However, the support of the WINP was largely confined to the north (with the partial exception of Pitt who won some support in San Fernando), while the Socialist Party dominated in the south, and there was no attempt to overcome these geographical divisions.

Labour and Politics, 1946–1950

In 1946, the first elections based on universal suffrage were held. As well as many independent candidates, there were five major parties, four of which claimed to represent labour. These were:

(i)   The United Front, led by Jack Kelshall, which included the West Indian National Party, the Indian National Council and the Negro Welfare Association (NWCSA) among its supporters;

(ii)   the Trades Union Council and the Socialist Party of Trinidad and Tobago, led by John Rojas, whose main support came from the OWTU, the Seamen's Union and, contrary to its position in the war, the FWTU;

(iii)   the Trinidad Labour Party which, after Cipriani's death in 1945, was led by Gerald Wight; and

(iv)   Butler's British Empire, Workers', Citizens' and Home Rule Party (Butler was released at the end of the war).

In the elections, political parties won eight of the nine seats, but the labour vote was fragmented: the United Front won three seats, the Butlerites three, and the Socialist Party two. The leaders of these three parties were all defeated by rival labour candidates. The divisions between the parties, and the dominant personalities enabled middle class politicians to dominate successive governments after 1946.

These differences were reinforced by the appointment of four of the elected members (Gomes, Joseph, Abidh, Roodal) to the Executive Council, in which they usually gave support to the governor. This was best exemplified by the debate on constitutional reform. In spite of the introduction of universal suffrage, the Legislative Council still had a majority of non-elected members. A Constitutional Reform Committee set up in 1947 outlined its Majority Report the following year and, despite recommending an elected majority in both the Executive and Legislative Councils, fell short of recommending responsible self-government. Some members resigned from the Committee, including Patrick Solomon who published a minority report recommending self-government. However, the Majority Report was accepted by the Colonial Office, with some modifications, and it formed the basis for the 1950 elections. Among the leading advocates of the report was Albert Gomes, who two years previously had strongly advocated self-government.

The continued problem of ethnic differences was also highlighted by a second Minority Report, drafted by the one successful independent candidate in the 1946 election, Ranjit Kumar. His report was similar to Solomon's, but Kumar's differed in that it did not support immediate responsible government. He argued that Trinidad was not an economically viable institution independent of Britain, and he expressed fears for the Indian minority if independence was achieved: "In Trinidad we have a minority problem, and it is the duty of the majority to gain the confidence of the minorities by showing them that in any proposal for self-government, the minorities would have equal rights. I am afraid that in this colony, the majority community has not yet done that" [Ryan 1974: 82].

Meanwhile, industrial unrest had returned after the interval in the war years. The major strike of this period took place in December 1946 over the oilfield employers' recognition of Butler's union. Although Butler's call for a strike led to an initially strong response, the strikers quickly drifted back to work. This strike showed the ideological differences in the trade union movement between Butler's conception of trade unions as a political instrument and the more conciliatory approach of other leaders. For instance, OWTU leader John Rojas consistently expressed his support for socialism and the Soviet Union at this time, but this was mere rhetoric and he was unwilling to support calls for strike action by oil workers. In this particular oilfield strike he actually cooperated with the employers and supplied them with labour during the strike.

Unrest persisted among Butler supporters until 1948 (when Butler went to England where he hoped to win an audience for his demand for home rule), but the trade unions as a whole remained weak. In 1948 there were as many as twenty-seven trade unions with a total membership of only 20 000 [Trinidad and Tobago 1950: 8], while the total population in 1946 was 557 970 [West Indian Census 1946: vii].

Ideological differences were reinforced by the segregation of the international trade union movement in 1949, caused by the cold war. According to the British TUC's adviser in Trinidad, Western trade unions (with some exceptions) left the World Federation of Trade Unions because of the Soviet bloc's attempts "to turn the WFTU into an instrument of the Cominform – the organ of Soviet Communist policy" [Dalley 1954: 5]. After 1949, on the one side there was still the pro-Communist World Federation of Trade Unions (WFTU); on the other was the new, pro-West International Confederation of Free Trade Unions (ICFTU). Within Trinidad, the Trades Union Council refused to adopt the British Trades Union Congress' advice to leave the WFTU and join the ICFTU. However, six trade unions, led by C.P. Alexander's Seamen's Union, split from the TUCo and formed the Trinidad and Tobago Federation of Trade Unions, which became an ICFTU affiliate in 1951 [OWTU 1986b: 16].

Attempts were also made to form a Pan-Caribbean trade union movement and in 1945 the Caribbean Labour Congress (CLC) was founded, which included the Trinidad and Tobago Trades Union Council among its affiliates. The CLC in turn affiliated to the World Federation of Trade Unions, and organized on the basis of a belief in an independent West Indies Federation and the need for a corresponding labour organization [Caribbean Labour Congress 1945a: 15]. However, efforts to develop the CLC as an influential political force were hindered by internal divisions over questions like anti-colonial attitudes and political unionism [CLC 1945a: 15-16; Harrod 1972: 239], and these were exacerbated by the split in the international trade union movement. The CLC remained affiliated to the WFTU, but the former had by this time become largely ineffective, and the resultant loss of membership that the CLC decision entailed, simply hastened its decline. In 1952, it was effectively disbanded as the Jamaican People's National Party adopted a pro-British stance on trade unionism.

This period also saw an increase in the direct involvement of the British TUC in the colonies, which was largely a response to the activities of Butler and his followers in 1946. The following year, at the request of the Secretary of State for the Colonies, a TUC adviser, Fred Dalley, was sent to Trinidad. He noted the continued existence of low wages, poor living conditions and casual labour, including unofficial child labour [Dalley 1947: 4, 27], but his major task was to "educate" the labour movement on the strategies of "responsible" trade unionism. Of particular concern was the strike prone and "impatient" nature of trade unions and Butler's refusal to separate industrial and political demands. His report concluded that "all the Trade Unions . . . should dissociate themselves from Uriah Butler and his methods. This is not a matter of 'lines of demarcation' or of trade union rivalry. Responsible Trade Unionism and 'Butlerism' cannot exist side by side; they are incompatibles, and the workers of Trinidad should be helped to realize this by all the responsible elements in the Colony". He also commented on Butler's alleged "mental abnormality" [Dalley 1947: 35].

While trade union influence extended beyond its small membership, its continued lack of strength in numbers both reflected and facilitated ideological divisions that hindered the development of working class political leadership before 1956. Four basic tendencies existed among those claiming to represent the working class and peasantry: first, there were those predominantly black workers who were inspired by the populist rhetoric of Butler; secondly, there were the more conservative elements that supported Gomes, the British government, and the British TUC, and were prepared for a gradual process of decolonization; thirdly, there were the East Indians in the rural areas who were conscious of ethnic differences and, despite Butler's attempts to revive "Afro-Indian" solidarity in 1947–48, were concerned about the consequences of black majority rule; and, fourthly, there were a number of more organized and more explicitly socialist (or labourist) parties, but these lacked stable support, especially in the trade union movement [Cross 1988: 295].

The Knox Street Quintet, Union Rivalry and further TUC Intervention, from 1950 onwards

The new constitution permitted competition for eighteen seats to the legislature. Divisions were once again common, particularly among those parties claiming to represent labour. The five main political organizations were: the Political Progress Group (PPG), a moderate party led by the increasingly conservative Gomes; the Trinidad Labour Party (TLP), now led by Raymond Hamel-Smith; the Caribbean Socialist Party (CSP), founded by Patrick Solomon after the collapse of the United Front, but which also suffered from internal divisions; the Trades Union Council (TUCo), which vainly called for labour unity; and the Butlerites, who stood on a platform of "Afro-Indian" unity, and for a break with the existing trade union movement.

The result was a minor triumph for Butler, whose party returned six candidates (four of whom were Indians), but the election was again inconclusive as the TLP, CSP and the PPG each won two seats, and six were won by Independents. The Butlerites won the support of two of the successful Independent candidates, but this only gave them eight out of twenty-six seats in the legislature (eight members were still unelected at this time). Butler's "radical" politics were clearly unacceptable to the Colonial Office which, together with manoeuvres by Governor Rance and the other parties, ensured that no Butlerite held a seat in the Executive Council.

A far more acceptable and conservative regime was instead established, which was based on collective leadership and known as the "Knox Street Quintet". This system lacked party discipline, but it had the great virtue (from the British viewpoint) that it would not challenge British (or US) interests in the region, whereas Butler advocated nationalization of the oil industry. The quasi ministerial regime implemented a far more conservative economic strategy. This bore the hallmarks of the Puerto Rican model discussed in the first chapter: efforts were made to attract foreign capital through tax incentives (the Pioneer Industries Ordinance 1952 for example), thereby (or so it was believed) facilitating the transition to an advanced capitalist economy.

Meanwhile, ideological and personal differences continued in the trade unions and were most clearly visible through the phenomenon of trade union rivalry. As well as two rival trade union federations after 1949, union competition existed in particular sectors. For example, in 1947, six unions competed for representation of the railway workers. In 1952, a similar number existed in the the sugar industry, and an uneasy "alliance" (secured in December 1953) between the ATSEFWTU and the Sugar Industry

Labour Union was broken after a strike was called at the Usine Ste Madeleine Estate in November 1954 [Dalley 1947: 7; Catchpole 1955: 3-4].

In 1954, concerned with what they regarded as the continued backwardness of trade unionism in Trinidad and Tobago, the British TUC again sent Fred Dalley to advise on the "proper" direction that trade unionism should take there. This visit was decisive in convincing Trades Union Council leaders such as John Rojas to leave the WFTU and affiliate to the ICFTU. In an attempt to establish trade union unity in the region, the ICFTU also set up a Caribbean Area Division of the Inter-American Regional Organization of Workers (ORIT) and most Caribbean unions affiliated to it (a notable exception was the Bustamante Industrial Trade Union in Jamaica).

This second report again expressed concern about the state of labour organization in Trinidad and Tobago, and cited three major problems for trade unions and labour parties. First, there were no established political parties; secondly, "politicians and political aspirants cultivate and sponsor certain trade unions . . . to further their own political careers [rather] than to assist the union and their members . . ."; and thirdly, voters did not give much support to trade union candidates anyway [Dalley 1954: 38].

The TUC also sent an adviser, Martin Pounder, to help sort out the problems of unionization in the sugar industry. He spent nine months in Trinidad, and with TUC financial help, the All-Trinidad union increased its membership from around 350 to 4000 [Roberts 1964: 39]. This reconstitution of the "All-Trinidad" as a "responsible" union failed to marginalize completely a group of "rebels" who quite legitimately demanded democracy in the union. However, trade union democracy was not one of the primary goals of TUC advisers; as Pounder said in his farewell speech, "what these rebels are doing is a lot of damned nonsense. It is a tragedy. While others try to build good relationship [sic] between the workers and the employers, the rebels who possess only nuisance value try to destroy it" [Trinidad Chronicle 1958]. So, for Pounder, the establishment of a moderate, "responsible" trade union took precedence over the establishment of a democratic one. The rebel movement, however, was not totally defeated and, in collaboration with the OWTU, it became an increasingly powerful force, as I show below.

The underlying premise of British TUC advice was the belief that there are separate industrial and political arenas and that trade unions should confine themselves to the former [Davies 1964]. (The "social scientific" equivalent of this view, held by Clark Kerr, was discussed in the opening chapter.) Dalley was concerned that trade unions should play a purely "economistic" role in the context of a voluntarist collective bargaining environment in which the state would abstain from intervention in the industrial sphere. Such a theory of trade unionism was hardly adequate from the point of view of the defensive interests of the nascent working class in a peripheral capitalist economy, as was discussed in the opening chapter. Moreover, such a view of trade unions hardly corresponded with the historical reality of British industrial relations; as Hyman has pointed out "trade union economism has always rested on certain historically contingent preconditions . . . Voluntarism had its roots in an era when unions were relatively weak (through limited membership and often high unemployment) and willing to exercise considerable self restraint in the use made of power they did possess" [1989: 46-47]. The TUC turned this "historical moment" into a dogmatic programme for trade unions in the colonies, which was important in steering trade unions into a "more acceptable" direction (again from the British and American viewpoints).

The Rise of the People's National Movement, the Trade Unions and Independence, 1956–1962

The Rise of the PNM

While the non-party government from 1950 to 1956 had shown a high degree of unity, the population generally felt that a united, nationalist, political party was needed to lead Trinidad to independence. In 1948, the prominent scholar Eric Williams returned to Trinidad as a deputy chairperson of the Caribbean Research Council (CRC) of the Caribbean Commission. By the early 1950s, he was giving public lectures throughout Trinidad and Tobago. At the end of 1954 he emerged on the centre stage of Trinidadian society as he engaged in a formal debate on education with Dom Basil Matthews. By this time he was involved with the People's Education Movement and in June 1955 he announced his dismissal from the CRC and formally launched his political campaign. After consultations with C.L.R. James, George Padmore and Arthur Lewis, the People's National Movement was officially founded in January 1956.

The elections of 1956 were fought by a large number of parties, and again included parties claiming to represent labour. As well as the PNM, there were three other new parties: the Caribbean National Labour Party (CNLP), the West Indian Independence Party (WIIP) and the People's Democratic Party (PDP). The CNLP was led by John Rojas and emerged from the failure of trade unions to win concessions from the PNM. At the inaugural conference of the PNM, union attempts were made to seek guarantees of candidates, but these were rejected. As Williams later stated, "With the experience of the British Labour Party before us, we were careful not to allow our movement to be dominated by the trade union block vote" [1969: 146].

Rojas and Williams were also divided over the issue of Texaco's takeover of Trinidad Leasehold Limited in 1956. Rojas opposed this and argued that the state should be the majority shareholder. Williams' support for the Texaco deal [*Trinidad Guardian* 1956] was important in convincing the British government that the PNM did not represent a threat to its interests, which by now had come to represent a close (but highly unequal) alliance with the USA and a growing political disinterest in the declining Empire.

As well as rejecting direct connections with the trade union movement, the PNM rejected a socialist strategy. Instead, Williams advocated the Puerto Rican model of industrialization and diversification in an attempt to move the economy away from an over-reliance on oil [Williams 1955: 16–21]. He acknowledged that the previous regime had given tax incentives to industry, but argued that increased tariffs were needed to allow industry to develop. Above all, he denounced politics based on religion, colour or class and called for "the united efforts of the entire population" [Williams 1955: 34]. However, the reality of the strategy was that it would promote the interests of already privileged groups and it was hoped that this would lead to the creation of a dynamic, indigenous capitalist class. In practice, such a strategy was compatible with the interests of sections of foreign capital and the political and strategic interests of Western countries playing the "cold war game".

The other new parties were the WIIP and the PDP. The former was a Marxist-oriented organization that had been created in 1952 and was led by Lennox Pierre and John La Rose. Its membership was always small and it only fielded one candidate in the 1956 election, advising its supporters to vote for the PNM. The PDP, on the other hand, was an Indian-based petty bourgeois party which appealed to Indians on the basis of their ethnic origins. Its leader was Bhadase Maraj, who was also a leading figure in the ATSEFWTU. Of the older parties, the Political Progress Group, the Trinidad Labour Party, and the Butlerites all stood. Butler's party began to decline almost immediately after 1950, when Butler went to Britain to agitate for the end of colonial rule. He believed that his party could win the 1956 elections but underestimated the appeal of Eric Williams and the PNM, and they won only two seats.

During the campaign it became clear that the two major parties competing for office were the PNM and the PDP. Both parties were of basically petty bourgeois origin and both had pro-capitalist programmes. By far the most divisive issue was that of race. With the absence of a united labour party alternative, the two parties appealed to labour according to its racial origin. The PNM effectively combined populism at the ideological level (in other words, the promotion of nationalism and a barely concealed racism) with clientelism at the organizational level (in other words, a highly restrictive recruitment of key political personnel, including, as I will show, trade union leaders). As Sudama states, "the method of selection of the top party personnel and the thinly disguised propaganda emphasizing the historical and continuing discrimination against Negroes, though at times couched in nationalist terms, was sufficient to keep the organization firmly in the hands of the Negro petty bourgeoisie and at the same time make an emotional appeal to the Negro working class" [Sudama 1983: 85]. Williams' claim to represent the whole population was therefore rather hollow. Instead, the PNM appealed to sufficient sections of the population to secure electoral victory, even if this was at the cost of further racial disunity in the country. The PDP, for its part, presented itself as the protector of the cause of East Indian cultural interests, and its leaders argued that such a "champion" was all the more necessary as Trinidad was close to independence and the prospect of black majority self-government.

Race was the most important and emotive issue in a bitter election campaign. The informal leader of the Knox Street Quintet captured the mood during the election campaign when he later stated that "the dismal fact is that exploitation of race had been the decisive factor in the elections, a fact which everyone recognized, even though, as with a guilty secret, people hesitated to make public mention of its existence" [Gomes 1974: 175].

The result of the election was not decisive. The PNM won 39 percent of the popular vote and thirteen of the twenty-four contested seats, while the PDP won five seats, with 20 percent of the popular vote. The TLP, the Butlerites and Independents each won two seats. The PPG, which largely represented the indigenous white and "off-white" population, clearly lacked a social base and failed to win any seats. This result did not give the PNM a majority in the Legislature, as seven seats were still non-elected. However, Governor Beetham was convinced that a PNM government was not incompatible with British or American interests (as the Texaco deal had shown) and successfully persuaded the Colonial Office to allow the PNM to form the government and guarantee it support among the appointed members. As a result, the PNM formed the government and Eric Williams became the Chief Minister [Ryan 1974: 166].

Trade Union Activity, 1956–1962

After the 1956 elections, the Trinidad Labour Party, the Political Progress Group and the People's Democratic Party united to form the Democratic Labour Party (DLP). The white and "off-white" population was numerically the smallest, while being economically the most dominant group in the country, but the 1956 election results demonstrated the necessity of entering into a political alliance with an organization that had wider popular appeal than the Political Progress Group. Whites were particularly concerned that black majority rule would threaten their economic interests so they were prepared to enter into an alliance with the PDP.

In 1958, elections for the West Indies Federation (a colonial experiment which collapsed in 1961) were held, thus providing the DLP with the first test of its popularity. To the dismay of the over-confident PNM, the DLP won six of the ten seats. Racial hostility became more overt as Williams denounced DLP appeals to the Indian nation and described Indians in Trinidad as a "recalcitrant and hostile minority masquerading as the Indian nation, and prostituting the name of India for its selfish, reactionary political ends" [Ryan 1974: 192]. The objective of such an attack was clear; as Sudama [1983: 87] states, "the Negro petty bourgeoisie was determined to mobilize the whole Negro working class behind it to maintain its power by projecting the racial threat of the East Indians".

The PNM therefore correctly perceived that the DLP was a serious electoral threat and took appropriate action. Changes were made to the electoral boundaries for the national elections of 1961 which would increase the PNM's chances of victory (although, in fairness to the PNM, the changes also made the results more representative of the national popular vote). Williams also combined a strategy of attracting black labour support through anti-Indian scaremongering with a pro-labour stance. He continued to reject any direct trade union base because he did not want to present the PNM as a party dominated by labour and a trade union bloc vote. The image put forward was one of a nationalist movement capable of uniting the "whole population" (which in practice actually meant the black population plus some secular Indians) in its movement towards independence. Nevertheless, the working class was by far the largest sector within the black population and so Williams gave his vocal support to a number of strikes in this period.

For instance, in March 1957 he supported workers who wanted union organization in a US firm which assembled office equipment. Williams said that "any industry coming here and behaving decently will be given decent treatment. If they do not like our action, let them pull out" [*Trinidad Guardian* 1957]. This support continued in June–July 1960, when oil workers at Texaco and Apex went on strike over threatened redundancies. By early July the strike had spread to Shell. There was also a shortage of cooking oil, the price of coal had increased, and public transport was affected. Despite mounting pressure on the government to intervene in the dispute, its only concession was to call a meeting between the parties, and secure an agreement to maintain essential services. The strike ended a few days later and Williams continued to defend the right of workers to withdraw their labour power. Williams also described workers as his "friends" and stated that "[i]f there is one group in the community which is going to defend democracy and self-government, that group is the workers" [Parris 1976: 14].

Williams also won popular support during his "left turn" in 1958–60, and in particular over the issue of the military base at Chaguaramas. This reached a peak in April 1960, as PNM leaders marched to Chaguaramas to demand that the United States of America return the land to the people of Trinidad and Tobago. The PNM later adopted a far more conciliatory attitude (the USA abandoned Wallerfield and Carlsen Field, but only part of

Chaguaramas), and Williams assured the Colonial Office of his support for the West. Once this guarantee was ensured (to the Secretary of State for the Colonies, Iain MacLeod, in 1960), Britain was prepared to let the PNM lead the country to independence [Ryan 1974: 220].

But the Chaguaramas issue showed that the PNM was committed to some, albeit rather tame, nationalist principles, and the black working class for its part was sympathetic to the nationalism of the PNM. The election campaign of 1961 had a distinctly populist tone as Williams, appealing "over the heads" of black trade union leaders, claimed that the old days of the plantation society were over, that "massa day done". The PNM also expressed its support for independence in the 1961 election, and relations with the black working class and the trade unions reached a peak. The Trinidad and Tobago Trades Union Congress (TTUC) which was created in 1957 out of the reunification of the two rival labour federations, noted that the DLP supported restrictive labour legislation, while the PNM claimed to oppose any policy of this kind. However, TTUC leaders rejected too close an allegiance to the PNM because they felt that "it would be dangerous for labour to become too closely identified with the PNM" [Ryan 1974: 256]. This was because they feared the consequences for labour should the PNM lose the election and, as Cohen (writing on Africa, but still of direct relevance) states, "[f]or the unions to stand consistently shoulder to shoulder with parties deriving their power base from traditional rulers or from members of the political class was tantamount to giving up any claim to represent the working class" [1974: 243]. In other words, Berg and Butler's contention that unions were apolitical in the transition to independence is incorrect in the case of Trinidad and Tobago (as well as in the case of several African countries, as Cohen points out), precisely because of the *absence* of this direct union–party link.

Even without this direct link, the TTUC still played a directly political role in the 1961 election campaign. The Civil Service Association, political dissenters in the TTUC, decided to organize demonstrations against the government. There were strong suspicions of collusion with the DLP, but the government decided to take no action and allowed the demonstrations to go ahead. This was important in the TTUC as the marches "provided the excuse which pro-PNM labour elements were looking for in order to get the [TTUC] to come out openly in support of the PNM" [Ryan 1974: 257]. Demonstrations in support of the PNM were organized and these probably contributed to the size of the PNM victory.

Racial tensions reached a climax during the election campaign as Indians were attacked and DLP leader Rudranath Capildeo incited racial violence [Ryan 1974: 266-70]. A major crisis was only averted by the declaration of a State of Emergency in some areas, and the willingness of both sides to hold back ultimately from full-scale confrontation. The outcome of the election was that the PNM won 58 percent of the popular vote and twenty seats, while the DLP won the other ten, thus establishing a two-party system (in which the two sides were divided by race). After the election, Williams decided to opt for independence for Trinidad and Tobago.

After consultations with the population, including sections of the trade union movement, independence was granted on 1 August 1962.

Trade Unions and Politics, 1962–1965 – "Political Confrontation" and the Industrial Stabilization Act

The PNM therefore won office and led Trinidad and Tobago to independence by "courting" the black working class independently of the official trade union movement. A year after independence, Williams attempted to carry out a coherent corporatist strategy of institutionally co-opting trade unions which would actually lead to their effective control. The National Economic Advisory Council was formed, consisting of representatives from business, labour and government, and in which the cooperation of (undemocratic but responsible) trade unions was secured. Control over the trade union movement was reinforced by a policy of incorporation of trade union leaders into the PNM hierarchy.

However, the ascendance of "responsible" trade unionism was not fully secured and the aforementioned "rebels", claiming allegiance to Uriah Butler, had increased their influence in a number of unions. Most significantly, in 1962 a new rebel leadership was established in the OWTU under the leadership of George Weekes. Bhadase Maraj's authoritarian leadership of the ATSEFWTU continued to be challenged, culminating in the creation of the

National Union of Sugar Workers in 1963. The conservative leadership of the Amalgamated Workers Union was challenged by workers at the Princes Town Bus Company, and this led to the formation of the radical Transport and Industrial Workers Union. So, by the time independence had been declared, there were two clear divisions in the trade union movement: on the one hand, there were the "responsible" trade union leaders who believed that the role of the trade union was based on a collective bargaining approach; on the other, there were the more radical unions whose leaders believed "we had to negotiate for improved wages and for better working conditions . . . but we also felt that the trade union had to politicize workers so that they could accept the view of a more just and equitable social order" [Young 1976: 164].

Rivalry between the PNM and these rebel leaders was visible from as early as 1960. For instance, the aforementioned oilworkers' strike of that year was significant in the long term for two principal reasons. First, it had been largely forced on the increasingly conservative John Rojas by the increasingly influential "rebel" group in the OWTU, and George Weekes later remarked that "[t]he 1960 strike marks the achievement of maturity and the realization that the workers are now powerful enough not only to seek, but to fight successfully for their rights" [Kambon 1988: 48]. Secondly, and not unconnected to the first point, Williams hinted at his later stance on labour relations when he wrote that "[i]rresponsible elements on the workers' side injected race into the strike, talked about emulating Castro, advocated nationalization of the oil industry . . ." [Kambon 1988: 46].

These radical trade union leaders enjoyed the support of a membership disoriented by the undemocratic practices of most trade unions, but they did not constitute a threat to the PNM or the DLP at the electoral level. These leaders were regarded by their members as trade union leaders only, and not (at least in the short term) as potential political leaders. Nevertheless, the rebels were still considered to be a "threat" because the PNM government was concerned that its inability to control some trade unions would discourage capital investment, and so weaken its industrialization strategy. In the 1960 strike, these differences were set aside as both parties shared the immediate goal of independence, and so the radicals largely supported the PNM (with some reservations) in the 1961 elections. After independence, this situation rapidly altered, and culminated in the PNM's decision to introduce the Industrial Stabilization Bill in 1965.

Hostilities between the PNM and the more radical elements of the trade unions became more visible in the context of an economic recession, increased post-independence expectations on the part of organized labour, and a consequent decline in the industrial relations climate after 1961. Economic growth had increased by an average of 10 percent a year from 1955 to 1961 [Thomas 1988: 280], but in 1961 and 1962 the world price of oil fell, sending the economy into a significant downturn. Economic growth slowed down to just one percent in 1962, and, with a population increase of three percent, it meant that per capita income actually fell and only grew very slowly in the following two years as well [Farrell 1975a: 46-47]. The government response was to blame the trade unions (Williams' "friends" in 1961) for the country's economic difficulties. During the passage of the Industrial Stabilization Bill through the House of Representatives in 1965 (see below), Williams outlined the strike statistics for the years 1960 to 1964: in this five-year period there were 230 strikes, involving 74 574 workers; the total number of work days lost was 803 899. Williams expressed particular concern at the disproportionately high number of days lost in the oil and sugar industries: 144 363 related to the sugar industry and 286 001 to oil [Thomas 1984: 49-50]. The number of work days lost in 1964 was actually less than for each of the previous four years, but by 1965 this hardly mattered to Williams. By this time "[w]hat was escalating was official hysteria about strikes and official identification of strikes with political subversion . . ." [Kambon 1988: 123].

The "honeymoon period" between the PNM and the trade union movement had, however, actually ended two years earlier. In February 1963, BP oil workers went on strike over the company's planned retrenchment of two hundred workers. The OWTU expected Williams to support the strike but he instead announced his intention to set up a Commission of Inquiry into subversive activities in the trade union movement. Williams was particularly concerned that the climate of labour unrest was discouraging foreign investment. Instead of attempting to respond to the demands of radical sections of organized labour, Williams tried to placate them. This clearly demonstrated the differences between the PNM's and the radicals' conceptions of nationalism. For the PNM, "nationalism was now subservience [*sic*] to the multinational corporations, in the national interest as they saw it. For Weekes and the OWTU, it was war against the multinational corporations, in the national interest as they saw it" [Kambon **1988: 70**].

The divisions in the trade union movement were formalized when the national Trades Union Congress, now led by George Weekes, boycotted Tripartite Committee talks in October **1964**. Weekes justified this position on the grounds that the government was now openly hostile towards the trade union movement, but a number of unions rejected this argument and resigned from the TTUC. The ATSEFWTU and the Amalgamated Workers Union (later joined by the Communication Workers Union, the Seamen and Waterfront Workers Trade Union and the Union of Commercial and Industrial Workers) set up an alternative federation, which they called the National Federation of Labour.

The Commission of Inquiry [Mbanefo **1965**] was set up in **1963** and its findings were laid before the House of Representatives on **18 March 1965**. It was particularly concerned with politically "subversive" activity in the trade union movement. A number of trade union leaders cooperated with the Inquiry, including Anthony Geoffroy and Rampatap Singh (ATSEFWTU), Daniel Reid (SWWTU), W. W. Sutton (AWU) and James Manswell (CSA). However, the most sensational (some would say sensationalized) evidence was given by the former OWTU President-General John Rojas, who repeated his allegations (first made in the Senate in August **1962**) that there was a plot by Marxist trade union leaders to lead a revolution in Trinidad and Tobago [Mbanefo **1965: 7**]. Rojas claimed that in **1962**, at the twenty-fifth anniversary celebrations of the OWTU, C.L.R. James had confided in him that "[t]he country is ripe for revolution" [Mbanefo **1965: 9**]. James Manswell of the CSA denied Rojas' allegations and the Commission politely dismissed the former OWTU leader's evidence [Mbanefo **1965: 10**]. In fact, given that the government was using the radical trade union leaders as a scapegoat for the failure of its development strategy, the findings of the Commission were surprisingly balanced. Although Weekes was described as a communist [**1965: 35**], the Commission argued, contrary to Williams' assertions, that "[t]he fact that the strikes [of **1962** and **1963**] were spread over all the major unions negatives the suggestion of subversion" [**1965: 45**].

Its specific contents were however less important than the general atmosphere in which the report was presented to the House of Representatives. Undemocratic practices in the sugar workers union continued, as the leadership failed to implement a pension plan in **1963** and agreed to a wage freeze without consulting its members. Sugar workers collected a petition calling for a Special

Conference of Delegates in accordance with ATSEFWTU rules, but the leadership refused to concede. The ATSEFWTU membership decided that there was only one course of action open to them. On 21 February 1965, a strike was called by sugar workers at the Ste Madeleine Factory. Industrial action quickly spread, and by 8 March the entire sugar industry had withdrawn its labour power, in a protest as much against the union as against the company, Caroni Ltd. The following day the OWTU leadership gave its support to the sugar workers. There were also strikes at the Lock Joint sewerage scheme, at Federation Chemicals, and in addition the Civil Servants Association was threatening to institute a go-slow over wage demands. The government's response was a request to the Governor-General to introduce a State of Emergency in the sugar belt (as he was entitled to do under the Emergency Powers Ordinance 1947). Emergency regulations were introduced the following day which restricted freedom of movement and banned public meetings in the sugar belt area, thus effectively banning contact between the oilfields and sugar belts.

New legislation was presented to the House of Representatives on 12 March, and after the presentation of the Mbanefo Commission's report on the 18 March, the Industrial Stabilization Bill was rushed through Parliament and received the Governor-General's assent on 20 March. The debate on the bill in the Senate clearly showed that the trade union movement was being blamed for the economic difficulties in the country. For instance, Senator Walke stated that "[t]he trade unions have brought this on themselves. They have been given a long rope in which to operate, and have succeeded in hanging themselves" [Trinidad and Tobago 1966a: 794]. Government Senator and trade union leader Carl Tull spoke of a communist plot in the OWTU and called on the workers "to eradicate these evil forces" [1966a: 852]. In introducing the bill in the Senate, the Attorney General stated what the new legislation had in mind: "the necessity to maintain a certain level of capital accumulation with a view to increasing the rate of economic growth; the necessity to maintain and expand the level of employment was necessary; the necessity to prevent gains in the wages of workers not being adversely affected by unnecessary and unjustified price increases" [1966a: 788]. The third and final consideration did at least place some limitation on the power of capital, and some measures for the establishment of price controls were undertaken in the Act [Trinidad and Tobago 1965: 6], but this part of the Act was never implemented (and was quietly dropped from the amendment in 1972).

The first two considerations are of more interest because they show that the government blamed the "irresponsible" trade unions for low capital investment. Williams himself believed that the problem was simply one of the impact of high wages "on the rate of investment in the whole economy and on the competitive position of exports" [Williams 1965a: 5]. However, as my discussion in chapter one suggested, it was the development strategy itself, rather than the capacity of the trade union movement to win high wages, which was at fault.

The Industrial Stabilization Act (ISA) broke with the tradition of voluntarism under which the state had played a restricted role in the field of industrial relations (the Boards of Inquiry set up since 1948 were the notable exceptions) and basically outlined provisions which restricted the right to strike. Strikes and lockouts were forbidden in essential services - electricity, fire, health, hospital sanitation, water services and sanitation. An Industrial Court was also established which functioned "to hear and determine trade disputes . . . [and] to register industrial agreements and to hear and determine matters relating to the registration of such disputes" [Trinidad and Tobago 1965: 6]. Any party to a dispute could report its existence to the Minister of Labour, who then had to certify that such a report had been made, and take steps to settle the dispute. If the Minister was unable to settle the dispute within twenty-one days, the matter had to be referred to the Industrial Court for settlement. A strike could only take place on the condition that the Minister had been given fourteen days' notice, and strikes (or lockouts) were prohibited if a dispute was before the Industrial Court or the Court of Appeal [Thomas 1984: 55-57]. The official justification for these limitations on the right to strike was that the interests of "the people" or the "general community" had to be protected [Trinidad and Tobago 1965: 10]. So once again Williams appealed "over the heads" of trade union leaders (particularly those who did not support the government) and used the inconvenience caused by strikes as the basis for an appeal to "the people".

On the day that the Industrial Stabilization Bill passed through the House of Representatives, a number of organizations, including trade unions, expressed their support by demonstrating outside the House. Most prominent among these were the Communication Workers Union and the Amalgamated Workers Union. Their leaders, Carl Tull and W.W. Sutton respectively, forcefully denounced the TTUC and successfully encouraged some unions to join their rival federation. Divisions also opened up in the TTUC and Weekes resigned from his position as President General later in 1965 [Weekes 1965].

The basic purpose of the ISA was "to depoliticize organized labour" [Parris 1976: 5]. Williams himself argued that trade union leadership "is not going to be able to utilize legitimate trade union activities, or to subvert them, for purely political ends" [Williams 1965a: 6]. He later described the ISA as "[m]y outstanding responsibility in Parliament in the second five-year period" and explained that it was necessary because "[t]he subversive elements in the society . . . were at work; the background was an open attempt to link the trade unions in oil and sugar" [Williams 1969: 311]. The ISA was introduced because the trade union movement had played a political role in the movement for independence, and precisely because the government, former allies of nearly all the trade unions, feared that this process might, at least in some cases, become uncontrollable. Williams had appealed to black labour before independence on the basis of their support for independence and as the major social group that represented "the national interest". After independence, the PNM government became concerned that sections of this group were a threat to the national interest, as embodied in the PNM's strategy of industrialization by invitation. Williams continued to appeal to black labour on a populist, non-class basis, arguing that the establishment of the Industrial Court was necessary to protect "the general community" (the third party in disputes presented to the Court) from "political subversives" in the trade union movement. He therefore simply bypassed those unions which challenged the government's development strategy, and appealed "over their heads" to the black masses (including many OWTU members).

These developments in turn altered the racial and class alliances that had occurred since 1956. Relations between the black and white petty bourgeoisies improved after the 1961 election, and by 1965 there were close consultations through employer bodies such as the Chamber of Commerce and the Manufacturers Association. This reflected the fact that the PNM was not concerned with radically threatening their interests. The East Indian petty bourgeoisie also played an increasingly ambivalent role, as some cooperated with, or chose to tolerate the PNM, and the DLP ceased to play an active role in opposition (see chapter four).

Conclusion

The events discussed in this chapter can be divided into three periods. First, from 1937 to 1956, several attempts were made to form a mass labour party out of the trade union movement. The failure of these endeavours can be attributed to the racial divisions among the labour force, and the diffuse nature of the class structure, which militated against the formation of a unified class-based organization. Added to this were the problems of trade union rivalry, conflicts of personalities, and official attempts to depoliticize trade unions. The second period, from 1956 to 1962, can be characterized as one in which a black middle class movement, eschewing direct links with trade unions, led the country to independence. In the third period, after 1962, the PNM became hostile to some trade unions and this led to anti-union legislation in 1965.

The absence of a trade union based party does not confirm the Berg–Butler thesis that labour was largely irrelevant in anti-colonial movements. The PNM was successful in capturing the support of the black working class on the basis of non-class politics, but trade unions were vocal in supporting the party in the 1961 election. Moreover, after independence trade unions continued to play a political role and this was a major determining factor in the government's decision to pass the Industrial Stabilization Act.

By 1965–66, non-black petty bourgeois opposition was largely vocal (the DLP still won its "safe twelve" seats in the 1966 elections, but it ceased to provide an effective parliamentary opposition), as it became increasingly clear that their interests were largely compatible with PNM policy. The only other significant challenge to the PNM, represented by the "political subversives", had been contained by the ISA and the split in the trade union movement.

The most immediate labour dilemma for the PNM concerned the administrative difficulties that were now faced in regulating industrial relations. The creation of the Industrial Court failed to resolve (on its own terms) the problem of unstable industrial relations, as it quickly became clear that the court was ill-equipped to deal with the large number of disputes referred to it [Okpaluba 1975: 70–71].

The absence of political opposition to the PNM was also short-lived, as I discuss in chapter four.

4

Race, Class and the "Informal Sector": The Black Power Revolt of 1970

Introduction

The increase in capitalist industrialization after 1950 intensified, rather than alleviated, uneven development, and so the size of the urban unemployed and "informal" sectors dramatically increased. These processes formed the economic and social framework for a new opposition to the PNM, centred in the urban, predominantly black areas, where unemployment and underemployment were high. Inspired by the Black Power struggles in the USA, new political organizations were established that challenged the direction taken by the PNM government since independence. These new organizations won widespread support for their ideas among the ranks of the dispossessed, and the new opposition took its grievances on to the streets, culminating in the uprising of February to April 1970.

On 26 February, students from the University of West Indies, St Augustine, led a march in Port of Spain to protest against the trial of West Indian students in Canada who had occupied the Sir George Williams University computer centre. After the march, the students staged a sit-in at a Roman Catholic Cathedral and later protested outside the Chamber of Commerce. The following day, nine of the protesters were arrested and various charges were made against them. This led to an escalation of unrest as students, some workers, and the unemployed sustained a fairly spontaneous protest against economic policies and social conditions.

A series of mass demonstrations was held throughout March, culminating in the "Long March" to Caroni, which was an attempt by radical black youths, through the most important organization of the period, the National Joint Action Committee (NJAC), to win the support of East Indian sugar workers and transcend traditional "racial" boundaries. The PNM government appeared to regain the initiative but on 6 April, the police shot a young NJAC supporter, Basil Davis, whose shooting provided the stimulus for further activity. From 6 to 21 April there were further marches, ministerial resignations, rumours of unrest in the armed forces, and an increase in organized labour movement involvement. Widespread strikes and marches were planned for 21 April, but they never took place as the government declared a State of Emergency, which restricted freedom of movement and led to the arrest of the leading figures in the revolt. While there was spasmodic opposition to Williams' decision, the most serious challenge to his authority came from a section of the army which initially regarded the seizure of state power as its ultimate goal. However, the mutineers eventually decided to negotiate with the government, and the mutiny came to an end on 1 May.

This chapter looks at the causes of the "February Revolution", and the role played in it by different sections of the working classes (and their organizations). It first examines the social effects of the economic strategy employed by the PNM government, and the new opposition that arose out of this. Secondly, it examines in more detail the movements and ideas behind the events of 1970, and assesses the degree to which they provided the basis for a long term political alliance of the working classes. Thirdly, the mutiny in the army is examined briefly and, finally, an evaluation is made of the unrest that persisted until the dramatic change in the government's economic fortunes in 1973.

The Economic and Social Background to the "February Revolution"

Government Economic Strategy and its Social Consequences

It became clear by 1969 that the "Lewis model" of economic development, discussed in chapters one and three, had not suc-ceeded. The average annual growth rate from 1955 to 1968 was high (8 percent), but the major objective of "balanced growth" had not taken place. Three weaknesses were particularly manifest by the late 1960s: first, tax incentives offered to attract foreign capital meant that the state lacked the resources needed for sus-taining a programme of economic expansion; secondly, manufac-turing had failed to provide the substantial increase in employment that was expected; thirdly, the industrialization strategy had led to a neglect of agriculture [Sandoval 1983: 252-55]. The capital intensive nature of investment was such that in 1967 it would have required more than three times the (second) Five-Year Plan development budget to provide employ-ment in pioneer manufacturing industries for the unemployed [Carrington 1971: 145]. According to official figures released in 1968, the 74 pioneer industries (those industries granted tax hol-idays, depreciation allowances and duty free imports) and 180 additional enterprises granted concessions (such as free import of raw materials and equipment) provided employment for only 7959 people [Ryan 1974: 385].

More generally, the strategy was also typical of the weaknesses of import-substitution-industrialization programmes. The internal market for domestically produced goods was too small to generate sustained economic growth, and the strategy was heavily depen-dent on importing foreign capital goods, which led to balance of payments difficulties [R. Ramsaran 1989: 115-17]. On the other hand, those industries that attempted to cater for the interna-tional market (such as the fertilizer industry) were effective enclaves under the control of foreign capital, and provided few linkages to the rest of the economy [Sandoval 1983: 255-56].

The strategy also failed to create the strong, indigenous capital-ist class that Lewis and the PNM had hoped for: in 1970, foreign investment in Trinidad and Tobago amounted to TT $2 billion, including over TT $500 million in oil; the seven major commer-cial banks were all foreign; almost half the land was owned by foreign capital; and perhaps most importantly (from the point of view of the PNM's economic strategy), 80 percent of manufacturing investment was made by foreign capital [Kambon 1988: 207]. Williams himself recognized the inadequacy of the programme and proposed a new "third way" between the Castroite and Puerto Rican models [Williams 1970: 111-12], which formed the substance of the third Five Year Plan in 1969. A draft of this plan expressed concern about the economic state of the nation and in particular criticized local business persons for their failure "to seize the numerous investment opportunities in agriculture, industry, fishing, tourism, and housing" [Sebastien 1985: 116].

So, to reiterate my discussion in chapter one, the basic problem of the PNM's economic strategy was that it was premised on the belief that there were "equalizing tendencies" within capitalism. If the government provided the right incentives, so it was believed, capital would be attracted to Trinidad and Tobago. When it became clear that this strategy was not working, the government blamed "political" trade unions for discouraging capital investment through their "excessive" wage gains and anti-capitalist politics. This view conveniently disregarded the fact that most foreign capital investment was concentrated in the sector – oil – in which these "problems" were most acute, but this counter-argument had failed to prevent the government from passing the Industrial Stabilization Act. However, despite this piece of legislation, foreign capital investment (outside of the oil sector) continued to be largely insignificant, and often (due to the product's high import content or failure to provide linkages to the rest of the economy), not particularly beneficial.

Nevertheless, the government's economic strategy had a major impact on the development of the working classes. From the 1940s to the 1960s there was a high rate of growth in, and important changes in the social structure of, the population. Between the two censuses of 1946 and 1960, there were "startling increases in the population of a few parts of the country . . . as people continued to move from the rural areas to rapidly growing urban centres at ever increasing rates" [Simpson 1973: 11]. In 1946, the proportion of the population that lived in urban areas was 23.25 percent; by 1960 this had increased to 36.39 percent [Simpson 1973: 15]. The proportion of the population involved in agriculture or agriculture-related activities declined from 27.5 percent in 1946 to 21.1 percent in 1960 [Harewood 1978: 77]. This process continued in the 1960s: the proportion of the population that lived in urban areas in 1960 was 40 percent; by 1970, this had increased to 53 percent [Cross 1979: 75]. The major reason for migration was the perception that urban areas could offer the advantages of employment and affluence, which were not readily available in the poorer rural areas. The emphasis placed by the government on industrialization meant that it was at the expense, and therefore further impoverishment, of the rural sector, which served to reinforce the growth of urban areas.

The problem with these developments was of course that industrialization failed to "deliver the goods". The proportion of the population involved in mining and manufacturing showed little change between the 1946 and 1960 censuses. In 1946, the figures were 3.2 percent for mining and 19.1 percent for manufacturing; by 1960, the proportions were five percent and 17.5 percent respectively [Harewood 1978: 77]. In the period up to 1970, the proportion for these two sectors may have actually declined to 21 percent of the total [Craig 1982b: 401]. There was also high unemployment, especially among the young. While the official rate of unemployment stood at 14 percent at the time of the crisis, among the 20–24-year age group the figure was 20 percent, and the rate for school leavers (in the 15–19-year age group) was as much as 30 percent [Sutton 1983: 119; Muschkin 1980: 50–51; Trinidad and Tobago 1975: 56]. Moreover, the official rate does not tell the whole story as a significant part of the labour force was only seasonally employed. The 1960 Census showed that 71 percent of the population was regularly employed, but the official rate of unemployment at the time was recorded at around 14 percent, which left another 14.5 percent as underemployed [Harewood 1978: 71]. According to one scholarly publication, by 1967 70 000 people (that is, one in every five employed persons) worked for less than thirty-two hours a week, and of these, 26 000 (7 percent) worked for less than sixteen hours a week [Tapia 1969].

The devaluation of the Trinidad and Tobago dollar in 1968 paved the way for further retrenchment, including the loss of 8000 jobs in the public sector. This came at a time when the PNM's expansion in education (introduced in 1961) began to take effect. Secondary school courses lasted for six years, but the recession in the late 1960s meant that a significant number of well educated people could not find employment. This process further discredited the government in the eyes of young people.

The PNM's industrialization strategy also largely failed to redistribute income among the population. The actual distribution of income was quite equitable by Third World standards: one study found that the upper 10 percent of income earners shared 33 percent of national income, compared to 43 percent in Jamaica (1958), 30 percent in the United States (1950), and 46 percent in Mexico (1957) [Ahiram 1966: 105-8]. It was generally felt, however, that income differentials remained too wide. According to the 1970 Census, the median income of professional and technical workers was TT $304 per month, compared to TT $158 for construction workers and TT $85 for service workers. The average monthly wage for women in the latter group was only TT $45 a month [Trinidad and Tobago 1973: 2-3]. Income was also unevenly distributed among the different ethnic groups, as I show below.

The problem of unequal income distribution was accompanied by another characteristic of the colonial era – racial discrimination. In an important article published in 1971, Acton Camejo examined the racial composition of executive and managerial staff in private firms employing more than a hundred people. He found that whites constituted 53 percent of this "business elite", "off whites" 15 percent, mixed 15 percent, Chinese nine percent, Indians nine percent and Africans four percent [Camejo 1971: 300]. He also found that of the seventy-one directors that inherited their position, 41 percent were white, 25 percent off white, 14 percent Indian, and seven percent mixed [1971: 301]. No director of African origin inherited his or her position. These figures suggest, but do not demonstrate, the existence of racial discrimination by private enterprise: for instance, they do not tell us anything about the educational qualifications of the elite. Most revealing then, are Camejo's findings concerning those with low educational qualifications who were appointed to top and middle positions in the business elite: of these, 71 percent were white, 24 percent off white, and five percent were mixed. No one of African or Indian origin had this easy access to managerial and executive positions [Camejo 1971: 302-4]. At this time, there were also frequent accusations that white, often foreign, managers discriminated against and abused black workers [Turner 1972: 125].

The distribution of income also cut across racial, as well as class, boundaries. According to the 1960 Census, the median monthly income for white male employees was over TT $500, compared with TT $104 for those of African origin, and a little less than TT $77 for Indians. Income distribution was also affected by a third factor – gender. The median monthly income for white women in the same period was TT $176, compared with TT $42 for Indian women and TT $38 for African women [Harewood 1971: 278].

So, industrial development led to major changes in the economy, but it failed to create a stable, "modern" economy with full employment and a relatively equal distribution of income. The old planter and merchant classes had been weakened by the rise of manufacturing and mining capitalists, generally of foreign origin, and a black, middle class, political elite. The problem, however, was that unequal income distribution, racial discrimination, and urban deprivation continued, the latter on an unprecedented scale. Nevertheless, some sections of the organized working class had managed to win a fairly privileged position for themselves. This was particularly true of the labourers in the oilfields, who enjoyed far higher wages than other workers.

The Resurgence of Opposition to the Government and the Rise of "Unconventional Politics"

The radical, "subversive" elements in the trade unions had been defeated by the introduction of the Industrial Stabilization Act, and effectively by George Weekes' resignation from the presidency of the TTUC in 1965. This defeat was reinforced by the dismal performance of the newly formed Workers and Farmers Party (WFP) in the 1966 election, in which all the candidates lost their deposits. The WFP was formed by radicals in response to the passing of the Industrial Stabilization Act. Its leaders included C.L.R. James, Weekes, Lennox Pierre and Stephen Maharaj, the latter of whom was formerly a leading parliamentary figure in the DLP. Its primary aim was to break the racial bases of the two major parties and create a "political organization based on politics not on race" [*Daily Mirror* 1965]. Apart from this appeal to African and Indian class unity, the WFP had a rather vague political programme which did not differ significantly from the PNM or the DLP. In its election manifesto, the WFP called for limits to ownership of the sugar estates and, more ambiguously, "planning", "control of public finance" and promotion of "local industry, commerce, labour" [Workers and Farmers Party 1966a: 2]. In the election campaign, both the major parties used the idea of a "hidden agenda" and "communist bogey" to discredit the WFP. The Minister of Home Affairs, Gerald Montano, claimed that all that the WFP "can offer is dictatorship" [*Daily Mirror* 1966]. Even more importantly, the PNM and the DLP once again successfully appealed to race for their respective constituencies. The WFP ultimately failed because it simply appealed to class unity and ignored the "social reality" of race. As Kambon argues, "[t]he tools of analysis put the racial realities out of focus instead of creatively seeking to come to terms with their implications" [Kambon 1988: 162]. After the 1966 election, the WFP quickly disintegrated as Maharaj became ill, James left Trinidad, and the other leaders appeared to lose interest.

Meanwhile, challenges from the official Opposition became equally mute, as the DLP was left in disarray over attitudes to the ISA and Maharaj's defection to the WFP. Its leader, Rudranath Capildeo, pushed the DLP in an ill-defined social democratic direction, while others maintained a strictly moderate (Vernon Jamadar) or even right wing (Ashford Sinanan) path. The party still won 34 percent of the popular vote in the 1966 election, and so continued to be the official Opposition, but ideological divisions, reinforced by a new crisis over who was to lead the party, weakened its effectiveness.

Williams had not, however, defeated all political opposition in the country. As I explained in the first section, his political victory over the radicals in the trade unions (which itself was short-lived – see below) was tempered by the fact that government economic strategy failed to "incorporate" large elements of the population in the way that he had in the case of the black working class.

This was obviously the case with the unemployed and under-employed, but it was also true of a radical intelligentsia based at the University of the West Indies. New organizations and newspapers were formed, such as *Moko*, which was started in 1968, and two years later became the official organ of James Millette's United National Independence Party (UNIP) and *Tapia*, the paper of Lloyd Best's Tapia House organization. These newspapers were run by university lecturers, but the ideas contained in them reflected a wider disillusionment with the outcome of independence at home, and, related to this, a challenge to North American imperialism in the Third World. In 1968 Millette debated with local business person Tommy Gatcliffe in the *Trinidad Express* on the nature of the transnational corporation and its effects in Trinidad and Tobago. This affair heightened public consciousness of the issues in a way not too dissimilar, at least in the short term, to the Williams–Matthews debate thirteen years earlier.

The challenge to the power of the USA did not only come from

Vietnam and other regions of the Third World, but also from within its own borders. The Black Power movement was a particularly potent symbol, and it served as an inspiration to the "underclasses" and their sympathizers (particularly students) in the West Indies. The first major rallying point for Black Power sympathizers occurred in October 1968, when the radical activist and scholar Walter Rodney was expelled from the Mona campus of the UWI in Jamaica. There was a major student and lecturer demonstration in support of Rodney, which, largely through the police's heavy handed tactics, became violent and led to fatalities.

A second major protest took place in Trinidad on 26 February 1969, this time over the visit of the Canadian Governor-General, two weeks after the arrest of eleven Trinidadian students at Sir George Williams University in Canada. On the evening of the demonstration, the NJAC was formed by two young radicals from the St Augustine campus, Dave Darbeau and Geddes Granger (now known respectively as Khafra Kambon and Makandal Daaga).

The NJAC was particularly important in the events of 1970 because, unlike the UNIP and *Tapia*, it won support for its views outside of the narrow confines of the university. Its views "struck a chord" with discontented urban youth, who were too young to be impressed by Williams' populist leadership. Most of them could not remember when the PNM had led the country to independence, and those who could remember were disappointed by the outcome. Populist nationalist appeals were meaningless to those that faced unemployment and urban slums.

The NJAC described the PNM government as "phoney nationalists", arguing that colonialism had been replaced by neo-colonialism, based on an alliance between the "Afro-Saxon" PNM government, international banking and transnational companies. In other words, the government was accused of failing to challenge the power of the white national and international capitalist class. Westminster style politics was also criticized for promoting racial divisions and corrupt, ineffective government and opposition. The precise relationship between race and class was unclear, as I argue below, but the NJAC placed heavy emphasis on a new black identity, which they called Black Pride. Black Power in the Trinidadian context therefore came to mean ownership and control of the economy by the black "majority". (The relationship with East Indians is discussed below.)

Meanwhile, radicals in the trade union movement had begun to recover some of their momentum. Trade disputes continued, albeit largely within the confines of the Industrial Court. In the oil industry, there were important disputes with Shell and BP in 1967 concerning plans to lay off workers. There was a 3 percent decline in the number employed in the oil industry between 1965 and 1969, and automation in the sugar industry also led to retrenchment [Turner 1972: 111]. Weekes led a "March of Resistance" of around 10 000 workers in June 1968, protesting against retrenchment in the industry. The government agreed to nationalization of part of the industry, through a National Oil Company, in 1968, but they were slow in carrying out their promises. There were, however, some challenges to the ISA, most notably when forty-five members of the Transport and Industrial Workers Union were charged with violating its regulations when they went on strike at Sissons Paints in September 1967. The union was fined TT $3000, but this did not stop its leader, Joe Young, from calling bigger strikes in public transport in June 1968 and May 1969. The second of these, despite its failure to save bus workers' jobs, was significant because different sectors of the working classes, including NJAC members, gave active support to the strike by bus workers.

Conclusion

The long-term causes of the "February Revolution" lie in the fact that the Williams government was unable to maintain its social base among the black labouring classes. The Industrial Stabilization Act tried to depoliticize those sections of the trade union movement which did not support the PNM, and who had challenged the disunity between the Indian and African labourer. This operation was a short-term success, but a new challenge was presented to the government from an increasingly "marginalized", young urban black population. This challenge was reinforced by the radicalization of university students and lecturers who were strongly influenced by international events and increasingly alienated from the PNM and DLP. These changes gave renewed confidence to the radicals in the trade unions, some of whom led strikes which contravened the regulations of the ISA. The government's development strategy after 1956 laid the framework for the forging of new alliances. The chief critics of the PNM in 1956 were local and foreign capital, the press and the Roman Catholic hierarchy; by 1970, they were its main supporters. The main supporters of the PNM in 1956 were black workers, progressive intellectuals and the unemployed; by 1970, progressive intellectuals and the urban unemployed, together with sections of the black proletariat, were its chief critics [Craig 1982b: 412].

Black Power, Race and Class and the "Alliance" of the Labouring Classes in 1970

One of the most important problems related to the study of social classes in underdeveloped societies concerns the prospects of an alliance between the (rural, as well as urban) working class, the urban marginals and the rural peasantry, and how the most progressive sections of these classes hope to achieve this unity. In this section, I highlight some of the difficulties of achieving such an alliance, which are compounded in the Trinidad case by the questions of race and ethnicity.

Black Power Ideology, its Trinidad and Tobago Context and the NJAC Leadership

Although the 1970 revolt won sympathy and/or active support from the progressive intelligentsia and sections of the working class, the leading social forces of the 1970 revolt were the urban marginals and radical students. These forces rallied behind the cry of Black Power. As I have already stated, this was a phenomenon which had its origins in the United States, and this led to a number of difficulties for the movement in Trinidad and Tobago.

The basic problem was that the context in which Black Power operated in the United States was bound to be different from that in the Caribbean. In the former, Black Power was a reaction by an oppressed black minority to urban squalor; in the West Indies, blacks were usually the majority of the population, or at least the largest ethnic group (as they were in Trinidad at the time). Moreover, the government was largely composed of black members. The NJAC attempted to deal with this problem by arguing that the political system was weak compared to the economic system, which was largely owned and controlled by whites.

While this argument was useful in that it transcended the limitations of "official" politics, it did not deal with the problem of an alliance of the oppressed. The difficulty with the slogan Black Power was not so much its applicability to the West Indies, as its inherent ambiguity. Indeed, this was (and still is) just as big a problem in the ethnically differentiated United States, as anywhere else. In Trinidad, the term Black Power was ambiguous because, like the United States, it was an ethnically heterogeneous society, and most importantly had a very large Indian population. In 1970, almost 43 percent of the population were of African origin, compared to figures of 40 percent Indian and 14 percent "mixed" [Trinidad and Tobago 1975: 6].

The slogan Black Power could therefore mean two different things. On the one hand, it could represent a movement of a particular section of society, organized along racial, but not class lines. Or it could mean "all" the oppressed of the Third World (although feminism had little impact at this time, and so in practice the term oppressed often did not explicitly include women). In other words, this position would combine a race and class analysis. After the death of Malcolm X in 1965, Stokely Carmichael (now known as Kwame Touré) emerged as the leading Black Power activist in the United States. In the last months of his life, Malcolm X appeared to be moving his political position from one of black nationalism and separatism, to one of black nationalism combined with a class analysis of the USA. Thus, he began to move away from the first position to an approximation of the second. Carmichael, however, continued to advocate a highly ambiguous position. In *The Running Man*, he stated that "we got brothers in Africa, we got brothers in Cuba, we got brothers all over the world" [Nicholls 1971: 444]. This may imply that a class analysis (albeit a crude one) which moved beyond skin colour was necessary, but it could also mean that the oppressed in the Third World constituted a homogenous mass in which internal conflicts did not occur. Carmichael appeared to accept this latter position during a visit to Guyana at the height of the rebellion in Trinidad, when he expressed admiration for the fact that the states in both Trinidad and Guyana were run by blacks and so argued that "the black man held position"; in other words, "Black Power" already existed [*Evening News* 1970a]. Furthermore, he said nothing about state repression, which was often directed against black people, and appeared uninterested in the population of Indian origin. On the other hand, in a speech to a crowd at Brooklyn, New York, less than one month later, Carmichael referred to the "heroic uprising" in Trinidad and Tobago [*Evening News* 1970b]. As well as these ambiguities, Carmichael at times betrayed a particularly distasteful attitude towards the role of women in the Black Power movement. In 1964 he is alleged to have said that "the only position for women in SNCC [Student Non-violent Coordinating Committee] is prone" [Solomon 1989: 84]. Such a view was apparently shared (according to its Public Relations Officer, Clive Nunez) by at least some NJAC sympathizers [*Express* 1970b].

The inconsistencies of Black Power ideology were not just a product of its leaders in the United States of America. The far more articulate and intellectual Walter Rodney was the leading exponent of Black Power in the West Indies, but he too had inadvertently demonstrated the vagueness of the term Black Power. In 1969 he wrote that Black Power in the West Indies meant three things: "(i) the break with imperialism which is historically white racist; (ii) the assumption of power by the black masses in the islands; (iii) the cultural reconstruction of the society in the image of the blacks" [Rodney 1969: 28]. Rodney recognized that the term Black Power was complicated by the variety of racial types and the processes of class formation in the West Indies (although this conclusion could equally be applied to the United States), but stated that "[n]evertheless, we can talk of the mass of the West Indian population as being black either African or Indian" [1969: 28]. However, he later refers to blacks almost exclusively in terms of African identity, and states that "[i]f we, the blacks of the West Indies, accept ourselves as African, we can make a contribution to the development of African culture, helping to free it from European imperialism" [1969: 52-53, 37]. Rodney also referred to the United States' "neocolonialist puppets in the West Indies" [1969: 52].

It should be clear then, that there were a number of problems with the ideology of Black Power. Nevertheless, given proper clarification it could have provided a useful rallying point for an alliance of the East Indian and black working classes in Trinidad. Indeed, I show below that there was the beginning of some unity among sections (from both major "racial" groups) of the organized working class, and that politics was as big a factor as race in explaining the defeat of the movement. Nevertheless, it remains the case that in Trinidad a large majority of support for the movement came from the black population. Attempts were made to forge "African–Indian unity", most notably through the "Long

March" to Caroni on 12 March, but, despite Geddes Granger's best efforts, this met with limited success. One observer present in Trinidad at the time has estimated that less than one percent of those attending the marches between February and April were of Indian origin [Nicholls 1971: 447]. Indian petty bourgeois groups were hostile to the movement and many Indian workers and peasants were ambivalent, regarding the Black Power versus government confrontation as "an affair which concerned Negroes" [Nicholls 1971: 455].

The problem with Black Power in Trinidad and Tobago was not the alleged inapplicability of a US ideology to the Caribbean, but the way that the leading organization in Trinidad (NJAC) reproduced the ambiguities of the general term Black Power. Many of the NJAC's critics argue that the organization borrowed too many ideas from the United States and falsely applied these to an inappropriate setting [La Guerre 1972b: 9]. My argument is that Black Power was as appropriate to Trinidad as it was to the USA, but I would question how this was articulated in both countries. The ideology of Black Power was unclear and even incoherent, but these problems, given the right leadership, were not insurmountable. The basic problem with the NJAC was that it did not attempt to overcome these ambiguities and indeed probably exacerbated them. On the question of racial unity, Granger argued that "Black Power has not turned against the Indian community . . . If you are not white you are black. Black Power is not confined to those of the African race. The Indian is the brother of the Negro" [*Express* 1970]. Similarly, in one of its most important political tracts, the NJAC stated that "African–Indian unity must be the basis for a new society" [NJAC 1971a: 34]. However, in practice the NJAC largely confined itself to propagating African history and culture, and at least some of its supporters (but not, it should be emphasized, the leadership) were openly hostile to the Indian population.

This problem of ambiguity extended beyond the question of racial alliances. While the populace had a reasonable idea what the NJAC was against (although even this was open to question), it was not clear what the NJAC was for. Moreover, this was a situation that the essentially populist NJAC openly encouraged: for example, in its April 1970 pamphlet "Why Black Power", its leaders wrote that "[o]ur demands are simple; we want our freedom, we want our manhood, and we want it now . . . what we are involved in is a Revolution. A Revolution knows no manifesto" [Riviere 1972: 25].

Aldwyn Primus led the Black Panther movement, a small and largely insignificant rival of the NJAC. In an otherwise bitter and sectarian attack on both the NJAC and the Tapia House Movement, he alluded to this fundamental weakness of NJAC: "The marches organized . . . represent a political confrontation with the government – the aim of which is forcing Williams and his gang to pack up and go . . . Nothing is wrong with that . . . but if that is the intention of the National Joint Action Committee and Lloyd Best, then for God's sake, Let The People Know" [*Express* 1970c].

It is not surprising that the question of state power was not posed by the NJAC because its leaders did not have a consistent political analysis of the PNM government. They tended to regard the government either as agents or as puppets of imperialism, which led to two conflicting political positions. If the PNM was a mere puppet, rather than a conscious agent, then there was some hope that they could change their policies for the benefit of the people of Trinidad and Tobago, and so the question of state power need not be posed. However, if the PNM consciously supported imperialism, the slogan of Black Power loses some of its potency, because the PNM leadership was predominantly black in composition. The NJAC described the government as "Afro-Saxon" because of its support for "neocolonialism", but this implies the need for a deeper class analysis than the NJAC allowed for. It was ironically the reformist Tapia House Movement that showed the contradictions of the NJAC's conception of Black Power in Trinidad, arguing that activists "ought not to be thinking that "black power" has to do with the colour of one's skin. If Castro is the blackest man in the Caribbean, the whitest, in these terms, are medieval figures such as Bradshaw of St Kitts or Bird of Antigua or Marie Antoinette Gairy of Grenada, the noted libertine who has now prescribed floggings for obscene language and obscene behaviour" [*Tapia* 1970: 2]. Race was a major issue, as I showed in the first section, but it was not the *only* issue.

To summarize: the NJAC's leadership of the Black Power mobilizations was weak because it failed to articulate clearly the links between race and class and, following on from this, it failed to challenge the power of the state, as embodied in the PNM government. As Turner notes, "NJAC engaged in a celebration of the creativity of the masses and a condemnation of the regime rather than a conscious directing of popular resources toward the seizure of power and its transfer from one class to another" [Turner

1972: 232]. The NJAC's leadership of the Black Power movement is one of two major reasons why the so-called February Revolution did not actually constitute a revolutionary or even pre-revolutionary situation. The other is discussed below.

The Role of Organized Labour in the Events of 1970

There were three central features of the 1970 rebellion. First, it was a spontaneous revolt by "marginalized" sections of the population, as I have attempted to show. Secondly, it was a period of marked industrial unrest, and thirdly, it was followed by a mutiny in the army.

It is the second of these features that I now want to discuss. However, before moving directly to an examination and assessment of organized labour's role in the rebellion, I want to first reiterate briefly why organized labour in general is so important a social force, even in situations where it is a small fraction of the size of the "informal sector" or peasantry. While this is not the case in Trinidad, it is true that in terms of numbers the urban unemployed and underemployed constituted by far the most important force in the rebellion. However, even though the proletariat did not play a revolutionary role, in a sense its numerically small contribution was more important, because the government's decision to introduce a State of Emergency cannot be comprehended without understanding the strategic significance of organized labour.

The revolt of 1970 took place against a general background of unrest throughout North and South America at this time. The "cult of the ghetto" existed in the United States, where the Black Panthers hoped to emerge as a major political force. Within the Third World, some writers believed that the traditional working class would not play the role assigned to it in traditional Marxist theory and that the urban marginals comprised the new revolutionary force. For instance, Frantz Fanon wrote that "[t]he lumpenproletariat, that horde of starving men, uprooted from their tribe, and from their clan, constitutes one of the most spontaneous and most radically revolutionary forces of a colonized people . . . It is within this mass of humanity, this people of the shanty towns . . . that the revolution will find its urban spearhead" [Fanon 1967: 103].

The evidence for such an assertion has been questioned [Cohen and Michael 1973: 33-35] and Fanon himself noted the necessity that they be "urged on from behind" by other agents of revolution [Fanon 1967: 103]. While Marx undoubtedly overemphasized the ease with which the organized working class would acquire revolutionary consciousness, there are still strong grounds for believing that its potential for radical political action is greater than that of the informal sector. The latter is too dispersed and disorganized to undertake political action without strong leadership from outside its ranks. The NJAC was not an organization which seriously challenged the PNM government. The organized working class is certainly not automatically revolutionary, but it is more likely to play a leading role in undertaking radical change. Moreover, its organizational strength makes it a much greater constant threat to any government and this was the basic reason why the government declared a state of emergency in 1970. Any examination of the 1970 events must therefore look at the role of organized labour.

The first important point to be made about the organized labour movement in 1970 is that it was a period when there was a marked increase in industrial unrest. There were 99 600 work days lost through strikes in 1970, a large increase on each of the previous five years since the ISA was passed [Turner 1972: 175]. Moreover, fewer grievances were being referred to the Industrial Court, which shows that more and more workers were willing to ignore the 1965 legislation. Given the wider Black Power context in which many of these strikes operated, it was likely that these "purely industrial" disputes could have wider implications. The question of the extent of proletarian support for the Black Power movement is therefore vital to an understanding of the reasons for its failure.

At a leadership level, some trade unions had close contact with the NJAC from the time of its formation. This was true of the Transport and Industrial Workers' Union (TIWU) and the Oilfields Workers' Trade Union (OWTU). However, at the start of the demonstrations in February there was little organized labour involvement. George Weekes quickly became associated with the Black Power movement, but there is no evidence to suggest that the OWTU membership followed his lead on any significant scale.

One trade union leader, Bhadase Maraj (the veteran of the ATSEFWTU - see chapter three) was openly hostile to Black Power ideology and publicly threatened NJAC leaders after they had announced their plan to march to Caroni. Bhadase Maraj was a popular cultural leader among the Indian community, and some writers have argued that his cultural hegemony over Hindus was a major factor in the lack of support that NJAC won from this section of the population [Gosine 1984: 27-28]. While there is a lot of truth in this assertion, its weakness lies in its underemphasis on the dynamics of how the situation developed in 1970. Such an approach assumes that Maraj's cultural hegemony was "total" and all embracing, and therefore incapable of being challenged. However, at the trade union level, he had faced persistent opposition to his leadership, most seriously in 1965. His threats to the NJAC should be seen in this light: his popularity among the Indian community notwithstanding, Maraj's authority as a trade union leader was continually under threat from a membership alienated by his undemocratic and corrupt practices. Indeed, significant links were established between sugar workers (who were mainly Indian) and the NJAC, albeit tentative and short-lived ones. This point is examined in more detail below.

As the momentum of the Black Power marches strengthened in both Trinidad and Tobago, developments were taking place in the trade union movement. There were some changes firstly in the OWTU. The day before Basil Davis was killed (6 April) by the police in Woodford Square, the OWTU General Council (rather than just Weekes) expressed its support for the Black Power struggle. More significantly, as it concerned the rank and file workforce rather than its politicized leadership, on 8 April, OWTU members at the Trinidad and Tobago Electricity Commission rejected management's wage offers. At this point, however, this development was entirely separate from the Black Power struggle.

These events were followed by the surprising decision of the Trinidad and Tobago Labour Congress to give its support to the Black Power movement. The Labour Congress had been established in 1966 by those conservative unions whose leaders had given support to the Industrial Stabilization Act. On 11 April 1970, its President, Clive Spencer, called for joint May Day celebrations between the Black Power movement and the Congress. He stated that in these planned marches the emphasis "shall be on the recognition and furtherance of Black Awareness. The Congress welcomes and invites all organizations and individuals to join with it in demonstrating on May 1 in the interest of overcoming oppression of the masses" [*Express* 1970d]. However, Spencer's statement also contained an implicit criticism of the NJAC, one which was to become more significant once the State of

Emergency was called. Echoing Williams' own limited support for "Black Power", Spencer argued that "Black Power can best be achieved by constructive planning, forceful persuasion and the transformation of ideas into activities which will create opportunities for the fulfilment of the aspirations of the Black Man" [*Express* 1970d]. In the event, Clive Nunez of the NJAC and the TIWU rejected Spencer's invitation on the grounds that the Labour Congress still supported the ISA and that "Congress leaders are being used by the power structure – as they always have been – to attempt to infiltrate the Black Power movement" [*Express* 1970d].

What is more significant is the extent to which many workers in Labour Congress unions were implicitly challenging the authority of their leaders by following the example of the "progressive unions" and going on strike. In mid March workers walked off their jobs at the construction firm George Wimpey, at Trinidad Cement and at a hotel construction project at Mount Irvine, Tobago. By mid April, industrial unrest had spread to postal workers, construction workers at the Hilton Hotel, pumping station workers at the Water and Sewerage Authority (WASA), and factory workers at Bottlers Ltd. The stoppages at the Hilton, WASA and Bottlers were important because they each involved members of the National Union of Government and Federated Workers. This union was formed in the late 1960s by a merger of the National Union of Government Employees and the Federated Workers Trade Union and so it became the largest union in the country and the backbone of the Labour Congress. These stoppages therefore struck at the heart of the Congress leadership which continued to support the strict limitations on strike activity embodied in the ISA. Strikes had also taken place since March at the docks, at Charles McEnearney, at Textile, at Battoo Brothers Ltd and among non-academic staff at the university [*Express* 1970e]. The majority of these strikes were carried out independently of NJAC but, given their context, were not regarded as completely autonomous from the events in the capital and the ideas of Black Power.

While some industrial action began to show signs of ending, most notably the strikes at the Hilton and Bottlers, the momentum of others increased. Members of the Trinidad and Tobago Postmen's Union demonstrated in Port of Spain and then moved on to the "People's Parliament" where the Union Vice President Albert Charles told Black Power supporters of their grievances. By 20 April, the union was threatening to turn its work-to-rule into a full-scale strike. Although there were moves to settle the dispute at WASA, around three hundred workers decided to continue their stoppage. At an OWTU rally on 15 April, President-General Weekes expressed the hope that "when we look forward for action from you the oilworkers, whenever it is necessary and when we give the call . . . you will come out" [*Trinidad Guardian* 1970]. Two days later the TIWU leadership called for a mass work stoppage on 21 April, and for workers to join in a mass protest demonstration against the refusal of Public Transport Service Corporation officials to reinstate workers who had lost their jobs in the 1969 bus strike. Members of this union also picketed the Industrial Court, calling for the repeal of the ISA.

Perhaps even more significant, at least from the point of view of unifying the two major racial groups, were the events in the sugar industry. On 19 April workers at the Brechin Castle sugar factory (owned by Caroni) stopped work in a protest against an Industrial Court decision which related to grievances dating back to January 1969. Although the Court awarded a wage increase, the workforce protested against the Court's rejection of union claims for pension and insurance plans, severance benefits, a guaranteed minimum wage and guaranteed employment throughout the year. ATSEFWTU leader Bhadase Maraj was called to the factory to appeal to the workers to return to their jobs, but his pleas were in vain. The following day the stoppage spread and, according to Caroni's public relations manager, over two thousand sugar workers were on strike [*Express* 1970e]. The same day over a thousand strikers marched in Couva with NJAC leader Geddes Granger and OWTU Research Officer Winston Leonard. This march then linked up with other demonstrations at the "People's Parliament" in Woodford Square. A delegation of workers at the Brechin Castle sugar factory also called on Weekes for help in their strike, and he promised to take up the matter at OWTU executive level.

So, by 21 April the country was in a state of industrial and social unrest, and there was the renewed threat (from the point of view of the government) of unity between sugar workers and the oil worker leadership. The situation was far more ominous for the government than in 1965, however, because, as the *Express* stated at the time, "these strikes are not isolated from the unrest which has swept this country since the 26 February invasion of the Cathedral of the Immaculate Conception" [*Express* 1970e]. It was therefore perceived that there was a danger that the "sectional" industrial unrest could be transformed into something far wider.

It was at this point that Williams decided that action had to be taken and a State of Emergency was declared on the night of 20 April. A curfew was imposed for twelve hours a day and the police were given wide powers of arrest and the right to restrict freedom of movement. Rioting followed and shops and banks were damaged. The Black Power leaders, including those in the OWTU, were arrested and sent to the remote Nelson Island prison. The strike in the sugar industry came to an end and a settlement at WASA was impending.

The momentum of the rebellion therefore came to an abrupt halt. While I do not want to suggest that the mobilization of organized labour was sufficiently politically conscious or widespread enough to carry out a social revolution (given the right leadership), the timing of the declaration of the State of Emergency is significant. Williams was certainly aware of the dangers of organized labour resistance and he justified the decision to introduce the State of Emergency by stating that "[i]t was only when the total breakdown of the trade union movement was imminent that I decided to act" [*Express* 1970g].

This statement becomes of greater import when one examines correspondence (revealed a year later) between Williams and Labour Congress leader Clive Spencer. At the 1971 PNM Party Convention, Williams revealed that Spencer presented Williams with an ultimatum on 20 April. According to Williams, Spencer's ultimatum was that

> [i]f immediate action was not taken by the Government to bring the whole situation under control, then the Labour Congress . . . would bring the whole community to a standstill by calling out the workers in the Port, the Airport, external and internal communications, the Civil Service and the daily paid workers . . . It was clear to the Ministers present and particularly the Prime Minister that the time had come for decisive action; it was no longer a problem of aimless marches and wild public statements; the whole labour movement was threatened [*Trinidad Guardian* 1971c].

An Emergency Cabinet session was called which gave the Prime Minister the power to declare a State of Emergency when he saw fit. Spencer denied that he had actually told Williams to declare a State of Emergency but he accepted that he complained to the Prime Minister about the latter's failure to take any action. He also disclosed that "members of the National Joint Action Committee had been engaged in activities at the Water and Sewerage Authority . . . and . . . had caused the workers to go on strike" [*Trinidad Guardian* 1971d]. It is clear from this statement that the leadership of the Congress, under challenge from sections of their membership, openly encouraged Williams to take "decisive action"; and after the declaration of the State of Emergency, Spencer told Williams that the right course of action had been taken.

In the absence of action by the government, Spencer was effectively calling for a mass strike by his members against Black Power and the progressive unions. Whether he would have won the desired response from them can only be a matter of conjecture. "Responsible" trade unionism and the "racial" disunity of the working class was under challenge, but this was confined to a minority of the labour movement. Moreover, the strikes that had arisen in March and April were quickly settled during the State of Emergency. The strikers' "confrontation" with their leaders' philosophy of trade unionism was short-lived (but it did have beneficial long-term effects, in that it paved the way for the emergence of younger leaders more willing to challenge sections of the bureaucratic leadership in the Labour Congress – see chapter six), and conflict with the government had hardly started. While sections of the proletariat had won higher wages and better working conditions, the momentum of these struggles had only just begun to be taken further, and it is unlikely that the NJAC could have provided the coherent leadership necessary to continue this task. The political legitimacy of the PNM had been undermined, but it was far from broken, most crucially in the eyes of many workers in a politically divided labour movement. The movement was therefore likely to fail "as long as the trade union movement itself remained bitterly divided, with one faction largely supportive of government policy and the other, in its leadership, alienated from it" [Sutton 1983: 126]. This is the second reason why the events of 1970 did not constitute a revolutionary or prerevolutionary situation.

Mutiny in the Army

An army mutiny may not appear to be of direct significance to a study of the politics of labour, but the mutiny from 21 April to 1 May is relevant for two reasons. First, because it placed the question of state power on the agenda, the mutiny constituted the most serious political challenge to the government in 1970.

Secondly, there were some informal links between the rebels in the army and individuals active in the organized labour movement. For these reasons, I now briefly examine the army mutiny.

The Trinidad and Tobago Defence Force had been formed in 1962 out of the West India Regiment that had collapsed along with Federation. The Officer Corps had been carefully selected by the former British commanders, largely on the basis of political reliability rather than military skill. After independence, political patronage continued and, in the words of the leading mutineer in 1970, Raffique Shah, "the senior officers had no military background whatever [*sic*]. They were what one might term political appointees who were appointed to such positions because they were loyal to the ruling party" [*Caribbean Dialogue* 1976: 22].

The army was therefore left as an inefficient force whose sole purpose was to suppress internal dissent, rather than repel external aggression. However, opposition to patronage and inefficiency arose, most conspicuously among the junior officer corps. Links were established with some of the former members of the WFP, including C.L.R. James (who had regularly lived in England, where many of the junior officers were trained) and activists involved in the production of the OWTU's newspaper, *Vanguard*. There were not, however, any ties with the NJAC [Shah 1990: 3].

Indeed, *Vanguard* appeared to know more about the problems of the military than the government. In an article published two weeks before the coup, an anonymous writer outlined the basic features of a "crisis in the army": "Inefficiency, mental oppression, victimization and threats, deplorable conditions of work, racism and black rebellion" [*Vanguard* 1970]. The writer described how the invasion of neighbouring Anguilla by British marines trained in the Caribbean had increased discontent among junior officers and the lower ranks and how the Black Power uprising had inspired them.

When the State of Emergency was declared on 21 April, the junior officers, led by Raffique Shah and Rex Lassalle, took control of the army. Shah later reasoned that "the one thing we could do was to prevent the government, which had obviously become unpopular at that point, from using the army against the people" [*Caribbean Dialogue* 1976: 23]. Some of the mutineers wanted to go to Port of Spain to challenge the government and it was at this point that the question of state power was posed. This is why the mutiny was a more serious threat to the government than the NJAC-led revolt on the street. There were undoubtedly some who (rather adventurously) believed that the road to socialist revolution lay in an army coup backed by radical leaders in the trade unions.

In the event, the young, inexperienced mutineers decided to settle their differences with the government by negotiation. The government's position was strengthened by the presence of US and Venezuelan battleships in Trinidad's territorial waters, and by the fact that two British frigates were placed on alert [Shah 1990: 5; *Express* 1970f]. The rebels were tricked into a negotiated settlement, and were then arrested and charged with treason. The government had therefore survived the most serious challenge to its authority.

The Consequences of 1970 and Continued Unrest, 1970–1973

The leaders of the Black Power rebellion were detained until November 1970, when the State of Emergency was lifted. (The leaders of the army mutiny were detained until they were tried for treason in 1971. Although they were found guilty, Shah and Lassalle were later freed on a technicality, and the former went on to play a very active role in labour politics in the 1970s – see chapter five for details.) Despite the government crackdown, and its defeat of the NJAC, industrial unrest continued and around 70 000 workdays were lost through strike activity in 1971 [Turner 1972: 175].

The most serious of these strikes involved members of the OWTU. Strikes took place at Dunlop and Federation Chemicals over delays in wage negotiations, the dismissal of six workers for insubordination (at Fedchem), and the employment of expatriates in senior positions (at Dunlop). The strikes, which involved around 600 people, rapidly spread as nearly 4000 oil workers came out in sympathy with their fellow workers [*Trinidad Guardian* 1971a, 1971b]. They were eventually settled but there was still a police raid (one had already taken place in 1970) at the OWTU headquarters. Documents were seized and four OWTU officials were detained [*Vanguard* 1971]. This raid showed that the mutual distrust that existed between the PNM and the OWTU leadership since independence had now developed into open hostility.

Two further developments led to the government calling a second State of Emergency in the space of eighteen months. The first involved the OWTU and three transnational companies: Texaco,

Badger Pan-American and Wimpey. Texaco contracted Badger to construct a desulphurization plant at its Pointe-à-Pierre refinery, and over a thousand workers joined the OWTU. Wage agreements were made, but Wimpey, which was also carrying out construction work at the plant, refused to pay a similar wage rate. Wimpey workers went on strike, and Badger workers followed in sympathy. However, Badger then responded by pulling out of Trinidad altogether.

The second factor involved relations between the leadership of the OWTU and the Labour Congress. Workers at WASA (active during the 1970 rebellion), the Telephone Company and in particular the docks, wanted to join the OWTU. The Labour Congress accused the OWTU, and in particular George Weekes, of poaching: according to one of its leaders, Nathaniel Critchlow, the consequences of Weekes' alleged action would be "the destruction of industrial peace in the country, the destruction of the investment climate, the creation of unemployment and discontent and the fomentation of political strife thereby making the country fertile ground for the propagation of an ideology of which he is a local protagonist" [*Express* 1971]. Critchlow warned that if Weekes did not stop his "poaching activity" the Labour Congress would respond by: calling for the expulsion of the OWTU from the ICFTU and the International Federation of Petroleum and Chemical Workers; requesting all maritime organizations to cease handling goods consigned to companies which gave recognition to the OWTU; instructing the SWWTU and the Caribbean Air Transport Trade Union to do the same to any goods entering the country which involved companies that recognized the OWTU; instructing unions in the communications and the postal services to do the same with goods produced, installed or repaired within the country [*Express* 1971].

However, Critchlow's claim that Weekes was poaching was probably erroneous – Weekes was still in prison when the dock workers requested representation by the OWTU. The OWTU Executive argued that the reality was that some dock workers

> have expressed dissatisfaction with the representation they got from the Seamen and Waterfront Workers' Trade Union and have individually applied to this union for membership. We have, of course, accepted them, as we believe that Trade Unions are in duty bound to uphold the constitutional right of all workers to choose the union of their choice to represent them . . . No organizers have been sent . . . to solicit membership [*Express* 1971].

Nevertheless, the government used the events at Badger and the claims of the Labour Congress to justify the declaration of another State of Emergency in October 1971. Under this particular State of Emergency, there was no curfew but public meetings were restricted and ten activists were detained. Those detained included George Weekes, OWTU legal adviser Jack Kelshall, Geddes Granger and the President of the Badger branch of the OWTU, Alain Campbell [*Trinidad Guardian* 1971e].

Despite the efforts of the Labour Congress to uphold the ISA, the events of 1970–71 had effectively destroyed it. The government, having decided that new legislation was necessary, introduced the Industrial Relations Bill shortly after the State of Emergency was declared. This bill became law in 1972, but it was less a replacement to the ISA than an amendment. The key limitations to the right to strike and the functions of the Industrial Court were retained. The provisions for price controls, which had never been implemented, were withdrawn and a new clause (aimed directly at the OWTU) stated that a trade union was not permitted to represent more than one group of workers in what were considered as essential industries. Public utilities, port operations, public transport, sugar and oil and related industries all came under this category.

Critchlow's statement above, and the events which followed it, showed that the political differences between "responsible unions" and "radical unions" still existed and that the former still adhered to their pre-ISA position that capital investment would be attracted if government and unions employed the correct policies. The radicals decided that an alternative trade union federation was necessary and in 1971 the Council of Progressive Trade Unions was established. At this time the federation was not aligned to any of the international trade union federations (it later affiliated to the World Federation of Trade Unions in 1980). Although the federation attracted several unions, the OWTU and TIWU were initially the only two of real significance.

Conclusion

In terms of the numbers involved, the Black Power rebellion of 1970 was the most serious challenge to the thirty years (1956–86) of PNM government. In a sense, however, it did not challenge the government at all because the urban poor and its NJAC leadership never posed the question of power. The rebellion of the black poor represented a challenge to the power base of the PNM, but it did not challenge the government's right to rule. It was only when the organized labour movement became a significant actor that Williams declared a State of Emergency. Therefore, the "danger" of an alliance between the organized working class (the proletariat), both Indian and African, and the urban poor, prompted Williams to act.

The question of unity among the working classes in 1970 is a difficult one to assess for two reasons. First, the "alliance", such as it was, had only just begun to be formed when the government acted. Secondly, and related to this first point, there was no organization that attempted to unite labour and go "beyond the fragments" of the disparate working classes.

Nevertheless, a few tentative conclusions and observations can be made. While race and ethnicity continued to divide the working classes, and the ideology of Black Power may have reinforced this, there were developments (the links between the NJAC, and African and Indian workers on strike) which suggest that unity on a scale similar to 1937 was not out of the question. Writers that "explain" the failure of the rebellion in terms of a timeless cultural divide between Indian and African (the plural society model) describe divisions of the greatest significance, but they do not explain either how these are rooted in history, or, related to this point, the dynamics of the 1970 events [La Guerre 1972b; Gosine 1984]. Racial and ethnic divisions were, along with politics, the most important reasons for the failures of 1970, but these divisions were constantly changing and never static. The changes that took place just before the crackdown indicate that relations between sections of the two ethnic groups were developing in a positive way. Secondly, notwithstanding the developments among sections of the rank and file within the Labour Congress, the proletariat itself remained divided by politics. Many workers remained loyal to the Labour Congress and to the PNM. This factor cannot be dismissed as "false consciousness" on the part of the working class, but can instead be attributed to the fact that the PNM had led the country to independence and had governed in a period when substantial numbers of workers had won material gains. Those workers that were alienated from their "responsible union leaders" and the PNM government were not necessarily in favour of their replacement by revolutionary means. And finally, the rank and file of the OWTU never followed the wishes of their leaders during 1970 and so never went on strike during the

February-April period. So long as this remained the case, the rebellion of 1970 was unlikely to develop into a revolution.

The period from 1970 to 1973 was one of intense unrest. By 1973 it appeared that Williams had threatened to resign, but the oil price rise (1973-74) led to a dramatic change in the country's economic fortunes, and with it the popularity of the government, which influenced the Prime Minister's decision to remain in office. The economic boom which followed also paved the way for a new period of labour history, and I turn my attention to this period in chapter five.

5

The Struggle for a Labour Party: The United Labour Front

Chapter three described the process by which trade unions unsuccessfully attempted to form labour and/or socialist parties that would win political office and lead the country to independence. It was, instead, the PNM that undertook this task. However, there remained a conflict of interest between the PNM's development strategy and the interests of the progressive trade unions, which culminated in restrictive labour legislation in 1965. There were renewed attempts to forge a new mass politics based on class rather than race in 1966 (namely, the WFP), and to some extent in 1970 (see chapter four). These were defeated, however, and the PNM continued to govern the country and promote a capitalist development strategy.

After 1974, the country entered a period of rapid economic growth which gave to the labour movement a new feeling of confidence that its demands could be met. An informal alliance of progressive trade unions was formed in 1975, which acquired the name of the United Labour Front (ULF). After government suppression the decision was taken to convert the ULF from a union-based interest group into a political party. Unlike its predecessors, the ULF had considerable initial electoral success and it won ten seats at the 1976 general election and control of the majority of local councils the following year. However, within twelve months of the general election, the ULF had split into two factions, and so the most serious attempt yet to form a popular labour and socialist-oriented party in Trinidad and Tobago fell into disarray.

In this chapter, I outline in four sections how the ULF emerged and rapidly disintegrated as a united political force. The first section briefly examines the basis for the emergence of the ULF by referring to the economic boom which gave the labour movement an unprecedented degree of confidence. Secondly, the formation of the ULF is examined and the reasons why it transformed itself into a political party are explained. In the third part of the chapter the divisions in the ULF are discussed and I assess the reasons for its failure. In this section, I take issue with a number of "Marxist–Leninist" analyses of the ULF which regard its failure as an inevitable manifestation of trade union "economism" and the lack of a political "vanguard". Instead, it is argued that the real reasons for the split were partly organizational, but were above all based on crude factionalism, the "politics of personality" and race. Finally, the outcome and the aftermath of the split are explored.

The Economic Boom

In 1973-74, the world price of oil sharply increased. The precise reasons for the increase are far more complex than the "third world challenge" to western hegemony that is often alleged by both neo-classicists and "third world nationalists". In fact, although they may not have instigated them, western oil companies played a leading role in maintaining high prices through limiting production and allocating markets, and the Third World as a whole lost more than it gained (through the increase in the price for oil imports). For oil exporting Third World countries such as Trinidad, however, the oil price rise provided an opportunity to finance new development projects and overcome its subordinate position in the world market.

In Trinidad the oil windfall between 1974 and 1978 was proportionately higher than for other oil exporting countries such as Ecuador, Venezuela and Nigeria; in this period it constituted the equivalent of 39 percent of non-mining gross domestic product

[Auty and Gelb 1986: 1163]. Government revenue from oil rose from US $33 million in 1972 to US $1.58 billion in 1980 [MacDonald 1986: 195]. These changes laid the basis for a revised government economic strategy which aimed to create large scale resource intensive export industries. The state played a major role in government economic policy. An industrial estate was developed at Point Lisas which included a chemical fertilizer industry and an iron and steel works. Government finance was used to improve roads, telecommunications, water and electricity supplies and other state services.

In the long term, the strategy was largely a failure and the reasons for this – and government and union responses to it – will be discussed in chapter six. For the moment, the short-term results and their effects on the working classes will be analysed. The social effects of the boom and the government's development strategy were contradictory. Per capita income increased from US$1,231 per annum in 1973 to US$3,168 in 1978. Unemployment declined to 8.8 percent by 1980 [MacDonald 1986: 191], and the amount of money in circulation ensured that many in the informal sector had a better standard of living than before 1973. Prime Minister Williams claimed that "Money is no problem", a slogan which acquired some popularity. The low income sectors of society were given some degree of protection as the government intervened (directly and indirectly) in the economy in order to ensure a supply of cheap essentials.

Nevertheless, poverty and inequality remained major problems. In a Household Budgetary Survey conducted in 1975-76, it was found that the bottom 50 percent of income earners earned 18.2 percent of total income [Harewood and Henry 1985: 48]. While there was some redistribution of income in this period, the main beneficiaries were the middle class and the highest paid members of the working class [Harewood and Henry 1985: 47-50]. The survey also found that 32.2 percent of the population lived below the poverty line, 32.7 percent did not have flush toilets, 41.4 percent did not have pipe-borne water in their homes, 23 percent did not have electricity, and 89.5 percent were without a telephone [Ryan and Jacobs c.1979: xx].

As the boom was sustained, the extent of poverty decreased and so it is very likely that there was a considerable improvement in these statistics. While uneven development continued and poverty remained a major social problem, improvements in living standards were still considerable. The economic climate helped to shape a renewed confidence in the PNM government and so any new political party, particularly a socialist one, was going to find it difficult to defeat the PNM in a general election. On the other hand, the boom provided the basis for a renewed vitality in the labour movement, as lower unemployment improved the bargaining position of the organized working class. The birth of the ULF was based on this premise.

The Birth and Early Development of the United Labour Front

The United Labour Front as an Alliance of Unions

The ULF was initially formed as an informal alliance of four trade unions: the OWTU, the ATSEFWTU, TIWU, and the Islandwide Cane Farmers Trade Union (ICFU). The leadership of both the OWTU and TIWU was still in the hands of "progressives" and in 1973-74 there were significant developments in the two sugar unions. Bhadase Maraj had died in 1971, but the ATSEFWTU, under the leadership of Maraj's deputy Rampartap Singh, remained undemocratic and corrupt. The other major sugar union was the pro-PNM Trinidad Islandwide Cane Farmers Association (TICFA), led by Norman Girwar. By 1973, a significant rival to TICFA had established itself – the ICFU, which was led by the former army mutineer, Raffique Shah. The ICFU executive also had strong representation from the explicitly Marxist UNIP. Rampartap Singh, rightly, saw this challenge to the TICFA as a challenge to his own union and so he recruited the charismatic Basdeo Panday as a bulwark against the ICFU. Panday had worked as a lawyer for the OWTU and had been a member of the WFP and so Singh was taking a gamble – one which he was soon to regret.

At the start of the sugar crop season, the increasingly popular ICFU inaugurated a no-cut campaign until employers recognized it as the sole bargaining agent for cane farmers. This campaign was supported by the ATSEFWTU as Panday staged an internal coup and established himself as its leader, and set about restoring democracy to the union. Panday then won a 100 percent wage increase and guaranteed work for the whole year for sugar workers, and these victories won him a strong loyalty among sugar workers.

In late 1974, Panday again called a strike at Caroni over the company's failure to negotiate a profit sharing scheme. Shah's union had still not won recognition from Caroni who argued that legislation passed in 1965 (the Cess Act) made the TICFA the only legitimate representative of cane farmers. Meanwhile, negotiations between the OWTU and Texaco over wage increases had reached a standstill and a strike seemed likely.

By early 1975 tension had increased and the government-owned radio station banned interviews with Shah, Weekes and Panday and dismissed journalists who publicly disagreed with this decision. The OWTU regularly called out members from work to attend mass union meetings and the sugar workers' strike spread to the government-owned Orange Grove Estate, and to Forres Park Estate and Caroni Distillers. Negotiations between TIWU and Neal and Massy were not progressing and a strike seemed likely. By March 1975 there were around 17 000 sugar workers on strike and 9000 cane farmers boycotting the sugar harvest [Baptiste 1976: 18; *Express* 1975b].

In an effort to reduce the industrial unrest, the Employers' Consultative Association (ECA) met with the two union federations. The ECA President, Ralph Rostant, repeated the arguments of senators before the ISA was passed in 1965 (and the leaders of the Labour Congress in 1970), when he stated that "[i]t is almost naive to believe that we can attract foreign investors in this situation. And we believe that it is almost impossible to correct the unemployment situation in this country without these investors". He was most critical of the OWTU and claimed that "[w]e don't believe that industrial relations should be used as a tool for political ends" [*Express* 1975a].

The talks were not successful and the four unions of what came to be known as the ULF made plans for a mass rally to be held on 18 March. The government claimed that any march would be illegal as no permit had been granted by the Police Commissioner, but the ULF argued that the rally was not a political meeting. It would in fact be a religious occasion where there would be prayers "for bread, justice and peace", and so a permit was not required.

The rally went ahead and the ULF leaders presented its six demands to the government in front of an unexpectedly large crowd of around 15 000 people:

1. To repeal Act no. 1 of 1965 – the Canefarmers Cess Act, and the immediate recognition of ICFTU.

2. To repeal Act no. 23 of 1972 – the Industrial Relation [*sic*] Act – IRA.

3. To protest the delay of Texaco, Caroni Ltd, and Neal and Massy Ltd, in concluding negotiations with the OWTU, ATSEFWTU and TIWU respectively.

4. To demand the withdrawal on Texaco's Writ and Injunction preventing the Recognition Board from pursuing OWTU's claim for recognition of the monthly paid workers of Texaco.

5. To demand withdrawal of the levy on sugar.

6. To let those who labour hold the reins [United Labour Front 1975: 1].

In the short term these demands were overshadowed by the response of the legal authorities as the police broke up the rally and arrested thirty-two ULF leaders [*Express* 1975c]. The specific grievances of the ULF as a union alliance were settled over the next few months by compromises on both sides. More significantly, the suppression of the march (which came to be known as "Bloody Tuesday") convinced the ULF leaders that the interests of the working class could only be served in the long run by the formation of a new political party. The ULF as an informal union alliance had won considerable industrial support from both African and Indian workers; its leaders hoped that this could be extended to politics.

The United Labour Front as a Political Party

After "Bloody Tuesday", there was widespread discussion about the form that a labour party should take. Some members (such as Lennox Pierre, Allan Alexander and John Humphrey) argued that the ULF should remain a union alliance and that there should be a separate (but organically linked) political party. There were also fears that ultra-left-wing organizations would use the ULF for their own ends (see below for details). Nevertheless, sufficient agreement was reached and "realizing the limitations of Trade Union Action the ULF held a COSSABO [Conference of Shop Stewards and Branch Officers] . . . on January 3 and 4, 1976 at which a decision was taken to bring into being the Party of the

Working Class" [TIWU 1976: 1]. At a further COSSABO a decision
was taken to hold the Founding Congress of the ULF on 21 March
1976.

The organizational structure that emerged out of this Congress
was complex and never stringently implemented, and it formed
the basis for a major division in the ULF. On the one hand there
was a tendency which wanted a highly centralized party structure
in which a Central Committee would play the leading role in the
running of the ULF. At the Founding Conference, this tendency
(led by old UNIP members James Millette and Richard Jacobs)
argued that the existing leadership should elect the Central
Committee. In other words, this tendency believed in an interpretation of the Leninist organizational principle of democratic centralism which placed the emphasis on centralism rather than
democracy. On the other hand, another tendency argued that the
party should be organized "from below" through party blocks,
which would be divided by region but could also be organized in
workplaces and other communities. This group recognized that
there would have to be some degree of centralization, but argued
as well that the Central Committee should be elected by the total
membership of the party. Lennox Pierre, the former leader of the
WIP (see chapter three), was the main figure in this group. In
practice, the Central Committee became the leading structure and
the party blocks were never properly instituted, and this factor
became a major point of contention in the 1977 split. At this
stage, Basdeo Panday and Raffique Shah, the two major protago-
nists in the split, did not take clear sides.

The organizational issue was complicated by the participation
of a number of tiny ultra-left-wing groups in the ULF. As well as
the UNIP these included the New Beginning Movement (NBM),
the National Liberation Movement (NLM) and the National
Movement for the Total Independence of Trinidad and Tobago
(NAMOTI). The NLM and NAMOTI were basically Maoist while
the NBM was a Jamesian inspired organization (and not Trotskyist
as is usually asserted – [Phillips 1984: 380]). NAMOTI was by
far the most significant of these organizations, and many "independents" in the ULF feared that it was being used as a battleground between Maoists (NAMOTI) and Stalinists (UNIP) to
promote their own interests at the expense of the ULF.

These issues of contention were originally controlled as the new
party set about drafting a constitution and political programme,
and preparing for the general election which was due some time

in 1976. A draft constitution was eventually agreed which set out the aims and objectives of the ULF:

> (a) To unite the working class as a class for political struggle and to struggle with the workers or any section of them for such political objectives as are immediately realizable and for the ultimate political objective of working class power;
>
> (b) To establish an economic system, a social order and a government consistent with the interests of the working classes and the people in general . . . [United Labour Front 1976b: 1].

The political programme of the ULF included proposals for national ownership and control of oil, natural gas, fertilizer plants, sugar, foreign trade, industrial monopolies such as motor vehicles, cement and rum, large distribution monopolies and financial systems. It also proposed a mixed economy of state and private capital for small and medium sized firms. Social legislation would include a minimum wage, the end of wage discrimination against women and a full social security system [United Labour Front 1976c: 14, 19].

There were some doubts expressed that the ULF should participate in "bourgeois" elections (there had been a widespread boycott of the 1971 elections in protest at a government imposed state of emergency) on the grounds that it might become an electoralist party, solely concerned with winning general elections at the expense of extra-parliamentary activity. The ULF leaders eventually decided that it was necessary to participate in the election on the principle that this was a means to an end, rather than an end in itself; the General Secretary argued that "the ULF has to contest the forthcoming elections . . . not because the ULF is an election machine, but because that is the role which the ULF is called upon, at this stage, to play" [Millette 1976: 2]. However, the party never adopted a clear political attitude towards parliament, as I argue below.

The party went into the general election in September 1976 without a clear leader and instead decided to uphold the principle of collective leadership. Allan Alexander, a radical lawyer of African descent, was nominated as the person who would become Prime Minister, possibly on the basis that the party did not believe that the country as a whole would accept an Indian leader. The electorate was however unconvinced by Alexander and regarded Panday as the real leader. The question of race quickly emerged as the major factor in the election campaign. ULF Central Committee member, Richard Jacobs later claimed that "it would be fair to say that we were actually blind to race . . . This mood, this tendency to ignore the racial factor, prevailed at all levels of the ULF" [Ryan and Jacobs c.1979: 271]. Jacobs' claim has, however, been strongly rejected by Panday at least [Panday interview 1990], and the decision to appoint Alexander as "Prime Minister in waiting" suggests that race was always an important consideration for the party. What is true is that the party overestimated the extent to which the industrial action ("class struggle") of 1971-75 had eroded historical racial divisions, and as a result, it failed to offer a challenge to the political hegemony of the black petty bourgeoisie. I will elaborate on this argument below.

During the election campaign, members of the "white" bourgeoisie presented the ULF as an Indian party and used racist arguments to appeal to the PNM's traditional African constituency. For instance, Jimmy Bain, director of numerous private companies and Chairperson of the state owned National Broadcasting Company, stated that "[s]hould this time come when the East Indian section owns most of the property, business and wealth of the country as well as control of the Government, an imbalance could develop in our society that would cause undesirable stresses and strains that would not be good for the nation. It is an urgent necessity therefore, that all of us give serious thought to these matters, and like sensible people make a conscious effort to counter any undesirable consequences that could develop from such a possible situation" [Trinidad Guardian 1976a].

The ULF was not successful in uniting the working classes across racial lines. Black members of the OWTU and the Labour Congress unions largely remained faithful to the PNM. In the last two weeks of the campaign, the party attempted to increase its profile in the north, along the East-West corridor, and it organized motorcades through the area. The effect of this strategy was counter-productive, because the strong presence of Indians on these motorcades convinced black proletarians and petty commodity traders and producers that the ULF was simply a new Indian party, a replacement for the DLP.

The result of the election demonstrated the problem for the party. The PNM won twenty-four seats, the Democratic Action Congress two seats (both in Tobago), while the ULF won the other ten. These seats were almost exclusively confined to the sugar producing areas, where the majority of the population was of

Indian descent. Allan Alexander actually failed to win his seat, and so Panday became Leader of the Opposition. Lloyd Best rightly argued, "[t]he ULF won the traditional DLP seats and the PNM won the traditional PNM seats with some slight change" [*Trinidad Guardian* 1976b]. The problem that the ULF faced was how to break out of this situation.

The Demise of the United Labour Front

The Factions and the Split

In August 1977, within one year of the general election, Panday was removed as Leader of the Opposition and the party had effectively been divided in two. On the one side, supported by a majority of parliamentarians but only by a small section of supporters outside of the House of Representatives, was the "Shah faction". On the other side was Panday, who had the social base of ULF support but was strongly distrusted by his colleagues in Parliament and the leadership of the party.

The split occurred against a background of increasing differences over organization and politics. The Shah faction was led by Pierre, Education and Research Officer and NAMOTI supporter "Teddy" Belgrave, Alexander, and Shah himself. This faction was opposed to the Soviet Marxism espoused by Millette and Jacobs, and the ULF became a breeding ground for left wing sectarianism. For instance, there was a lot of discussion about Cuba's role in Angola and the "correct" response to the death of Mao [Millette interview 1990]. There were also differences over the most appropriate socialist strategy for Trinidad and Tobago. Millette accused NAMOTI of having its own agenda and of advocating a Maoist "people's war" strategy, based on armed conflict, rather than the ULF policy of consolidating a mass base through electoral means [Millette 1976: 18].

Panday was aware of the divisions but was only interested in them insofar as they constituted a threat to his own perception of the ULF. This differed from both factions, because Panday was an essentially electoralist politician opposed to all ideologies, except his own. He basically advocated unity between the two races and some degree of workers' participation [Panday interview **1990**], but his concrete proposals to achieve these were vague and he was a populist who had established a strong social base in the sugar areas during the industrial unrest of **1973** to **1975**.

It was Panday's populism that was so objectionable to the Shah faction and, together with the ULF's commitment to working class unity across race lines, these factors above all others explain why the party split in two. The election result had reproduced the very pattern of race based, two-party politics that the ULF had set out to destroy. After the election, Shah in particular came to believe that there should be a concerted strategy of campaigning in the north, and in particular in the all important East–West corridor, even if this was at the expense of existing support in the sugar areas. The Shah faction quickly came to believe that Panday's politics reinforced the status quo at the expense of principled, class-based, socialist politics. They believed that Panday, like Bhadase Maraj before him, had come to represent a political demagogue who was basically happy to represent one section of the community. As the Shah faction's political organ *Classline* asked, "[w]as the ULF to practise the maximum in democracy or were we to sink into political opportunism and one-manism" [*Classline* 1977]. The faction then went on to make some specific allegations: each of the unions that made up the ULF had more than one union leader on the Central Committee except for the sugar workers' union which had only Panday, who had instead insisted that his friend John Humphrey be a CC member; he had chosen former members of the PNM (Sonny Khayadat) and DLP (Mulchan Seuchan) and close political colleagues (Faizal Mohammed) for the 1977 local government elections instead of members of his union (such as radical shop steward, Omar Khan). For Shah and his colleagues, these men "represented the old – opportunism, racism and contempt for the poor people of our country" [*Classline* 1977]. Panday was also accused of deviating from party policy on issues such as self-government for Tobago, and of introducing a motion of no confidence in the government without consulting any colleagues. Perhaps most seriously, Panday was accused of racism because he publicly condoned to his constituents in Couva a statement that he was letting the Africans in the ULF ride his back and that he should get rid of them [*Classline* 1977]. As a result of these divisions, on **9** August **1977**, the Party Central Committee removed Panday as parliamentary leader of the ULF [*Express* 1977b]. Shah had the support of six of the ten ULF MPs and, after some constitutional questions were resolved, he replaced Panday as Leader of the Opposition on 19 August [*Express* 1977c, 1977g].

Panday's response was to appeal to the social base that he had, and Shah did not have. Within three days of his expulsion, all four of the ULF controlled councils had given their support to Panday and "No Panday! No ULF!" banners were common in the sugar producing areas [*Express* 1977h]. The cane farmers' union gave their support to Panday, despite the fact that it was led by Shah [*Express* 1977d]. Panday held public meetings to put forward his own version of why he was removed as leader. Before his removal, he had talked of a "bunch of traitors and stooges" that were out to destroy the party [*Express* 1977a]. Panday's appeal to his social base became increasingly nationalist as well as populist: he complained that NAMOTI "wanted to destroy the foundations of the working class ideology [and] to impose a foreign radical view which had no relevance to our situation" [*Express* 1977e]. He also claimed that he was not particularly interested in leadership but went on to say (in a classically populist manner) that "if the people call on me to lead I will not flinch one hair's breadth from this sacred trust" [*Express* 1977f].

In November Panday called a "Party Congress" of the ULF which demonstrated that there were by now effectively two parties claiming the party banner. On the one side was Shah and his supporters who were the official Opposition but had little support outside of Parliament, and on the other was Panday and his supporters in the sugar belt. By the end of March 1978, Shah resigned as Opposition Leader because he was disillusioned with the processes of parliamentary politics and after a quite blatant piece of PNM-sponsored, state-judicial victimization of the ULF (Shah faction) MP Boodram Jattan [Ryan and Jacobs *c*.1979: 312]. In his farewell address as Opposition Leader, Shah spoke of a "plot to plunge the country back into racial politics" [*Trinidad Guardian* 1978].

Panday's initial removal was followed by the resignation of James Millette as General Secretary. He blamed the ultra-left (NAMOTI and the Shah faction) for splitting the party, and using it as "a battleground on which rival factions and jejune ideas could joust for the triumph of their own version of purity in the working class movement". He argued that the task of the ULF was to "consolidate the Party as a united national movement of working people and to equip it with the resources necessary for the accomplishment of the task of taking power and using it in the interests of all the people" [ULF 1977 no.19].

So, by September 1977 the party had divided into two factions led by Panday and Shah, plus a "semi-faction" led by Millette. Shah's faction saw Panday as a threat to the "new politics" proposed by the ULF, while Panday and his supporters argued that Shah was simply a figurehead for a NAMOTI "coup" within the party. Millette was critical of aspects of Panday's behaviour but basically took the view that Panday was removed because "the others wanted to take the leadership" [Millette interview 1990]. While the two main factions regarded the split as in many ways a good thing, Millette saw it as a disaster.

Economism, Vanguardism and the Split in the ULF

Most of the assessments of the ULF, particularly those written by socialists, argue that the split was a consequence of two related factors: the party's trade union roots, and the resultant failure to organize the party as a vanguard of the working class. Phillips [1984: 367, 409] has written that the factors that led to the formation of the party were "based in 'mere economism' " and that the "ideological monolithic direction which is characteristic of a vanguard did not exist in the ULF". She goes on to argue that the ULF "may have been useful in the context of the subjective social circumstances within Trinidad . . . [b]ut [it] was not a mass party that was properly constructed" [1984: 410]. History has shown that "[m]ass organizations of a pro-socialist nature have existed as a forerunner to a Vanguard Party, but always with a core vanguard among the leadership of the mass organization" [1984: 409-10]. She argues that a specific analysis of Trinidad and Tobago (rather than an inflexible line) was needed, but also that a "vanguard party would be selective and monolithic, (if only at the leadership core of the mass party), and would guide the working class struggle to the realization of change in its interests. The ULF was not this kind of party" [1984: 411]. For Phillips then, the basic problem of the party was organizational – the ULF was not a vanguard of the working class, and it instead represented a conflict between two strands of Marxism: reactionary Maoism and the far more preferable "Marxism–Leninism" [1984.: 392].

The supporters of Millette's "semi-faction" (which became known as the February 18 Movement) took a more flexible approach but similarly rejected trade union "economism" and advocated vanguardism. Millette's journal, *Workers Tribune*, established after the split, was very hostile to NAMOTI and its influence in the progressive trade union movement. It argued that "even within the ranks of the 'progressive' trade union movement economism is rampant. It is disguised only in the fact that the 'progressive' trade unionists talk all the time of working class politics and the need for working class parties" [*Workers Tribune* 2 (2): 1]. Instead of trade union economism, "[w]hat the Revolution needs are revolutionaries. What the Revolution needs is a truly revolutionary party. What the Revolution does not need is another trade union party" [*Workers Tribune* 1 (1)]. In other words, according to Millette, NAMOTI's "Maoism" (in actual fact this part of NAMOTI's politics was closer to the thought of C.L.R. James rather than Mao Zedong) led it to advocate loose organizational principles based around communities and workplaces rather than the centralized vanguard that was required.

The problem with this approach is twofold: first, it is based on a one-sided approach to both the limitations of trade unionism and the virtues of vanguardism (and in fact has more in common with Clark Kerr than Lenin); and secondly, it ignores the very real obstacles that the ULF faced in winning support among a highly divided labour force, problems which would not have "magically disappeared" had the party's organizational structure been different. These problems were never adequately dealt with by Shah and NAMOTI and I discuss them (and the "problem" of Panday) below. First I will discuss the question of trade unions and political vanguardism.

The "Marxist" view that trade unions are economistic is derived from a misreading of Lenin, as I discussed in chapter one. Trade unions are not an obstacle to socialist revolution; rather, they should be seen as "a limited form of class consciousness representing the very social forces and interest upon which a revolution can be built" [Wood 1968: 192]. Ultra-left views that trade unions are purely economic actually converge with right wing "labourist" theories of trade unionism. For instance, Phillips is very supportive of the approach of the Bank and General Workers' Union, whose leader (Michael Als) formed the Stalinist People's Popular Movement, which consciously separated "bread and butter" union issues from "politics" (and has consistently failed, as a supposed "vanguard" party, to win any support among the working class). Phillips writes that "[i]t is evident that Mr Als and other members of the union executive engage their union in strictly 'trade union issues' and not overtly in political issues. They have been able to separate the two". She later states that "[t]he mature realization by the leadership of BGWU of the dichotomy between the role of a trade union and the role of a political party in a capitalist dominated social formation is instructive, and is in fact reflective of a level of consciousness not found among the leaders of any other union" [Phillips 1984: 281, 497].

This approach is contrasted with the leaders of TIWU where "some of its promising leaders have reverted to handling issues which are mainly of an outright 'trade union' nature" [Phillips 1984: 497]. But, according to the logic of Phillips' argument, this is precisely what the Bank and General Workers' Union does (at the trade union level at least). What Phillips appears to be saying is that TIWU (and by implication, the Shah faction in the ULF) concentrated too much on "strictly union" issues, at the expense of political party organization; she therefore sets up a false dichotomy between trade unions and politics. It may be true that TIWU and the ULF neglected the limitations of trade unions as agencies for social change, but the dichotomy is hers and not the union's. A trade union can never simply be "economistic" in a capitalist social formation for the simple reason that the power of capital is by its nature political. Ownership of private property is a relationship of power and trade unions, for all their weaknesses, represent a restraint (and therefore a partial challenge) to this power. All attempts to depoliticize trade unions are therefore political "projects" which have more in common with F.W. Dalley (see chapter three) and Clark Kerr (chapter one), than they do with socialist politics.

It is true that the ULF failed to win the widespread support of trade unionists in the Labour Congress or the OWTU, but this has more to do with the wider problems that the party faced, rather than the limitations of trade unionism per se. These problems would include the question of the divisions of the working classes, and the problem of attracting the support of higher paid workers (especially oil workers) who benefited most from the economic boom. Again it should be stressed that this had nothing to do with the OWTU leadership's commitment to "purely trade union issues" (a ludicrous claim) and everything to do with the state of class consciousness of the oil workers at this time.

The false dichotomy of trade unions and politics is carried over into the belief that a vanguard was necessary for the ULF to become a party of the working class. Phillips' claim that mass organizations of the working class have always had a monolithic vanguard at their core is simply untrue. The Bolsheviks were divided over the "small matter" of whether to seize the Winter Palace in October 1917. And, despite Phillips' claims to the contrary [1984: 410], the Sandinista National Liberation Front in Nicaragua (which won power in the 1979 revolution) was not a monolithic organization but in fact was made up of three factions, each with its own "line" on revolutionary strategy [Weber 1981: 38-60; Black 1981: 175-78].

The commitment to vanguardism and "Marxist purity" was shared by both the Stalinists (Millette) and the Maoists (Shah, Belgrave et al.) in the ULF. NAMOTI may not have advocated "democratic centralism" (with the emphasis on the latter) as an organizing principle but it still placed as much emphasis on "the right line" as its Stalinist adversaries. For instance, while the Stalinists accused the Maoists of "left economism" [Sebastien 1981: 59], the Maoists argued that "[t]he problem of the mass movement has been the problem of leadership. Just when it seems that the mass movement is poised to fulfil its mission, some leader sells it out or causes it to split. The most recent example was the ULF experience with people like Panday and Millette" [NAMOTI 1976]. In other words, the problem of the ULF was simply a question of leadership; once the "correct line" (often on obscure international issues over which any Trinidad government would have no say) was obtained, the issue of "the masses" would take care of itself.

The vanguardist approach was also carried over to the party's attitude to Parliament. Shah and Panday's differences were often characterized as an irreconcilable conflict between revolutionary and electoral politics, but this perspective is based on too rigid a contrast between the two types of politics. As Millette recognized, parliamentary politics could be used as a means to an end, rather than an end in itself. However, ULF MPs quickly became frustrated with parliamentary procedure, and this came to a head in November 1976 during the debate on the 1977 budget, when they walked out of Parliament and later staged a motion of no confidence in the Speaker. While there was undoubtedly collaboration between the PNM and the media, which led to discrimination against the ULF, the response of the party was often counterproductive. At one point, Shah summoned a meeting of the Central Executive to determine whether MPs should continue attending Parliament [Ryan 1989b: 169]. This attitude was indicative of the party's black and white, vanguardist approach to politics.

The issue of factions in the ULF is therefore an important one, but not for the reasons given by Phillips. What was needed in the ULF was not a monolithic ideological direction but an organizational structure that allowed for divergence of views and "lines". It was precisely the commitment to dogmatic, vanguardist politics (something Phillips advocates) which provided the organizational basis for the split which occurred. The split should therefore be seen as a response by competing factions to break out of the party's narrow social base. Contrary to Phillips' claims, factionalism and vanguardism compounded rather than alleviated this problem.

The consequence of this elite vanguardism was that the Marxists were tied up in their own sectarian debates and so they never seriously tackled the problem of winning widespread support among the working classes. The historical divisions of the labour force in terms of class fractions (proletariat, peasantry, informal sector and so on), race, gender and politics were never properly addressed. The Shah faction's attitude to Panday is particularly instructive. Panday may have been an opportunist politician who used race to guarantee his own political base, but the implication of this (and indeed the same applies to the PNM's appeal to the African population) is that the question of race cannot be ignored. Panday at least addressed the race factor, even if his motives in doing so were at best confused, and at worst dishonourable. (This question continues to be at the forefront of Trinidadian politics and I will address it again in the context of the 1980s recession in chapter six.) This faction also failed to tackle the question of PNM and liberal democratic hegemony. Liberal democracy may have been limited by the wider economic system and PNM corruption and repression, but Shah and his comrades failed to see that the political system still guaranteed certain rights (won by working class struggle) which made "adventurist" politics inappropriate.

What was therefore needed was a greater awareness by the party of the concrete conditions in Trinidad and Tobago. Of all the socialists in the ULF, James Millette showed the greatest sensitivity to the immediate task of consolidation in the party, but this awareness was hindered by his own (Stalinist) vanguardism and his ultra-left view of trade unions (see above). Furthermore, he underestimated the race problem and may have therefore been

too charitable towards Panday's opportunism. A long-term
"counter hegemonic" strategy was necessary to challenge the domination of the PNM and racially based politics, rather than sterile
debates (which were often full of half truths and inaccuracies)
about Maoism and Stalinism. Of all the people who have written
about the ULF, it is the non-Marxist Selwyn Ryan who has most
accurately described what the ULF did not do and should have
done – "What was missing was a willingness on the part of the
actors involved to learn from the history of working class politics
in Trinidad and Tobago. What was clearly needed was for Indian
and African workers to get used to the idea of working together
politically to help overcome the suspicions and prejudices inherited from the past" [Ryan 1989b: 176-77]. This may be an unre-
markable conclusion, but it is a far more realistic one than those
proposed by the socialists in the ULF.

The Factions after the Split

After the split in the party, Panday's faction, after successfully
winning the right to the party's name, continued its shift to the
right and supported the government over the constitutional question of parliamentary representation in cases where MPs had left
their original party and "crossed the floor" [*Classline* 1978]. In a
local government by-election within Shah's constituency, the pro-
Panday candidate easily beat the Shah supporter. Panday's party
did badly in the 1980 local government elections and so the decision was taken to enter into an alliance with the Democratic
Action Congress and the Tapia House Movement for the 1981
elections. Panday's opportunism extended to an alliance with the
Organization for National Reconstruction, the ONR (a party with
politics considerably to the right of the PNM) in the 1986 general
election. This alliance will be examined in more detail in chapter
six.

Shah's faction refused Panday's offer of a renewed alliance and
did not participate in the 1981 election [Panday interview 1990;
Shah interview 1990]. Although Shah advocated armed struggle
as late as 1981, the faction began to take a far more realistic
approach from this period. NAMOTI was dissolved and the faction's doctrinaire Maoism was gradually abandoned. The

Committee for Labour Solidarity (CLS) was formed in 1981 and its leaders described it as a "preparatory political party". It began to concentrate on building support at the grassroots level, especially through the trade union movement. In other words, as well as rejecting Panday's opportunism, it also consciously tried to avoid the excessive vanguardism of the Marxist factions in the ULF. By the late 1980s, the CLS had converted itself into a political party called the Movement for Social Transformation (see chapter six for more details).

Finally, Millette's "faction" became the February 18 Movement. This tiny organization regretted the split in the ULF and argued that Panday's faction had degenerated into a new DLP, and that the CLS repeated the old economism of NAMOTI [Millette 1981: 11; *Workers Tribune* 2 (2)]. This movement has had little impact on working class politics and, given its dogmatic allegiance to Stalinist politics and organizational principles, this situation is unlikely to change.

Conclusion: A Lost Opportunity

Electoral contests in Third World societies are relatively infrequent events, but the Caribbean region provides some examples of changes in the ruling party through parliamentary contests (for instance in Jamaica). In the case of Trinidad it was always going to be difficult to challenge the hegemony of the PNM because of its success in leading the country to independence, the racial nature of politics and voting behaviour, and its control of patronage. Given that the ULF was largely a race-based party and was divided by ideology, it was unlikely to form a government.

The ULF split because it was divided on the questions of race and factionalism. Race became a major issue as soon as one Marxist faction (around Raffique Shah) attempted to break out of the party's existing social base. The disputes over political strategy were not successfully contained, not because the ULF lacked a vanguard approach to politics, but because the factions themselves were "overcommitted" to vanguardism. As a result, important questions such as winning the support of trade unionists in Labour Congress unions, the support of the "informal sector", and the question of race itself, were all trivialized. Therefore, while the attempt by Shah's faction to extend the ULF's social base was itself correct, the manner in which it was done was problematic. The left in the Caribbean saw the disastrous consequences of vanguardism six years later in Grenada when one faction murdered the leaders of a rival faction [Marable 1987: 265–67].

Despite its undeveloped politics, factional infighting and short political life, the ULF represented the most serious attempt to form a popular working class, socialist political party. It can be said with hindsight that its disintegration was disastrous for the working classes (of both ethnic groups), because it left them ill-prepared for the recession in the 1980s. The recession, and the response of the labour movement to it, will be the subject of chapter six.

6

Uneven Development Revisited: Labour and the Recession of the 1980s

The contradictions of Trinidad's peripheral capitalist development discussed in chapter one became readily visible after the country entered an economic downturn in 1982. The responses to the recession sharpened the tensions between capital and organized labour as the former called for cutbacks in the state sector and a return to a leading role in the economy for the private sector. George Chambers' PNM government initiated a move in this direction, but it was with the election of the "multiracial" National Alliance for Reconstruction (NAR) government (in December 1986) that the twin processes of state sector cutbacks and privatization really accelerated. As a result, the labour movement was forced to face the worst crisis in its history. Unemployment increased and union membership sharply declined and workers in the public sector faced wage cuts and freezes. Other sections of the working classes similarly suffered as unemployment, poverty and serious crime all dramatically increased. The social crisis also become a political one as the NAR government split in 1988, ethnic tensions increased and in 1990 there was a vain attempt to overthrow the liberal democratic system itself through an Islamic coup.

This chapter examines the impact of the recession on the working classes and how they resisted the demands of employers and government. It shows that the factors that have traditionally divided labour (race, gender, uneven class formation and politics/trade union disunity) remained pervasive, and in some respects more acute, but that there was also some tentative movement towards a recognition (at leadership level) that labour unity is vital to represent the interests of the working classes. This was seen most clearly by the increased awareness that there is a need for one trade union federation and a move away (by at least some Labour Congress unions) from purely collective bargaining mechanisms to "social movement unionism". These questions are examined by looking, first, at the causes of the recession and its impact on the working classes, and, secondly, by exploring the changing nature of politics and trade unionism in this period, looking in particular at renewed attempts to introduce trade union unity, the development of a conception of social movement unionism, and the renewed quest for a mass labour party.

The Recession and its Impact on the Working Classes

The Crisis in the Economy

The economic crisis of the 1980s had its origins in Trinidad's continued dependence on oil and the state revenues that are derived from taxation in this industry. By 1980, oil production and refining constituted 42 percent of gross domestic product (GDP), directly provided 65 percent of government revenues, and accounted for TT $9.17 billion of the country's total export earnings of TT $9.72 billion [Yelvington 1987: 12]. After the oil "shocks" of 1973-74 and 1979-80, the price of oil on the world market began to decline and in December 1985, the Organization for Petroleum Exporting Countries (OPEC) announced that it would abandon efforts to maintain a high price for oil. OPEC instead embarked on a new strategy which would concentrate on recapturing its dominance of world oil production.

This changing strategy had its roots in the competition between OPEC and non-OPEC oil producing countries [Farrell 1985b: 390-92], a conflict which had a particular impact on Trinidad's "open petroleum economy" [Seers 1964]. Although Trinidad had benefited greatly from the rise in world oil prices, the foundations of the recession could be found in the boom period. From 1978 onwards, national oil production steadily declined and the refineries were operating at well below full capacity. After the first oil shock, the United States, Trinidad's major oil market, reduced its dependence on imported oil, and in particular residual fuel oil, which is Trinidad's main oil export. US refineries also began to refine more residual fuel oil than they had done before 1973, and the Trinidad refineries began to outlive their usefulness to North American transnational corporations [Farrell 1985b].

By the early 1980s the Trinidad economy had to face a decline in the market, and a decline in the price per barrel for its principal export. Nevertheless, the boom had provided the government and the private sector with an opportunity to diversify so that the country was no longer so dependent on the fluctuations of the world oil market. The 1973 oil price rise had, for instance, led to a windfall oil revenue of TT $24 billion [Farrell 1985a: 8]. However, this opportunity was wasted for at least three reasons: the government undertook overambitious and expensive development projects; the private sector continued to show little interest in substantial domestic investment (see chapter one, which refers to the export of capital in this period); and money was wasted on corruption.

The result of this particular conjuncture of international and domestic forces was devastating for the economy. From 1982 to 1989, the country experienced negative growth rates in every single year, and by 1987 real GDP was about 28 percent lower than it had been in 1982 [Trinidad and Tobago 1984; 1985; 1986; 1989; Yelvington forthcoming: 16]. Gross domestic product fell from US $6229 million in 1984 to US $5610 million in 1987, and the external debt stood at US $1.41 billion in 1987 [LARR 1988b]. The external debt service ratio rose from 2 percent in 1982, to 24.3 percent in 1987 [Trinidad and Tobago 1986: 46; Farrell 1989: 9].

Both the PNM and the NAR governments introduced strong measures in trying to halt the decline. In December 1985, the Chambers government announced a 50 percent devaluation in the Trinidad and Tobago dollar and a new 10 percent tax on some consumer goods [*Express* 1985]. In August 1988, a further devaluation was announced by A.N.R. Robinson's NAR government [LARR 1988a]. Further measures were also carried out which had a direct impact on industrial relations, and these are examined below.

Perhaps the most visible feature of the crisis was the rise in unemployment and the consequent increase in poverty, vagrancy and the size of the informal sector. Unemployment increased from 10 percent in 1981 to 18 percent by 1986, and an estimated 23 percent by the late 1980s [Hunte 1988: 10, 13]. The problem was most serious among young people: in the first quarter of 1987, the unemployment rate was 42 percent for males and 54 percent for females in the 15–19-year-old age group; among 20–24-year-olds, the figures were 39 percent for males and 38 percent for females [Hunte 1988: 11].

The Impact on the Labour Movement and the Working Classes

Cecil Paul, the General Secretary of the Council of Progressive Trade Unions (CPTU), claimed that the economic situation, and the response of successive governments to it, laid the framework for "the collapse of collective bargaining" in the country [Paul *c*.1986: 1; Paul interview 1990]. He identified a number of symptoms: employers no longer honouring terms of collective agreements and introducing conditions without consulting trade unions; the continued (one is tempted to say, after twenty-five years, eternal) backlog of cases at the Industrial Court; employers failing to honour Industrial Court agreements; employers' use of lockouts to subvert collective agreements and their subsequent offering of individual contracts (or strike-breaking labour) to workers. Paul argued that "[a]t present in Trinidad and Tobago, we are witnessing . . . a development of weak and immobilized Trade Unions, the underselling of labour, the subversion of the trade unions, the surplus of labour (unemployment) and as a result, the pauperization of large sections of . . . society" [Paul *c*.1986: 1].

The trade union movement suffered accordingly. The last survey of the whole trade union movement conducted at national level (in 1985) suggested that between 1982 and 1985, over 70 000 workers (16 percent of the total labour force) were retrenched. In the period from 1981 to 1985, trade union membership declined from approximately 142 000 workers to 100 000 [CPTU 1985a]. From 1985 to 1990, there are no published fig-

ures on the size of the national trade union movement, but esti-
mates (below) by leaders of the two federations, and individual
unions, suggested that the size of the trade union movement continued to contract.

Table 6.1 Trade union membership in Trinidad and Tobago, 1990

Trade Union/Federation	Membership 1990	Peak Membership	
Council of Progressive Trade Unions (Federation)	30 000	38 000	(1980-82)
Labour Congress (Federation)	80 000	120 000	(1982)
National Union of Government and Federated Workers	44 000	76 000	(1983-84)
All-Trinidad Sugar and General Workers Trade Union	10 000	18 000	(1980-82)
Oilfields Workers Trade Union	11 000	16 000	(1980-82)

Source: Interviews with Cecil Paul 28.3.1990; Carl Tull 1.5.1990; Selwyn John 30.4.1990; Sam Maharaj 12.4.1990; Errol McLeod 30.3.1990.

The accuracy of these figures is questionable, not least because
the claims made for the size of the two federations conflict with
the more precise survey carried out by the CPTU in 1985.
However, while these figures may be overestimates made by hope-
ful, rather than accurate, trade union leaders, they are useful
because they show that there was an almost universal trend
towards declining trade union membership since the end of the
boom in the early 1980s. Each interviewee also stated that a
major reason for the decline in union membership was retrenchment of the workforce. There are two exceptions to this trend –
the Trinidad and Tobago Unified Teachers' Association and the
Public Services' Association – but in both cases the increase in
membership was explained by changes in the internal structure of
the union rather than a favourable bargaining position with

employers (which in both cases was the state) [Ramnanan interview 1990; Rennie interview 1990].

Since the election of the NAR government in late 1986, it was
the public sector unions that suffered most. The new government
was committed to a leading role for the private sector and
"rolling back" the economic functions of the state. In its 1987
budget, the government suspended the cost of living allowance
(COLA), which had effectively acted (since the Second World
War) as an automatic wage increase tied to inflation. The following year a 5 percent "mobilization for economic independence"
tax was introduced, the top rate of income tax was reduced from
70 percent to 50 percent, and there were price increases for
basic goods. Prime Minister Robinson also announced his intention to ask the International Monetary Fund (IMF) for finance to
compensate for falling export earnings. After ignoring an
Industrial Court decision of July 1988 to increase wages and
restore the COLA, the government introduced its most austere
budget in 1989, which included a 10 percent cut in public sector wages, which was ratified by the Public Sector Emolument
Act [LARR 1989; *Express* 1989b]. Finally in 1990, the indirect
and therefore regressive value added tax (VAT) was introduced
for many basic but "non-essential" goods at the standard rate of
15 percent.

The situation in the publicly owned sugar industry (Caroni) was
equally desperate for the workforce. In early 1987, the Caroni
board of directors, which included five workers' and farmers' representatives, submitted a Directional Plan for the industry to the
Minister of Planning, Winston Dookeran, who had close ties with
the sugar union. The plan made provisions for those affected by
rationalization of the industry and it was envisaged that all workers laid off would be offered land and/or cash as compensation.
All workers who opted for land would be assisted in forming agricultural cooperatives and would supply cane to the main company, but they would also be free to grow other crops (and
thereby help to reduce the nation's food import bill). However,
the government rejected the Directional Plan and introduced its
own which would reduce sugar production, close the sugar factory
at Brechin Castle, and, according to the union, retrench 7000
workers without any compensation in land or cash [Maharaj
interview 1990].

The public sector (and so – significantly – the Labour Congress
unions) therefore suffered most amongst the organized working

class since 1986. There was widespread retrenchment, particularly among daily rated and public work scheme workers (the public works system, DEWD, was closed in 1987, leaving 8000 jobless), attrition (non-replacement of workers who had emigrated or retired), and wage cuts and loss of benefits [John interview 1990; Rennie interview 1990]. However, there were also many job losses in the private sector (which itself challenged the economic philosophy of the NAR government) and from 1982 to 1986, total employment in this sector contracted by 20 percent [Hunte 1988: 9]. The collapse of Kirpalani's in 1986, one of the "Big Four" national conglomerates, was the most dramatic of all the bankruptcies of private enterprise [*Express* 1986a].

The most visible result of retrenchment was an increase in unemployment and in the size of the petty commodity sector. The number of vendors in the towns, and in particular in Port of Spain and San Fernando, soared, and this in turn led to new conflicts with the government – for instance, over the area that street vendors were allowed to sell their goods [*Express* 1990b]. It was also likely that poor women have suffered most from the recession due to a sharp fall in real wages, a reduction in public spending for services on which women rely [Safa: 3], and an intensification of their dual role as wage earners and unpaid domestic workers. Moreover, the government's economic strategy also included the promotion of export processing zones, which often rely on the employment of low paid female labourers working in very poor conditions.

Labour Unity in the 1980s

The unfavourable situation facing the organized working class led to major changes in the labour movement. On the one hand, fear of unemployment led to low morale and a general unwillingness on the part of the workforce to strike. Between 1984 and 1987, there were very few officially recorded major strikes (these involved strikes which resulted in the loss of at least 2000 workdays): in 1984, there were 10; in 1985, there were 5; in 1986, there were 4; and in 1987, only 2 [Trinidad and Tobago 1989a: 89]. There have been a number of stoppages since then (see below for details), but these were rarely long term and in this respect conformed with the pattern of labour resistance from 1984 to 1987. On the other hand, the economic and social difficulties faced by the trade union movement (and the working classes more generally) led to significant changes among the attitudes of the leaders of organized labour. In this section, I look first at the gradual (but still limited) movement towards trade union unity. Secondly, I examine new moves to unify the working classes as a whole through a community and trade union based organization (the Summit of People's Organizations) and through labour-based political parties (the United National Congress and the Movement for Social Transformation). Thirdly, I show how this has been linked to an explicitly political critique of government (and International Monetary Fund and World Bank) policy.

Trade Union Unity

The movement toward trade union unity was tentative, but a new national TUCo was created in June 1991. The two predecessor federations were divided over ideological issues, reflected in their respective international affiliations; the Labour Congress was aligned to the International Confederation of Free Trade Unions, while (since 1980) the Council of Progressive Trade Unions was aligned to the World Federation of Trade Unions [Tull interview 1990; Paul interview 1990]. The extent to which these ideological issues (and other "local problems" – not least, the question of personality differences among trade union leaders) were overcome is discussed below.

Political differences notwithstanding, the majority of trade unions recognized that the crisis in the trade union movement could only be challenged by closer ties between both the federations, and the non-aligned (the teachers' and sugar workers') unions. Before the 1986 general election, trade union unity was of a basically informal nature but met with little success. After the NAR entered office, most trade unions moved closer to each other, albeit on specific issues rather than on the question of one trade union centre. At the formal level, the first joint Labour Day celebrations were held in 1982 and some labour unity resolutions were held. On this basis, the CPTU in particular tried to initiate talks about one trade union centre, but these actions were not welcomed by a Labour Congress leadership suspicious of the CPTU's "communist" sympathies [OWTU 1986b: 20]. A Labour Congress team prepared a draft discussion document on labour unity in 1986, but this went no further in either of the two federations [Trinidad and Tobago Labour Congress 1986].

More informally, the Joint Trade Union Grouping was set up in December 1983 by unions from both federations and the non-aligned sections [OWTU 1986b: 21]. Conferences of shop stewards were held and the Grouping mobilized a picket outside Parliament on the day that the 1984 budget was presented to the House of Representatives. An alternative economic programme was presented which demanded an immediate moratorium on retrenchment and a small wage increase "that recognizes that workers, no less than management, have the right to maintain their standard of living" [*Trinidad Guardian* 1984]. This argument – that the working classes were being forced to pay a disproportionate share of the economic pain in the recession – became a common conviction of the trade union movement, especially after the NAR was elected (see below).

The Joint Trade Union Grouping (later renamed the Concerned Group of Trade Unions) remained a purely informal grouping which united on concrete issues, which in practice meant that it organized annually around the time of the Budget. Its 1986 programme outlined as its main objective the development of "unity in action of all Trade Unions around concrete issues . . . through activities that are acceptable to Unions and agreed upon in an 'informal' body that can best achieve consensus, thereby laying the foundation for Formal Unity" [Concerned Trade Unions 1986b: 1]. The problem, however, was that the Group failed to deal with the long standing divisions in the trade union movement and never enjoyed the full support of those Labour Congress union leaders that had close ties with the PNM. The result was that in practice the trade union movement often remained as divided as ever (at leadership level, at least) on concrete issues.

The TIWU dispute with Neal and Massy in 1986 is a case in point. This particular conglomerate, the largest in Trinidad, has led the offensive against organized labour since 1983. The parent company unilaterally declared a wage freeze, withdrew the COLA, reduced the working week and contracted out work at some of its subsidiary companies [*Socialist Worker* April/May 1986]. When these actions were followed by lockouts at other subsidiaries (Polymer Caribbean, Neal and Massy Motors, Edgar Borde, Electrical Industries and Automotive Components), TIWU called for a boycott of two food and drink subsidiaries (Cannings food and drink and Hi-Lo supermarkets) in April 1986. This call was supported by thirteen trade unions, but was strongly criticized by the most important Labour Congress union, the National Union of Government and Federated Workers [*Express* 1986b].

The election victory of the NAR paved the way for a new period of attempts to unify the trade union movement. The momentum of the struggle for trade union unity increased for two reasons. First, the defeat of the PNM meant that there were no longer the close ties of patronage between government and conservative trade union leaders that had existed since the early 1960s. Secondly, there was the question of government policy itself. The government's commitment to cutting back the economic role of the state and promoting private enterprise meant that Labour Congress unions (especially the NUGFW and the Public Services' Association) suffered most from government policy.

The new government created institutional structures in which (so it was claimed) the trade union movement would enjoy genuine representation and a chance to promote its own particular demands as representatives of labour. The most important of these was the Joint Consultative Council. Both the trade union centres and the non-aligned unions were dismayed when the COLA was withdrawn from public sector workers in the 1987 budget. The Council of Progressive Trade Unions responded by presenting a paper to the Joint Consultative Council which criticized the government's policies of promoting "free enterprise". The paper argued that "the Private Sector was only called upon to make minimal sacrifices through the national recovery impost . . . And in spite of this, their contribution to the national reconstruction effort so far has been minimal" [CPTU 1987: 2]. The CPTU called for a reduction in the salaries of company directors, a price freeze, increased taxation on capital exports and the establishment of funds for the provision of social services [1987: 3-4]. This paper was subsequently adopted by the Labour Congress, which also proposed a similar revenue-raising alternative budget [Trinidad and Tobago Labour Congress 1987]. The Congress also claimed that labour had taken more than its share of the required sacrifice, arguing that while, between 1983 to 1986 real income for the country as a whole had fallen by almost 30 percent, labour income in the public sector had fallen by 44 percent [*Trinidad Guardian* 1987]. In 1965 and 1970, conservative trade union leaders had blamed the "political" trade unions for the country's economic problems.

By 1987, the Congress was arguing that the

> fundamental structural problem . . . lies with the business community,
> and with the manner in which our businessmen have elected to provision
> the economy. The determination of the business community to earn their
> livelihood through imports, the reluctance of these citizens to reinvest
> their profits in this country, and the reluctance of these entrepreneurs to
> take any major investment initiative except [if] it is in some way under-
> written by the government, have all added up to what exists today; an
> economy that remains heavily dependent upon foreign investment, an
> economy whose fortunes remain very sensitive to the conditions of the
> government's budget [*Trinidad Guardian* 1987].

Despite the Labour Congress' implicit "conversion" to the notion of
uneven capitalist development, there were still some differences
between the two centres on the question of the economy. The
major issue was whether the government should ask the IMF for a
loan and accept conditionalities in order to retain the confidence
of external creditors. The CPTU was against any such policy,
while (in 1987) the Labour Congress was concerned about the
social effects of IMF conditionalities, but not yet completely
opposed to the government's expected course of action [Trinidad
and Tobago Labour Congress 1987: 6-7]. However, this potential
area of disagreement had rapidly disappeared, as by early 1988
the Congress was describing the government's courting of the IMF
as "dangerous and extremely serious" and stated that it was "vehe-
mently opposed to the outdated conditions of the Fund" [*Express*
1988a].

The government's decision to approach the IMF was first officially announced at the presentation of the budget in early 1988,
and this was followed by the submission of a Letter of Intent to
the IMF the following November [Farrell 1989: 15], despite accusations by a former IMF official that the organization had been
deliberately inaccurate in its assessment of the Trinidad economy
[Ryan 1989c: 321]. In late 1988 and early 1989, two IMF loans
(plus one from the World Bank) were secured, and, more importantly, the IMF "seal of approval" was given to bankers to continue
to lend money to the country. The usual conditionalities applied,
especially to the second loan: these included a reduction in the
budget deficit, a periodic review of the exchange rate, and a
reduction in import and price controls.

It was against this background that the first IMF-influenced
budget was introduced in early 1989, in which the aforemen-

tioned salary cuts were made. In anticipation of a harsh budget, the trade union movement planned a national day of resistance for March. By this time the informal alliance of trade unions had evolved into the Joint Trade Union Movement (JTUM), which, given the context in which it operated, was far more unified than its predecessors. Before the Day of Resistance, the Labour Congress demanded the recall of the 1989 budget, arguing that its fiscal measures "will have the effect of damaging the economic system of the country, while at the same time instituting a level of poverty and suffering such as the society will not be able to bear. This is a Budget which has attacked workers by cutting their pay, by reducing their jobs [sic] security . . . In our view the Government of this country has every reason to reopen negotiations with the IMF and to seek to get better terms for the people of this country" [Express 1989a].

The Day of Resistance was held on 6 March 1989. The intention was that the whole of the country's workforce would stay away from work for one day. The response to this call by the JTUM was strong in the public sector, especially among teachers, public transport workers and public servants, but workers employed by private enterprise were far less supportive [Trinidad Guardian 1989a; 1989b].

The immediate response of the government to the protest action was negative. NAR General Secretary Bhoe Tewarie, criticized the trade union movement that "is now being led astray by a callous clique whose actions are prompted by political ambitions. Indeed, the trade union movement itself may well be in jeopardy because of the callous and irresponsible attitude of these political players in the trade union movement" [Express 1989b]. This attack, reminiscent of Eric Williams in his prime, was ill advised because the trade union leadership of the late 1980s was very different from what it had been in the mid 1960s. Prime Minister Robinson therefore took a more conciliatory line and set up a technical team which would make proposals for a medium-term economic programme.

This technical team met in May 1989 and had representation from both union federations. Through the JTUM, demands were made for a moratorium on some of the 1989 budget measures, on retrenchment and on the Cabinet plan for the sugar industry (see above) [Express 1989c]. However, a split developed between the two federations over the talks. According to Labour Congress representative Selwyn John, progress was made on the issues of retrenchment, but not on the issue of a 10 percent cut in public salaries. However, CPTU leaders claimed that they "accomplished nothing" [*Express* 1989d]. This division became serious as the CPTU withdrew from the technical team, which effectively destroyed the unity of the Joint Trade Union Movement. In a media announcement, the Congress stated that it regretted "the move by its sister Federation, the CPTU, to resist all attempts to arrive at a united position in relation to further talks with the Government" [*Express* 1989e]. Although Congress encouraged the CPTU to re-enter dialogue with Congress and the government, the old political divisions were resurrected. Congress stated that it was not a political football "to be used and misused when it suits the interests of those who are bent on carving out some space in an increasingly difficult political environment. We therefore have no intention of letting our guard down" [*Express* 1989e]. The CPTU was also accused of having an agenda and finance organized by "foreign forces" [Paul interview 1990; John interview 1990].

The technical team continued without CPTU representation and so unity was once again undermined. However, by the end of 1989, two factors helped to restore a limited degree of unity. First, there was industrial action at the oil refineries, the WASA and the Public Service Transport Corporation (PSTC). The strike involving the oilworkers was successful in winning a (realistically small) wage increase along with better pension schemes and medical benefits for workers [*Express* 1989f]. In a public statement, the OWTU argued that the strike was of wider significance because it "re-established without a doubt the respect and regard by employers (private and state) managers and Government for the Trade Union Movement in general and the OWTU in particular" [*Express* 1989g]. There were also sit-ins and work stoppages at WASA and the PSTC in response to retrenchment orders (later partially withdrawn) [*Express* 1989h; *Trinidad Guardian* 1990a]. The WASA stoppage was particularly important because it involved workers in the largest Labour Congress affiliated union (the NUGFW). Secondly, and related to the WASA stoppage, the Labour Congress became disoriented with the government's attitude to the technical team and in particular to the role of the trade union movement in it. The leadership claimed that in meetings with the IMF and the World Bank, the government had ignored the Labour Congress [*Trinidad Guardian* 1989c].

This breakdown of negotiations was reflected in the 1990 budget. The introduction of 15 percent VAT was strongly criticized by both federations and it provided the basis for renewed impetus in the Joint Trade Union Movement and the creation of a wider, community-based organization, the Summit of People's Organizations (SOPO) [Rennie interview 1990; Paul interview 1990]. Demonstrations were organized against the budget and the June 1990 Labour Day celebrations were reunited under one banner at Fyzabad [*Express* 1990c].

The prospects for trade union unity in the 1990s are greater than they have been since the last major split in 1965 - as the creation of the new national TUCo in 1991 demonstrates. At the same time, however, the scale of the problems facing the movement has never been greater and the new unity is potentially fragile. While some Labour Congress unions regularly attended JTUM meetings, the federation itself was not affiliated to it [Tull interview 1990]. Moreover, those unions affiliated to Congress that did attend were not as fully committed to the JTUM as the CPTU unions. There were basically two levels of criticism made by Labour Congress affiliated unions against the Joint Trade Union Movement. On the one hand, the well-worn criticism (see chapters one and three) made by older leaders that the progressive trade unions are too political: according to NUGFW President Selwyn John, "[the] difficulty that has come up in the trade unions within the last year, maybe two years, is that the left wing forces have attempted to take most, if not all the trade unions, and in doing so they undermine these bodies . . . It is our view that this was an international left wing cause - that in order to gain power they must have not only trade union power but political power" [John interview 1990]. On the other hand, some younger leaders, who were far less critical of the CPTU and not so closely associated with the Labour Congress' "old guard", rejected this false separation of trade unions and politics, but criticized the JTUM on the more realistic basis that there has been a long-term separation of leaders from workers. According to the Bank Employees' Union General Secretary (and Labour Congress Deputy General Secretary) Patrick Rabathaly, while the JTUM was a worthwhile endeavour (in that it at least recognizes the need for trade union unity), "we have not been communicating well with workers" and so the JTUM "will only really get the credibility it deserves if people can see that the labour movement is united". He regarded the JTUM as too much of a "top down", leadership-oriented initiative [Rabathaly interview 1990]. The two non-aligned unions were active in the JTUM, but were sceptical about the prospects for long-term unity, arguing that the

major obstacle was one of personality conflicts [Ramnanan interview 1990; Maharaj interview 1990].

Only time will tell whether or not the new federation can overcome a number of problems. First, there is the resistance of
some old but highly influential trade union leaders [Tull interview 1990; John interview 1990] opposed to "political
unionism". Secondly, there is the wide gap that exists between
trade union leaders and rank and file members which must be
narrowed. This is all the more important in the current period
because the recession has lowered the morale and the confidence
of organized labour. Perhaps the most promising development in
this regard has taken place in some of the Labour Congress
unions (the PSA and the Bank Employees Union, among others)
where old, often corrupt, leaders have been replaced by a
younger leadership which rejects so-called responsible unionism
and is broadly sympathetic to the aims (if not the methods) of
the old CPTU. I examine this in more detail below, in the context of "social movement unionism", the SOPO and new labour
parties.

Labour Parties and Social Movement Unionism

There are currently two political parties claiming to represent
the cause of labour, and these essentially reflect the split in the
ULF in 1977. On the one hand, there is Basdeo Panday's United
National Congress (UNC), which established itself as the official
Opposition after the attempted Islamic coup in July 1990 [LARR
1990] while, on the other, there is MOTION, which has its origins in the old Shah faction of the ULF.

After the split in the ULF, Panday's party entered various
alliances (see chapter five), culminating in the NAR. The problem with this coalition was that it contained such a diversity of
political views that it never really constituted a positive alliance
– its only unifying feature was a desire to end twenty-five years
of PNM government. Once the party entered office, divisions
quickly arose. Panday and some of his followers felt that the
government was not sufficiently challenging the entrenched state
bureaucracy, especially on the issue of public works schemes
[Ryan 1988b: 69-76]. They felt that this was indicative of a
wider government failure to challenge anti-Indian racism in society. Within a year of the NAR's election victory, the party was in

open conflict. By February 1988, Prime Minister Robinson was talking of forces "bent on destruction within the party – some of them functioning at the highest levels" [*Express* 1988b]. He argued that the "splitters" were using race, and in particular the government's refusal to allow the Indian government to build an Indian cultural centre, to divide the party [Ryan 1989: 160-62]. Panday, who was by now holding open meetings of NAR dissidents, argued that the divisive factors were a combination of class and race: "Sugar workers are owed $125 million in back pay and they cannot get a word on that, and they are now saying that the centre is the issue? The fact that the centre was mentioned as an issue demonstrates the road which they wish to travel and that is to divide us again . . . They are trying to do exactly what the PNM used to . . . [T]hose who seek to divide the country will feel the wrath of the people. Only our people will never go back to the racial syndrome. That is a mistake they making [*sic*]" [*Express* 1988c]. On 8 February Robinson dismissed Panday, Kelvin Ramnath and Trevor Sudama from the Cabinet [*Express* 1988d], and in April 1989, the UNC was founded [*Express* 1989e].

The new party attracted a social base similar to the old ULF (although some old ULF members stayed loyal to the government). To become a mass party it faced the basic problem of attracting black working class support. The party has placed much emphasis on the persistence of racial discrimination in society, which has led to renewed accusations that Panday is a racist [*Express* 1988f; *Trinidad Guardian* 1990d]. However, raising the question of race where racism exists is not itself racist, and the political left in Trinidad have continued to ignore race as a mere epiphenomenon of capitalism. What is questionable about Panday and his followers is the zeal with which he condemns anti-Indian racism but the comparative reluctance to condemn racist comments made by some Indian leaders [*Trinidad Guardian* 1990b]. So, while Panday quite rightly emphasizes the continued significance of the race factor, the manner in which he raises it is questionable and not dissimilar to the style of the old DLP.

The second party claiming to represent the working classes is MOTION, which was formed in September 1989 out of the Committee for Labour Solidarity. It is an independent socialist party committed to a mixed economy [MOTION 1989: 8] and is critical of the record of the "socialist" countries [Abdulah interview

1990]. The decision was taken in 1988 to transform the CLS into a full political party because of the changing political climate – in particular, the rise of the NAR and the associated demise of racially based voting. After the subsequent problems of the government, CLS activists believed that there was a sufficient change in the political atmosphere to justify the formation of a new labour-based party. In the words of its interim political leader, David Abdulah, "the mood had changed . . . The people were ready for a new kind of politics, not just a new kind of party" [Abdulah interview 1990].

The problem with this perspective is that it underestimates the resilience of ideologies like racism. The divisions that existed between African and Indian workers were not created by the PNM and are therefore unlikely to simply disappear now that a different party is in office. Moreover, recessions are a fertile breeding ground for scapegoating, and there has been a marked increase in racial tensions in the last two years. For instance, government plans for a national service have led to a moral panic that the races will become "mixed" [*Trinidad Guardian* 1990b]. While MOTION undoubtedly recognizes the persistence of racism [Abdulah interview 1990], the party still tends to regard it as an epiphenomenon of capitalism or a capitalist conspiracy. For instance, its political programme contains relatively progressive sections on women's rights, education, and young and old people but there is no section on race or ethnicity. A section on sport and culture does not mention the historical divide between Indian and African [MOTION 1989: 30-37].

The second major problem that MOTION faces is that it may come to be regarded as yet another isolated socialist party which involves a few CPTU leaders but few rank and file trade unionists or unorganized workers. A more credible alternative might have been the creation of a progressive labour party out of those unions in both federations, which would have shown to workers (organized and unorganized) that the trade union movement is capable of achieving some unity. In the long term, the creation of such a party would lead to a conflict in the Labour Congress between the new, younger leaders and the "old guard", but this would eventually aid unity as the latter group remains the biggest obstacle to one trade union centre.

The final important organizational development among the working classes is the creation of the SOPO. This was formed in February 1990 in response to the burden of IMF and World Bank-influenced government policy. The organization was set up on the initiative of trade unions from both federations (but again, with less support from some Labour Congress affiliated unions) but is a wider body than a "pure" (or "responsible") trade union. It includes religious and cultural organizations (among these, before July 1990, was the Jamaat-Al-Muslimeen, the organization behind the coup attempt), feminist groups (the Caribbean Association for Feminist Research and Action) and various political parties, including elements of the PNM and MOTION [SOPO 1990: 1].

The basic inspiration for SOPO is the success of "social movement unionism" in countries such as Brazil and South Africa. This phenomenon is based on an alliance of organized labour with other social movements, and its motivation is the belief that "there is a growing confluence of interests and a gradual overcoming of previous social and political barriers" [Munck 1988: 117]. This conception rejects the distinction between economic and political unionism, and the crude Marxist notion (discussed in the opening chapter) that the class struggle is the major (or only) source of conflict in society. As Waterman states, in this conception

> worker struggles are neither condemned as 'economic/reformist', nor glorified as 'political/revolutionary', but recognized as representing one front or site of political struggle that must be articulated intimately with others if the 'present state of things' is to be abolished . . . In our increasingly diverse, complex but interdependent economies, polities and cultures . . . it is not unity but diversity that is strength. It is, in other words, not so much a matter of trying to reduce all the increasing variety to one 'primary', 'fundamental' contradiction (class, nationality or – for that matter – gender). It is rather one of recognizing within the many movements (which thus include the labour one) the common democratic thread [Waterman 1990: 8, 11].

The immediate demands of SOPO included a halt to retrenchment at Caroni and PSTC, the reinstatement of the COLA and the 10 percent of salaries that were cut from teachers and public servants, a halt to cutbacks in social services, the withdrawal of the VAT and an immediate programme of job creation [SOPO 1990: 1-2]. While some of these demands are of more immediate concern to the trade union movement, others (such as stopping the cuts in social services and abolishing the VAT) are of relevance to all sections of the working classes and therefore represent a move towards social movement unionism. However, this move remains tentative and at the time of writing is largely confined to trade union leaders and activists.

Summary and Conclusion

Uneven Development Revisited and the Rise of Social Movement Unionism

The nature of government economic policy, especially since 1986, has forced the trade union movement, and in particular the Labour Congress unions, to rethink the relationship between trade unionism and politics. This in turn has led to a protracted debate over economic policy, which echoes my discussion of uneven development presented in the opening chapter.

The trade union movement's criticisms of the government have addressed economic policy per se, and the social consequences of these policies on the organized working class and the poorest sections of the population. The basic philosophy behind government, IMF and World Bank policy is the neo-classical theory which I challenged in chapter one. In order to revive the economy, the IMF typically proposes cutbacks in the state sector, privatization and the liberalization of imports. This equilibrium model also expounds the view that foreign investment will be attracted to a country if the government provides the right incentives. These views are undoubtedly shared by the NAR government's Minister of Finance, Selby Wilson [*Express* 1990a], and in 1990, the country's first export processing zone was established at Point Lisas [*Trinidad Guardian* 1990c). However, as I argued in chapter one, this equilibrium model is seriously flawed, as it fails to examine the agglomeration tendencies of international capitalism, and the weakness of the private sector in developing countries (and its related tendency to export capital). Furthermore, Export Processing Zones do not provide a great deal of employment or linkages with the rest of the economy, and they generally rely on the super-exploitation of cheap, usually female labour [Jenkins 1987: 123–43; Elson and Pearson 1981]. The union movement has therefore correctly predicted that government policy (at least in the absence of a massive oil price rise) will lead to a worsening of the recession and a redistribution of wealth away from the poor towards the rich. Such a process is common in many Third World countries, in which austerity protests occur where debt and IMF pressure are most pronounced [Walton and Seddon 1994: 324].

Government economic policy has laid the framework for a substantial revision of trade union practice and most of the movement's leaders have recognized the necessity for greater unity. Moreover, there is now a widespread belief that trade unions should link up with other organizations, so that non-unionized sectors of the working classes can be represented. The success of social movement unionism and mass labour party politics will depend on the extent to which the trade union movement can bridge the gap between leaders and members (or non-members), and the divisions of race, gender and class fractions.

7

Conclusion

The history of Trinidad is incomprehensible without an examination of the history of labour. The economic development of the island over the last five centuries must be understood as the simultaneous evolution of different methods of labour control. Existing mainstream theories of development and underdevelopment lack such a labour–based approach.

In the twentieth century, the working classes have played a major role in the history of Trinidad – the struggles of **1937** helped to pave the way for the process of decolonization, and although the official labour movement was marginalized at independence, it still played an important role, which led to anti–labour legislation in **1965**. Furthermore, less organized sections of the working class played a crucial role in the Black Power struggles of **1970**, and the "cultural revolution" which developed out of this struggle.

Nevertheless, uneven development and racialization have meant that the working class has rarely acted as a homogenous force, but this is no more true in Trinidad than in other capitalist societies. A focus on class struggle is important, not because there is a "true" or "false" consciousness (or because such a focus can predict how people will behave – clearly it cannot), but because it explains the specificity of capitalist development, and the resistance that has arisen out of this process. Thus, a history of the working classes is vital, irrespective of the undoubted fact that it has remained fragmented throughout its history.

Nevertheless, the question of why the working class is so fragmented must be addressed. It should be clear from my discussion in chapters two and three that the thesis of cultural pluralism, based as it is on a timeless ethnic essentialism, should be rejected. "Race" is socially constructed through concrete processes of history, and is therefore constantly subject to changing meanings. Too often scholars influenced by this school of thought have taken the pronouncements of (often racist) politicians at face value, and failed to place such rhetoric in a historical context. On the other hand, any attempt to move "beyond the fragments" of the working class and the different experiences of its members, must constructively engage with, rather than ignore, the diversity within the working class. Clearly, the Marxism–Leninism of the ULF in the 1970s failed in this process. It is at this point that the pessimistic 1980s may also provide some lessons for the future. In the past, political parties have attempted to subsume the particular experiences of the working class, in the name of a universalism defined by the leaders of self-styled "vanguard parties". In the late 1980s, the tentative beginnings of a social movement unionism suggest that Trinidadian labour may be attempting to construct a genuine universalism, constructed from the bottom up, which takes full account of the diversity of experiences of working class people, and on that basis attempts to develop a genuinely collective identity.

Bibliography

Abdulah, Norma. 1977. *The Labour Force in the Commonwealth Caribbean: A Statistical Analysis.* St Augustine, Trinidad: Institute of Social and Economic Research, Univ. of the West Indies.

Abel, Christopher, and Michael Twaddle, eds. 1982. *Caribbean Societies.* London: Univ. of London, Institute of Commonwealth Studies.

Action Group of Dedicated Citizens. 1970. *The Road to Freedom.* Trinidad: Action Group of Dedicated Citizens.

Ahiram, E. 1966. "Distribution of Income in Trinidad and Tobago and Comparison with Distribution of Income in Jamaica". *Social and Economic Studies* 15, no. 2: 103–20.

Alavi, Hamza. 1976. "The State in Post-Colonial Societies: Pakistan and Bangladesh". *New Left Review*, no. 74: 59–81.

Albert, Bill, and Adrian Graves. 1984. *Crisis and Change in the International Sugar Economy 1860–1914.* Norwich: ISC Press.

Allen, C.H. 1975. "Union Party Relationships in Francophone West Africa: A Critique of 'Teleguidage' Models". In *The Development of an African Working Class*, edited by Richard Sandbrook and Robin Cohen, 99–125. London: Longman.

Allen, V.L. 1975. "The Sociology of Industrial Relations". In *Industrial Relations and the Wider Society*, edited by E. Barrett, E. Rhodes and J. Beishon, 35–39. London: Collier-Macmillan.

Als, Michael. N.d. *Is Slavery Again! Some Factors Leading Up to the Introduction of the Industrial Stabilization Act (ISA) 1965, in Trinidad and Tobago.* Port of Spain: Cacique.

_____ . 1977. "The AIFLD – Multinationals Hopes in Trade Unions". In *Trade Union Conference 20/21 July 1977*, Oilfields Workers' Trade Union", 1–7. San Fernando: Oilfields Workers' Trade Union.

Ambursley, Fitzroy L. 1978. *The Working Class in the Third World: A Study in Class Consciousness and Class Action in Jamaica, 1919–1952.* St Augustine, Trinidad: Univ. of the West Indies.

Ambursley, Fitzroy L., and Robin Cohen, eds. 1983. *Crisis in the Caribbean.* London: Heinemann.

Anderson, Perry. 1978. "The Limits and Possibilities of Trade Union Action". In *Trade Unions under Capitalism*, edited by Tom Clarke and Laurie Clements, 333–50. Hassocks: Harvester.

Annamunthodo, Walter. 1962. *The OWTU Elections 1962.* San Juan: Vedic Enterprises.

_____ . *c.*1963. *Labour: A Review.* San Juan: Vedic Enterprises.

Auty, R., and A. Gelb. 1986. "Oil Windfalls in a Small Parliamentary Democracy". *World Development* 14, no. 9: 1161–75.

Baptiste, Fitz A. 1978. *The United States and West Indian Unrest, 1918–1939.* Mona, Jamaica: Institute of Social and Economic Research, Univ. of the West Indies.

_____ . 1988. "The Exploitation of Caribbean Bauxite and Petroleum, 1914–1945". *Social and Economic Studies* 37, nos. 1 & 2: 107–42.

Baptiste, Owen, ed. 1976. *Crisis.* St James, Trinidad: Inprint Caribbean.

Barrett, E., E. Rhodes, and J. Beishon, eds. 1975. *Industrial Relations and the Wider Society.* London: Collier-Macmillan.

Barry, Tom, Beth Wood, and Deb Preusch. 1984. *The Other Side of Paradise: Foreign Control in the Caribbean.* New York: Grove Press.

Basch, Linda Green. 1978. *Workin' for the Yankee Dollar: The Impact of a Transnational Petroleum Company on Caribbean Class and Ethnic Relations.* New York: New York Univ.

Basdeo, Sahadeo. 1981. "The Role of the British Labour Movement in the Development of Labour Organisation in Trinidad, 1919–29". *Social and Economic Studies* 30, no. 3: 21–41.

_____ . 1982. "The Role of the British Labour Movement in the Development of Labour Organisation in Trinidad 1929–1938". *Social and Economic Studies* 31, no. 1: 42–73.

_____ . 1983. *Labour Organisation and Labour Reform in Trinidad 1919–1939.* St Augustine, Trinidad: Institute of Social and Economic Research, Univ. of the West Indies.

Battlefront. 1978. Paper of the All-Trinidad Sugar and General Workers Trade Union.

_____ . 1979.

_____ . 1980.

_____ . 1981.

_____ . 1985.

Bauer, P.T. 1981. *Reality and Rhetoric*. London: Weidenfeld and Nicholson.

Bauer, Raymond A., and Alice H. Bauer. 1942. "Day to Day Resistance to Slavery". *The Journal of Negro History* 28, no. 4: 388-419.

Beckford, G. 1972a. "Aspects of the Present Conflict between the Plantation and the Peasantry in the West Indies". *Caribbean Quarterly* 18, no. 1: 47-58.

_____ . 1972b. *Persistent Poverty*. London: Oxford Univ. Press.

Beckford, G., ed. 1975. *Caribbean Economy*. Mona, Jamaica: Institute of Social and Economic Research, Univ. of the West Indies.

Beckford, G., and M. Witter. 1982. *Small Garden, Bitter Weed: Struggle and Change in Jamaica*. London: Zed Books.

Bennett, Karl. 1988. "External Debt, Capital Flight and Stabilization Policy: The Experiences of Barbados, Guyana, Jamaica and Trinidad and Tobago". *Social and Economic Studies* 37, no. 4: 57-77.

Berg, Elliot J., and Jeffrey Butler. 1964. "Trade Unions". In *Political Parties and National Integration in Tropical Africa*, edited by James S. Coleman and Carl G. Rosberg, 340-81. Berkeley: Univ. of California Press.

Bergquist, Charles, ed. 1984. *Labour in the Capitalist World Economy*. Beverly Hills: Sage.

Bernal, Richard. 1982. "Transnational Banks, the IMF and External Debt of Developing Countries". *Social and Economic Studies* 31, no. 4: 71-101.

_____ . 1984. "The IMF and Class Struggle in Jamaica 1977-1980". *Latin American Perspectives*, no. 42: 53-82.

Bertrand, Louis, Karl Theodore, and Roy Thomas. 1983. "Public Enterprise in Trinidad-Tobago". *Studies in Caribbean Public Enterprise* 1: 51-84.

Besson, J., and J. Momsen, eds. 1987. *Land and Development in the Caribbean*. Basingstoke: Macmillan Caribbean.

Best, Lloyd. 1968. "A Model of Pure Plantation Economies". *Social and Economic Studies* 17, no. 3: 283-326.

_____ . 1971a. "Independent Thought and Caribbean Freedom". In *Readings in the Political Economy of the Caribbean*, edited by Norman Girvan and O. Jefferson, 7-28. Trinidad: New World Group.

_____ . 1971b. *A Short Biography of the Labour Market in the Caribbean*. St Augustine, Trinidad: Univ. of the West Indies.

_____ . 1974a. *Black Power and National Reconstruction: Proposals Following the February Revolution*. Tunapuna, Trinidad: Tapia House Publishing.

_____ . 1974b. "Lloyd Best on Race, Class and Power". *Tapia* 4, no. 5: 5 & 8.

_____ . 1979. *The Choice of Technology Appropriate to Caribbean Countries*. Montreal: Centre for Developing Area Studies, McGill Univ.

_____ . 1980. "International Cooperation in the Industrialisation Process:

The Case of Trinidad and Tobago". In *UNIDO, Industry 2000*, New Perspective.

Best, Lloyd, and Kari Levitt. 1969. *Externally Propelled Growth and Industrialization in the Caribbean*. Montreal: Centre for Developing Area Studies, McGill Univ.

Black, George. 1981. *Triumph of the People: The Sandinista Revolution in Nicaragua*. London: Zed Books.

Blomstrom, Magnus, and Bjorn Hettne. 1984. *Development Theory in Transition*. London: Zed Books.

Blum, William. 1986. *The CIA: A Forgotten History*. London: Zed Books.

Bolland, O. Nigel. 1981. "Systems of Domination After Slavery: The Control of Land and Labour in the British West Indies after 1838". *Comparative Studies in Society and History* 23, no. 4: 591-619.

Boodhoo, Ken I. 1979. "The Multinational Corporations, External Control and the Problem of Development: The Case of Trinidad and Tobago". In *The Restless Caribbean*, edited by R. Millett and W. Marvin Will, 62-70. New York: Praeger.

Bourne, Compton. 1982. "Notes on Financial Changes in Trinidad and Tobago: 1966-1978". *Social and Economic Studies* 31, no. 4: 171-91.

_____ . 1985. "Banking Booms and Bust Economies: Lessons from Trinidad and Tobago and Jamaica". *Social and Economic Studies* 34, no. 4: 139-63.

Boyd, Rosalind, Robin Cohen, and Peter C.W. Gutkind, eds. 1987. *International Labour and the Third World*. Aldershot: Gower.

Braithwaite, Lloyd. 1968. "Social and Political Aspects of Rural Development in the West Indies". *Social and Economic Studies* 17, no. 3: 264-75.

_____ . 1975. *Social Stratification in Trinidad*. Mona, Jamaica: Institute of Social and Economic Research, Univ. of the West Indies.

Brass, Tom. 1988. "Slavery Now: Unfree Labour and Modern Capitalism". *Slavery and Abolition* 9, no. 2: 183-97.

Brenner, Robert. 1977. "The Origins of Capitalist Development: A Critique of Neo-Smithian Marxism". *New Left Review*, no. 104: 25-92.

Brenner, Philip. 1984. "Waging Ideological War: Anti-Communism and US Foreign Policy in Central America". *The Socialist Register 1984*, 230-60. London: Merlin.

Brereton, Bridget. 1974. "The Foundations of Prejudice: Indians and Africans in 19th Century Trinidad". *Caribbean Issues* 1, no. 1: 15-28.

_____ . 1979. *Race Relations in Colonial Trinidad 1870–1900*. Cambridge: Cambridge Univ. Press.

_____ . 1981. *A History of Modern Trinidad 1783–1962*. London: Heinemann.

_____ . 1984. "Post Emancipation Protest in the Caribbean: 'The Belmanna Riots' in Tobago, 1876". *Caribbean Quarterly* 32, nos. 3/4: 110-23.

Brett, E.A. 1983. *International Money and Capitalist Crisis*. London: Heinemann.

_____ . 1988. "States, Markets and Private Power: Problems and Possibilities". In *Privatisation in Less Developed Countries*, edited by Paul Cook and Colin Kirkpatrick, 47–67. Brighton: Wheatsheaf Books.

Brewster, Havelock. 1969. *Wage–Policy Issues in an Underdeveloped Economy: Trinidad and Tobago*. Mona, Jamaica: Institute of Social and Economic Research, Univ. of the West Indies.

_____ . 1972. "The Growth of Employment Under Export Biased Underdevelopment: Trinidad". *Social and Economic Studies* 21, no. 2: 153–69.

_____ . 1973. "Economic Dependence: A Quantitative Interpretation". *Social and Economic Studies* 22, no. 1: 90–5.

Brewster, Havelock, and Adlith Brown. 1974. "A Review of the Study of Economics in the English Speaking Caribbean". *Social and Economic Studies* 23, no. 3: 48–68.

Brewster, Havelock, and Clive Y. Thomas. 1967. *The Dynamics of West Indian Economic Integration*. Mona, Jamaica: Institute of Social and Economic Research, Univ. of the West Indies.

Bruce, C.J. 1972. "The Open Petroleum Economy: A Comparison of Keynesian and Alternative Formulations". *Social and Economic Studies* 21, no. 2: 125–52.

Bryans, Robin. 1967. *Trinidad and Tobago*. London: Faber.

Buhle, Paul. 1988. *CLR James: The Artist as Revolutionary*. London: Verso.

Burawoy, Michael. 1974. "Race, Class and Colonialism". *Social and Economic Studies* 23, no. 4: 521–50.

_____ . 1985. *The Politics of Production*. London: Verso.

CADORIT. 1955. *Report of the Second Conference*. Bridgetown: CADORIT.

Calder-Marshall, Arthur. 1939. *Glory Dead*. London: Michael Joseph.

Camejo, Acton. 1971. "Racial Discrimination in Employment in the Private Sector in Trinidad and Tobago: A Study of the Business Elite and the Social Structure". *Social and Economic Studies* 20, no. 3: 294–318.

Caribbean Dialogue. 1976. Vol. 2, nos. 3/4: 22, 23, 42.

Caribbean Issues. 1974. "Industrial Relations", Vol. 1, no. 2: 84.

Caribbean Labour Congress. 1945a. *Official Report of Conference*. Barbados: Caribbean Labour Congress.

_____ . 1945b. *Report of Conference by the Antigua Delegates*. Barbados: Caribbean Labour Congress.

_____ . 1947. *Report – Population Edition of Second CLC*. Kingston: Caribbean Labour Congress.

Carrington, S. 1971. "Industrialization in the Caribbean". In *Readings in the Political Economy of the Caribbean*, edited by N. Girvan and O. Jefferson, 140–47. Trinidad: New World Group.

Catchpole, F.C. 1955. *Report of the Board of Inquiry into the Causes and Circumstances of the Dispute between the All-Trinidad Sugar Estates and*

Factories Workers' Trade Union and Sugar Industry Labour Union, Trinidad.
Port of Spain: Government Printing Office.

Charles, Wendy. 1978. *Early Labour Organisation in Trinidad and the Colonial Context of the Butler Riots.* St Augustine, Trinidad: Univ. of the West Indies.

Chase, Ashton. 1964. *A History of Trade Unionism in Guyana 1900 to 1961.* Demerara: New Guyana Company.

Clarke, Tom, and Laurie Clements, eds. 1978. *Trade Unions under Capitalism.* Hassocks: Harvester.

Classline. 1977. 1978.

Cockcroft, James D. 1978. "Recent Caribbean Development and Need for Theoretical Expansion". *Latin American Perspectives* 5, no. 2: 29-36.

Cohen, David W., and Jack P. Greene. 1972. *Neither Slave nor Free.* Baltimore: Johns Hopkins Univ. Press.

Cohen, Robin. 1972. "Class in Africa: Analytical Problems and Perspectives". *The Socialist Register 1972,* 231-55. London: Merlin.

———. 1974. *Labour and Politics in Nigeria* London: Heinemann.

———. 1982. "Althusser Meets Anancy: Structuralism and Popular Protest in Ken Post's *History of Jamaica*". *The Sociological Review* 30, no. 2: 345-57.

———. 1983. "Theorising International Labour". Draft paper, Univ. of Warwick.

———. 1987. *The New Helots: Migrants in the International Division of Labour.* Aldershot: Gower.

Cohen, Robin, and David Michael. 1973. "The Revolutionary Potential of the African Lumpenproletariat: A Sceptical View". *Bulletin of the Institute of Development Studies* 5, nos. 2/3: 31-42.

Cohen, Robin, Peter C.W. Gutkind, and Phyllis Brazier, eds. 1979. *Peasants and Proletarians: The Struggle of Third World Workers.* London: Hutchinson.

Coleman, James S., and Carl G. Rosberg, eds. 1964. *Political Parties and National Integration in Tropical Africa.* Berkeley: Univ. of California Press.

Commission for Racial Equality. 1978. *Five Views of Multi-Racial Britain.* London: Commission for Racial Equality.

Concerned Group of Trade Unions. 1986. "Letter to Minister of State Enterprises", 19 February.

Concerned Trade Unions. 1986a. "Some Notes on the Economic Crisis of Trinidad and Tobago and its Effects on Working People, Farmers, Youths, Unemployeds and Housewives". Unpublished document.

———. 1986b. "Programme of Joint Activity for all Trade Unions – 1986". Unpublished document.

———. 1986c. "The Collapse of Collective Bargaining". Unpublished document.

Connell, R.W. 1984. "Class Formation on a World Scale". In *For a New Labour Internationalism,* edited by Peter Waterman, 176-209. The Hague: International Labour Education Research and Information Foundation.

Cook, Paul, and Colin Kirkpatrick. 1988. "Privatisation in Less Developed Countries: An Overview". In *Privatisation in Less Developed Countries*, edited by Paul Cook and Colin Kirkpatrick, 3–44. Brighton: Wheatsheaf Books.

_____ , eds. 1988. *Privatisation in Less Developed Countries*. Brighton: Wheatsheaf Books.

Council of Progressive Trade Unions. N.d./a. "The Circumstances Surrounding the Enactment of Labour Legislation in 1965". Unpublished CPTU position paper.

_____ . N.d./b. "A Brief Overview of the Development of Trade Unions and Trade Union Activity in Trinidad and Tobago". CPTU position paper.

_____ . N.d./c. "Industrial Relations". CPTU position paper.

_____ . N.d./d. "Circumstances Surrounding the Split in the National Trade Union Congress of Trinidad and Tobago". CPTU position paper.

_____ . 1985a. "Labour – A Review 1984–85". Unpublished paper.

_____ . 1985b. "A Sectoral Review of Labour Issues since the Economic Downturn". Unpublished paper.

_____ . 1985c. "Statistical Report of Organised Labour (Trinidad and Tobago) 1981–1985". Unpublished paper.

_____ . 1986. "History of Cost of Living Allowance". Unpublished paper.

_____ . 1987. "Paper Presented to Joint Consultative Council on Contributions to be Made by the Private Sector to National Reconstruction in Trinidad and Tobago". Unpublished document.

Cox, Oliver Cromwell. 1959. *Caste, Class and Race*. New York: Monthly Review Press.

Craig, Alton W.J. 1975. "A Framework for the Analysis of Industrial Relations Systems". In *Industrial Relations and the Wider Society*, edited by E. Barrett, E. Rhodes, and J. Beishon, 8–20. London: Collier-Macmillan.

Craig, Susan. 1974. *Community Development in Trinidad and Tobago 1943–73: From Welfare to Patronage*. Mona, Jamaica: Institute of Social and Economic Research, Univ. of the West Indies.

_____ .1977. Afterword to *Labour in the West Indies*, by W. Arthur Lewis, 57–84. London: New Beacon.

_____ . 1982a. "Sociological Theorizing in the English-speaking Caribbean: A Review". In *Contemporary Caribbean: A Sociological Reader*, 2 vols., edited by Susan Craig, 143–80. Maracas and Port of Spain: College Press and Paria.

_____ . 1982b. "Background to the 1970 Confrontation in Trinidad and Tobago". In *Contemporary Caribbean: A Sociological Reader*, 2 vols., edited by Susan Craig, 385–423. Maracas and Port of Spain: College Press and Paria.

_____ . 1988. *Smiles and Blood: The Ruling Class Response to the Labour Rebellion in Trinidad and Tobago*. London: New Beacon.

Craig, Susan, ed. 1981/1982. *Contemporary Caribbean: A Sociological Reader*, 2 vols., Maracas and Port of Spain: College Press and Paria.

Craton, Michael. 1982. *Testing the Chains: Resistance to Slavery in the British West Indies*. London: Cornell Univ. Press.

Cross, Malcolm. 1968. "Cultural Pluralism and Sociological Theory: A Critique and Re-evaluation". *Social and Economic Studies* 17, no. 4: 381–97.

————. 1971. "On Conflict, Race Relations and the Theory of the Plural Society". *Race* 12, no. 4: 474–94.

————. 1979. *Urbanisation and Urban Growth in the Caribbean*. Cambridge: Cambridge Univ. Press.

————. 1988. "The Political Representation of Organised Labour in Trinidad and Guyana: A Comparative Puzzle". In *Labour in the Caribbean*, edited by Malcolm Cross and Gad Heuman, 285–308. London and Basingstoke: Macmillan Caribbean.

Cross, Malcolm, and Arnaud Marks, eds. 1979. *Peasants, Plantations and Rural Communities in the Caribbean*. Guildford: Univ. of Surrey.

Cross, Malcolm, and Gad Heuman, eds. 1988. *Labour in the Caribbean*. London and Basingstoke: Macmillan Caribbean.

Cumper, G.E. 1961. "Labour and Development in the West Indies: Part I". *Social and Economic Studies* 10, no. 3: 278–305.

————. 1962. "Labour and Development in the West Indies: Part II". *Social and Economic Studies* 11, no. 1: 1–33.

————. 1974. "Dependence, Development and the Sociology of Economic Thought". *Social and Economic Studies* 23, no. 3: 465–82.

Dabydeen, David, and Brinsley Samaroo, eds. 1987. *India in the Caribbean*. London: Hansib.

Daily Mirror. 1965. 1966.

Dalley, F.W. 1947. *Trade Union Organisation and Industrial Relations in Trinidad*. Colonial No. 215. London: HMSO.

————. 1954. *General Industrial Conditions and Labour Relations in Trinidad*. Port of Spain: Government Printing Office.

Davies, D.I. 1964. "The Politics of the TUC's Colonial Policy". *The Political Quarterly* 35, no. 1: 23–34.

David, Wilfred L. 1968. "Democracy, Stability and Economic Development". *Caribbean Quarterly* 14, no. 4: 7–24.

Dietz, James L. 1984. "Destabilization and Intervention in Latin America and the Caribbean". *Latin American Perspectives*, no. 42: 3–14.

Dunkerley, James, and Chris Whitehouse. 1980. *Unity is Strength: Trade Unions in Latin America – A Case for Solidarity*. London: Latin America Bureau.

Dunlop, J.T. 1958. *Industrial Relations Systems*. Carbondale: Southern Illinois Univ. Press.

————. 1975. "Industrial Relations Systems". In *Industrial Relations and the Wider Society*, edited by E. Barrett et al., 1–32. London: Collier-Macmillan.

Dupuy, Alex. 1985. "French Merchant Capital and Slavery in Saint Domingue". *Latin American Perspectives*, no. 46: 77–102.

Durkheim, Emile. 1964. *The Division of Labour in Society*. London: Collier-Macmillan.

Eastern Caribbean Region. 1960. *Population Census 1960 – Administration Report*. Vol. 1, Part A. Port of Spain: Central Statistical Office.

Edwards, C. 1985. *The Fragmented World*. London: Methuen.

Edwards, S. Hylton. 1982. *Lengthening Shadows: Birth and Revolt of the Trinidad Army*. Trinidad: Inprint Caribbean.

Elkins, W.F. 1969. "Black Power in the British West Indies: The Trinidad Longshoremen's Strike of 1919". *Science and Society* 33, no. 1: 71–75.

Elson, Diane, and Ruth Pearson. 1981. "Nimble Fingers Make Cheap Workers: An Analysis of Women's Employment in Third World Export Manufacturing". *Feminist Review*, no. 7: 87–107.

Evening News. 1970a. 1970b.

Express. 1969.

_____ . 1970a (7.3).

_____ . 1970b (11.3).

_____ . 1970c (9.4).

_____ . 1970d (11.4).

_____ . 1970e (21.4).

_____ . 1970f (23.4).

_____ . 1970g (4.5).

_____ . 1971 (11.10).

_____ . 1975a (9.3).

_____ . 1975b (11.3).

_____ . 1975c (19.3).

_____ . 1976.

_____ . 1977a (1.8).

_____ . 1977b (11.8).

_____ . 1977c (15.8).

_____ . 1977d (16.8).

_____ . 1977e (17.8).

_____ . 1977f (19.8).

_____ . 1977g (20.8).

_____ . 1977h (13.9).

_____ . 1985 (18.12).

_____ . 1986a (6.8).

_____ . 1986b (7.8).

_____ . 1987.

_____ . 1988a (23.1).

_____ . 1988b (7.2).

_____ . 1988c (8.2).

_____ . 1988d (9.2).

_____ . 1988e (1.5).

_____ . 1988f (15.11).

_____ . 1989a (15.1).

_____ . 1989b (4.3).

_____ . 1989c (2.5).

_____ . 1989d (3.5).

_____ . 1989e (15.6).

_____ . 1989f (17.10).

_____ . 1989g (22.10).

_____ . 1989h (30.12).

_____ . 1990a(18.3).

_____ . 1990b (10.4).

_____ . 1990c (22.6).

Fanon, Frantz. 1967. *The Wretched of the Earth*. Harmondsworth: Penguin.

Farrell, Terrence W. 1979. "The Structure, Organisation and Performance of Manufacturing Industry in Trinidad and Tobago". PhD diss. Univ. of Toronto.

_____ . 1989. "The IMF and the Trinidad and Tobago Letter of Intent". *Asset* 7, no. 2: 8–19.

Farrell, Trevor. 1974. "The Multinational Corporations, the Petroleum Industry and Economic Underdevelopment in Trinidad and Tobago". PhD diss. Cornell Univ.

_____ . 1975a. *The Economics of Discontent*. San Fernando: Oilfields Workers' Trade Union.

_____ . 1975b. *The Petroleum and Petro-Chemical Industries*. Trinidad: Oilfields Workers' Trade Union.

_____ . 1978a. "A Tale of Two Issues: Nationalisation, the Transfer of Technology and the Petroleum Multinationals in Trinidad and Tobago". *Social and Economic Studies* 27, no. 1: 234–81.

_____ . 1978b. "The Unemployment Crisis in Trinidad and Tobago: Its Current Dimensions and Some Projections to 1985". *Social and Economic Studies* 27, no. 2: 117–52.

_____ . 1982. "The CARICOM Oil Market. Unpublished paper. Univ. of the West Indies, St Augustine.

_____ . 1985a. The Facts about the Trinidad Oil Crisis. Unpublished paper. Univ. of the West Indies, St Augustine.

_____ . 1985b. "The World Oil Market 1973–1983, and the Future of Oil Prices". *OPEC Review* (winter): 388–415.

February 11th Defense Committee. *c*.1971. *Sir George Rebellion and Caribbean Revolution*. Montreal: February 11th Defense Committee.

Forster Commission. 1938. *Trinidad and Tobago Disturbances 1937, Report of Commission Presented by the Secretary of State for the Colonies to Parliament*. Cmd. 5641. London: HMSO.

Fox, Alan. 1985. *Man Mismanagement*. London: Hutchinson.

Frank, André Gunder. 1969a. *Capitalism and Underdevelopment in Latin America*. New York: Monthly Review Press.

_____ . 1969b. *Latin America: Underdevelopment or Revolution*. New York: Monthly Review Press.

Froude, James Anthony. 1888. *The English in the West Indies*. London: Longmans, Green.

Frucht, R. 1967. "A Caribbean Social Type: Neither a Peasant nor Proletarian". *Social and Economic Studies* 16, no. 3: 295–300.

Furtado, Celso. 1970. *Economic Development in Latin America*. Cambridge: Cambridge Univ. Press.

Gamble, Andrew. 1985. *Britain in Decline*. Basingstoke: Macmillan.

Genovese, Eugene D. 1970. *The World the Slaveholders Made*. London: Allen Lane.

_____ . 1979 *From Rebellion to Revolution: Afro-American Slave Revolts in the Making of the Modern World*. Baton Rouge: Louisiana State Univ. Press.

George, Susan. 1988. *A Fate Worse than Debt*. Harmondsworth: Penguin.

Giddens, Anthony. 1971. *Capitalism and Modern Social Theory*. Cambridge: Cambridge Univ. Press.

Girvan, Norman. 1970. "Multinational Corporations and Dependent Under-development in Mineral Export Economies". *Social and Economic Studies* 19, no. 4: 490–526.

_____ . 1973. "The Development of Dependency Economics in the Caribbean and Latin America". *Social and Economic Studies* 22, no. 1: 1–33.

Girvan, N., and O. Jefferson, eds. 1971. *Readings in the Political Economy of the Caribbean*. Port of Spain: New World Group.

Gomes, Albert. 1974. *Through a Maze of Colour*. Port of Spain: Key Caribbean.

Gordon, D. 1978. "Working Class Radicalism in Jamaica: An Exploration of the Privileged Worker Thesis". *Social and Economic Studies* 27, no. 3: 313–41.

Gosine, Mahendra. 1984. "Culture and Ethnic Participation in a Social Move-ment: The Case of the East Indians and the Black Power Movement in Trinidad". Paper presented at the Third Conference on East Indians in the Caribbean, Univ. of the West Indies, St Augustine.

Green, Andy. 1983. "The Caribbean's Stolen Jewel". *Marxism Today* 27, no. 12: 11–13.

Greene, J.E. 1974. "A Review of Political Science Research in the English Speaking Caribbean: Toward a Methodology". *Social and Economic Studies* 23, no. 1: 1–47.

_____ . 1984. "Challenges and Responses in Social Science Research in the English Speaking Caribbean". *Social and Economic Studies* 33, no. 1: 9–46.

Griffin, Keith. 1978. *International Inequality and National Poverty*. Basingstoke: Macmillan.

Guillebaud, C.W. 1957. *Report and Arbitration Award in Dispute between the Seamen and Waterfront Workers Trade Union and Chaguaramas Terminals Limited*. Port of Spain: Government Printing Office.

Hall, Douglas. 1978. "The Flight from the Estates Reconsidered: The British West Indies 1838–42". *Journal of Caribbean History* 10/11: 7–24.

Hall, Stuart. 1977. "Pluralism, Race and Class in the Caribbean". In *Race and Class in Post-Colonial Society*, 150-82. Paris: UNESCO.

_____ . 1978. "Racism and Reaction". In *Five Views of Multi-Racial Britain*, 23-35. London: Commission for Racial Equality.

Halliday, Fred. 1983. "Cold War in the Caribbean". *New Left Review*, no. 141: 5-22.

Haraksingh, Kusha. 1987. "Control and Resistance among Indian Workers: A Study of Labour on the Sugar Plantations of Trinidad 1875-1917". In *India in the Caribbean*, edited by David Dabydeen and Brinsley Samaroo, 61-77. London: Hansib.

Harewood, Jack. 1963. "Population Growth of Trinidad and Tobago in the Twentieth Century". *Social and Economic Studies* 12, no. 1: 1-26.

_____ . c. 1963. "Employment in Trinidad and Tobago − 1960". *1960 Population Census Research Programme No. 5*. St Augustine, Trinidad: Institute of Social and Economic Research, Univ. of the West Indies.

_____ . 1971. "Racial Discrimination in Employment in Trinidad and Tobago". *Social and Economic Studies* 20, no. 3: 267-93.

_____ . 1972. "Changes in the Demand for and Supply of Labour in the Commonwealth Caribbean 1946-60". *Social and Economic Studies* 21, no. 1: 44-60.

_____ . 1978. *Unemployment and Related Problems in the Commonwealth Caribbean*. St Augustine, Trinidad: Institute of Social and Economic Research, Univ. of the West Indies.

Harewood, Jack, and Ralph Henry. 1985. *Inequality in a Post-Colonial Society: Trinidad and Tobago 1956–1981*. St Augustine, Trinidad: Institute of Social and Economic Research, Univ. of the West Indies.

Harrod, Jeffrey. 1972. *Trade Union Foreign Policy*. London and Basingstoke: Macmillan.

Hart, Richard. N.d. *Origin and Development of the Working Class in the English Speaking Caribbean Area: 1897 to 1937*. London: Community Education Trust.

Harvey, Franklyn. N.d. *On Revolution*. Trinidad: New Beginning Movement.

_____ . 1974. *Rise and Fall of Party Politics in Trinidad and Tobago*. Toronto: New Beginning Movement.

Henry, Frances, and Pamela Wilson. 1975. "The Status of Women in Caribbean Societies: An Overview of their Social, Economic and Sexual Roles". *Social and Economic Studies* 24, no. 2: 165-98.

Henry, Ralph. 1988. "Job Creation, the Trade Union Movement and a Declining Economy". *Asset* 7, no. 1: 35-44.

Henry, Z. 1972. *Labour Relations and Industrial Conflict in Commonwealth Caribbean Countries*. Port of Spain: Columbus.

Heuman, Gad. 1986. Introduction to *Out of the House of Bondage*, edited by Gad Heuman, 1-8. London: Frank Cass.

Heuman, Gad, ed. 1986. *Out of the House of Bondage*. London: Frank Cass.

Hilton, Rodney. 1987. Comment in *The Transition from Feudalism to Capitalism*, edited by Rodney Hilton, 109–17. London: Verso.

Hilton, Rodney, ed. 1987. *The Transition from Feudalism to Capitalism*. London: Verso.

Hinds, Ronald. 1987. "The Domestic Debt Crisis". *Asset* 6, no. 1: 9–19.

Hintzen, Percy C. 1985. "Ethnicity, Class and International Capitalist Penetration in Guyana and Trinidad". *Social and Economic Studies* 34, no. 3: 107–63.

Hobsbawm, E.J. 1968. *Industry and Empire*. Harmondsworth: Penguin.

_____ . 1984. *Worlds of Labour*. London: Weidenfeld and Nicholson.

_____ . 1988a. *The Age of Revolution*. London: Cardinal.

_____ . 1988b. *The Age of Capital*. London: Cardinal.

_____ . 1988c. *The Age of Empire*. London: Weidenfeld and Nicholson.

Hold the Fort. 1981. Organ of the Committee for Labour Solidarity.

Hope, Kempe R. 1986. *Economic Development in the Caribbean*. New York: Praeger.

Hope, Kempe R., and R.M. Walters. 1980. *Recent Performances and Trends in the Caribbean Economy and Imperialism*. St Augustine, Trinidad: Institute of Social and Economic Research, Univ. of the West Indies.

Howe, Darcus, and Bukka Rennie. 1982. "The Unemployed and Special Works". In *Contemporary Caribbean: A Sociological Reader*, 2 vols., edited by Susan Craig, 127–36. Maracas and Port of Spain: College Press and Paria.

Hoyos, F.A. 1974. *Grantley Adams and the Social Revolution*. Basingstoke: Macmillan.

Humphrey, John D. N.d. "The Trinity Manifesto". Curepe: Manifesto for the Revolutionary Party of Trinidad and Tobago.

Hunte, Desmond. 1988. "Current Trends in Employment/Unemployment in Trinidad and Tobago". *Asset* 7, no. 1: 7–18.

Hyman, Richard. 1975. *Industrial Relations: A Marxist Introduction*. London: Macmillan.

_____ . 1978. "Marxism and the Sociology of Trade Unionism". In *Trade Unions under Capitalism*, edited by Tom Clarke and Laurie Clements, 383–403. Hassocks: Harvester.

_____ . 1979. "Third World Strikes in International Perspective". *Development and Change*, no. 10: 321–37.

_____ . 1989. *The Political Economy of Industrial Relations*. Basingstoke: Macmillan.

Insurgent Sociologist. 1980. "Race and Class in Twentieth Century Capitalist Development". *Insurgent Sociologist* 2, no. 10: 2–128.

Jacobs, William Richard. 1969. "The Role of some Labour Movements in the Political Process in Trinidad 1937–1950". MSc thesis, Univ. of the West Indies, Mona.

_____ . 1971. "Factors Affecting Trade Union Organisation and Development in Trinidad and Tobago". Department of Government seminar paper. Univ. of the West Indies, St Augustine.

_____ . 1975a. *The History and Philosophy of the Trade Union Movement – A Caribbean Perspective*. Trinidad: Oilfields Workers' Trade Union.

_____ . 1975b. *Socialism is the Answer*. Port of Spain: Transport and Industrial Workers Union.

_____ . 1976. "Trade Unionism in Multi-Racial Societies and its Impact on the Political Economy – A Comparative Analysis of Malaya, Trinidad and Zambia". *Labour and Society* 1, no. 1: 79–94.

Jacobs, William Richard, ed. 1976. *Butler versus the King*. Port of Spain: Key Caribbean.

James, C.L.R. N.d. *Party Politics in the West Indies*. San Juan: Vedic Enterprises.

_____ . 1932. *The Life of Captain Cipriani*. Nelson, Lancashire: Coulton.

_____ . 1960. *Dr. Eric Williams: A Biographical Sketch*. Port of Spain: PNM Publishing.

_____ . 1964. *Lenin, Trotsky and the Vanguard Party: A Contemporary View*. Facing Reality pamphlet, Detroit.

_____ . 1970. "The Caribbean Confrontation Begins". *Race Today* 2, no. 9: 311–14.

_____ . 1980. *Spheres of Existence*. London: Allison & Busby.

_____ . 1984. *At the Rendezvous of Victory*. London: Allison & Busby.

_____ . 1986. *Beyond a Boundary*. London: Stanley Paul.

_____ . 1989. *The Black Jacobins*. London: Allison & Busby.

James, Winston. 1983. "The Hurricane that Shook the Caribbean". *New Left Review*, no. 138: 85–91.

Jenkins, Rhys. 1984a. *Transnational Corporations and the Industrial Transformation of Latin America*: Basingstoke: Macmillan.

_____ . 1984b. "Divisions Over the International Division of Labour". *Capital and Class*, no. 22: 28–57.

_____ . 1987. *Transnational Corporations and Uneven Development*. London: Methuen.

Jeyifo, Biodun, Darcus Howe, and Tim Hector. 1984. *Africa, Europe,Caribbean*. Trinidad: Oilfields Workers' Trade Union.

Johnson, Howard. 1987. "Oil and Imperial Policy". In *The Trinidad Labour Riots of 1937*, edited by Roy Thomas, 141–81. St Augustine, Trinidad: Univ. of the West Indies.

Jones, Chester Lloyd. [1916] 1970. *Caribbean Interests of the United States*. Reprint, New York: Arno Press.

Kambon, Khafra. 1988. *For Bread, Justice and Freedom*. London: New Beacon.

Kelly, John. 1988. *Trade Unions and Socialist Politics*. London: Verso.

Kerr, Clark, John T. Dunlop, Frederick H. Harbison, and Charles A. Myers. 1962. *Industrialism and Industrial Man*. London: Heinemann.

Klass, Morton. 1988. *East Indians in Trinidad: A Study in Cultural Persistence*. Illinois: Waveland Press.

Klein, M., and S. Engerman. 1987. "The Williams Thesis Reconsidered". In *British Capitalism and Caribbean Slavery*, edited by B. Solow and S. Engerman, 350–52.

Knight, Franklin W. 1978. *The Caribbean*. New York: Oxford Univ. Press.

Knowles, William H. 1959. *Trade Union Development and Industrial Relations in the British West Indies*. Berkeley and Los Angeles: Univ. of California Press.

La Guerre, J.G. 1972a. "The General Election of 1946 in Trinidad and Tobago". *Social and Economic Studies* 21, no. 2: 169–204.

⸻ . 1972b. *The Tyranny of Concepts*. St Augustine, Trinidad: Univ. of the West Indies.

⸻ . 1974. "Afro-Indian Relations in Trinidad and Tobago". *Caribbean Issues* 1, no. 1: 49–61.

⸻ . 1975. *The Politics of Unity*. St Augustine, Trinidad: Univ. of the West Indies.

⸻ . 1978. "Socialism in Trinidad and Tobago". *Caribbean Issues* 4, no. 2: 16–29.

⸻ . 1979. *The Politics of Communalism – The Agony of the Left in Trinidad and Tobago 1930–1950*. St Augustine, Trinidad: Pan-Caribbean Publications.

⸻ . 1982. "The General Election of 1981 in Trinidad and Tobago". *Journal of Commonwealth and Comparative Politics*, 21: 132–57.

⸻ . 1988. "Race and Class in the Caribbean". Unpublished paper. Institute of Social and Economic Research, Univ. of the West Indies, St Augustine.

La Guerre, J.G., ed. 1985. *From Calcutta to Caroni*. St Augustine, Trinidad: Univ. of the West Indies.

Lal, Deepak. 1983. *The Poverty of 'Development Economics'*. London: Institute of Economic Affairs.

Latin American Regional Report. 1988a (29.9.88), 1988b (8.12.88), 1989 (30.3.89), 1990 (20.4.90)

Laurence, K.O. 1963a. "Colonialism in Trinidad and Tobago". *Caribbean Quarterly* 9, no. 3: 44–56.

⸻ . 1963b. "The Settlement of Free Negroes in Trinidad before Emancipation". *Caribbean Quarterly* 9, nos. 1/2: 26–52.

Lemoine, Maurice. 1985. *Bitter Sugar*. London: Zed Books.

Lengerman, P.M. 1971. "Working Class Values in Trinidad and Tobago". *Social and Economic Studies* 20, no. 2: 151–63.

Lenin, V.I. 1988. *What is to be Done?* London: Penguin.

Levitt, Kari, and Lloyd Best. 1975. "Character of Caribbean Economy". In *Caribbean Economy*, edited by George Beckford, 34–60. Mona, Jamaica: Institute of Social and Economic Research, Univ. of the West Indies.

Lewis, Arthur. 1950. "The Industrialisation of the British West Indies". Reproduced from *Caribbean Economic Review*.

⸻ . 1954. "Economic Development with Unlimited Supplies of Labour". *The Manchester School of Economic and Social Studies* 22, no. 2: 139–91.

⸻ . 1955. *The Theory of Economic Growth*. London: Allen and Unwin.

_____ . [1939] 1977. *Labour in the West Indies*. Reprint, London: New Beacon.

Lewis, Gordon K. 1968. *The Growth of the Modern West Indies*. New York: Monthly Review Press.

_____ . 1987. *Main Currents in Caribbean Thought*. Baltimore and London: Johns Hopkins Univ. Press.

Lewis, Vaughan. 1970. "Comment on Girvan's 'Multinational Corporations and Dependent Underdevelopment in Mineral Export Economies' ". *Social and Economic Studies* 19, no. 4: 527–33.

Lowenthal, David. 1972. *West Indian Societies*. London: Oxford Univ. Press.

Lubeck, P. 1979. "The Value of Multiple Methods in Researching Third World Strikes: A Nigerian Example". *Development and Change* 10, no. 2: 287–300.

MacDonald, Frank. 1970a. *Trinidad: The February Revolution*. Institute of Current World Affairs, FJM–23.

_____ . 1970b. *Trinidad: Black Power and National Reconstruction*. Institute of Current World Affairs, FJM–24.

MacDonald, Scott B. 1986. *Trinidad and Tobago: Democracy and Development in the Caribbean*, New York: Praeger.

Maharaj, Stephen. 1966. *A New Domination*. San Fernando: Stephen Maharaj.

_____ . 1976. *An Open Letter to George Weekes and other Leaders of ULF*. Trinidad: Stephen Maharaj.

Malik, Yogendra. 1971. *East Indians in Trinidad*. London: Oxford Univ. Press.

Malloy, James, and Eduardo A. Gamarra, eds. Forthcoming. *Latin American and Caribbean Contemporary Record*, Vol. 8. New York: Holmes and Meier.

Mandle, Jay. 1972. "The Plantation Economy: An Essay in Definition". *Science and Society* 36: 49–62.

_____ . 1984. "Caribbean Dependency and its Alternatives". *Latin American Perspectives*, no. 42: 111–24.

Mann, Michael. 1987. "The Social Cohesion of Liberal Democracy". In *Society and the Social Sciences*, edited by David Potter, 255–68. London: Routledge and Kegan Paul.

Marable, Manning. 1987. *African and Caribbean Politics*. London: Verso.

Mars, Perry. 1984. "Destabilization and Socialist Orientation in the English Speaking Caribbean". *Latin American Perspectives*, no. 42: 83–110.

_____ . 1985. "Political Mobilization and Class Struggle in the English Speaking Caribbean". *Contemporary Marxism*, no. 10: 128–47.

Marshall, W.K. 1968. "Peasant Development in the West Indies since 1838". *Social and Economic Studies* 17, no. 3: 252–63.

_____ . 1972. "Aspects of the Development of the Peasantry". *Caribbean Quarterly* 18, no. 1: 30–46.

Marx, Karl. 1976. *Capital*. Vol. 1. Harmondsworth: Penguin.

_____ . 1984. *Selected Writings*. London: Oxford Univ. Press.

Marx Delson, Roberta. 1981. *Readings in Caribbean History and Economics*. New York: Gordon and Breach.

Massiah, Joycelin. 1986. "Women in the Caribbean Project: An Overview". *Social and Economic Studies* 35, no. 2: 1-29.

———. 1986. "Work in the Lives of Caribbean Women". *Social and Economic Studies* 35, no. 2: 177-239.

Mbanefo Commission. 1965. *Report of the Commission of Enquiry into Subversive Activities in Trinidad and Tobago*. House Paper no. 2. Port of Spain: Government Printing Office.

McClelland, David. 1967. *The Achieving Society*. New York: Free Press.

McIntyre, Alister, and Beverly Watson. 1970. *Studies in Foreign Investment in the Commonwealth Caribbean, No. 1: Trinidad and Tobago*. Mona, Jamaica: Institute of Social and Economic Research, Univ. of the West Indies.

McLeod, Errol K. 1987. *Presidential Address to the 48th Annual Conference of Delegates*. Trinidad: Oilfields Workers' Trade Union.

McLeod, Marian B., ed. 1983. *Tradition, Change and Revolution in the Caribbean*. Florida: Association of Caribbean Studies.

Meeks, Brian. 1976. "The Development of the 1970 Revolution in Trinidad and Tobago". MSc thesis, Univ. of the West Indies.

Mentor, Ralph. 1944. *Trade Unionism in Trinidad*. San Fernando: *Vanguard*.

Miles, R. 1987. *Capitalism and Unfree Labour*. London: Tavistock.

———. 1989. *Racism*. London: Routledge.

Millett, R., and W. Marvin Will, eds. 1979. *The Restless Caribbean*. New York: Praeger.

Millette, James. 1971. *The Black Revolution in the Caribbean*. Curepe, Trinidad: United National Independence Party.

———. 1973. *Race and Class: Factors in the History of Protest Movements in the West Indies since 1789*. St Augustine, Trinidad: Univ. of the West Indies.

———. 1976. *Our Present Tasks*. Trinidad: United Labour Front.

———. 1981. "National Political Formation and the Forthcoming Elections". *Tribune* 1, no. 1: 1-35.

———. 1985. *Society and Politics in Colonial Trinidad*. London: Zed Books.

Mills, Charles W. 1987. "Race and Class: Conflicting or Reconcilable Paradigms?" *Social and Economic Studies* 36, no. 2: 69-108.

Mills, C. Wright. 1959. *The Sociological Imagination*. New York: Oxford Univ. Press.

Mills, G.E. 1981. "The Administration of Public Enterprise: Jamaica and Trinidad-Tobago". *Social and Economic Studies* 30, no. 1: 45-74.

Mintz, Sidney. 1978. "Was the Plantation Slave a Proletarian?" *Review* 11, no. 1: 81-98.

———. 1979. "The Rural Proletariat and the Problem of Rural Proletarian Consciousness". In *Peasants and Proletarians: The Struggle of Third World Workers*, edited by Robin Cohen, Peter C.W. Gutkind and Phyllis Brazier, 173-97. London: Hutchinson.

_____ . 1984. *Caribbean Transformations*. London: Johns Hopkins Univ. Press.

_____ . 1988. Foreword to *Labour in the Caribbean*, edited by Malcolm Cross and Gad Heuman, xiii–xvii. London and Basingstoke: Macmillan Caribbean.

Mintz Sidney W., and Sally Price, eds. 1985. *Caribbean Contours*. Baltimore and London: Johns Hopkins Univ. Press.

Mohammed, Patricia. 1985. *The Women's Movement in Trinidad and Tobago since the 1960s*. Cave Hill, Barbados: Women and Development Unit, Extra-Mural Department, Univ. of the West Indies.

Moreno Fraginals, Manuel. 1976. *The Sugar Mill*. London: Monthly Review Press.

Moreno Fraginals, Manuel, Frank Moya Pons, and Stanley L. Engerman, eds. 1985. *Between Slavery and Free Labour: The Spanish Speaking Caribbean in the Nineteenth Century*. Baltimore: Johns Hopkins Univ. Press.

Morrissey, Marietta. 1981. "Towards a Theory of West Indian Economic Development". *Latin American Perspectives*, no. 28: 4–27.

MOTION. 1989. *Political Programme*. Trinidad: MOTION.

Munck, Ronaldo. 1988. *The New International Labour Studies*. London: Zed Books.

Munroe, Trevor. 1983. *The Politics of Constitutional Decolonization: Jamaica, 1944–62*. Mona, Jamaica: Institute of Social and Economic Research, Univ. of the West Indies.

Murray, Robin. 1972. "Underdevelopment, International Firms, and the International Division of Labour". In *Towards a New World Economy*. Papers and Proceedings of the Fifth European Conference of the Society for International Development, 159–247. Rotterdam: Rotterdam Univ. Press.

_____ . 1981a. Introduction to *Multinationals Beyond the Market*, edited by Robin Murray, 1–14. Brighton: Harvester Press.

_____ . 1981b. "Transfer Pricing and its Control: Alternative Approaches". In *Multinationals Beyond the Market*, edited by Robin Murray, 147–76. Brighton: Harvester Press.

Murray, Robin, ed. 1981. *Multinationals Beyond the Market*. Brighton: Harvester Press.

Muschkin, Clara G. 1980. "Public Policy, Labour Force, and Employment in Trinidad and Tobago". MSc thesis, Santiago, Chile.

NAMOTI. 1976. *Special Labour Day Bulletin no. 1: Support the Just, Anti-Imperialist and Democratic Struggles of the United Labour Front*. Trinidad: NAMOTI.

National Joint Action Committee. 1971a. *Conventional Politics or Revolution?* Belmont, Trinidad: National Joint Action Committee.

_____ . 1971b. *Slavery to Slavery*. Belmont, Trinidad: National Joint Action Committee.

_____ . 1983. *NJAC 1970–1983*. Trinidad: National Joint Action Committee.

National Union of Sugar Workers. 1963. *A Betrayal of the Sugar Workers: An Analysis of the Agreement Made by the Sugar Manufacturers Federation and* the *All-Trinidad Sugar Estates and Factories Workers Trade Union in December 1963*. San Fernando: National Union of Sugar Workers.

Nevadomsky, Joseph. 1982. "Social Change and the East Indians in Rural Trinidad". *Social and Economic Studies* 31, no. 1: 90–126.

_____ . 1984. "Economic Organisation, Social Mobility and Changing Social Status among the East Indians in Rural Trinidad". *Social and Economic Studies* 33, no. 3: 31–62.

New Beginning Movement. 1974. *16 Questions on Socialism*. San Fernando, Trinidad: New Beginning Movement.

_____ . 1976a. *Bulletin No. 1: What ULF Can Be and How*. Tunapuna, Trinidad: New Beginning Movement.

_____ . 1976b. *ULF: The Alternative Government: What it Must Mean*. Tunapuna, Trinidad: New Beginning Movement.

New Dawn — Paper of the National Union of Government and Federated Workers. 1985, 1986.

Nicholls, David. 1971. "East Indians and Black Power in Trinidad". *Race* 12, no. 4: 444–59.

_____ . 1973. *The Three Varieties of Pluralism*. New York: St Martin's Press.

Nicholson, Marjorie. 1976. *The TUC and the West India Royal Commission*. London: Univ. of London, Institute of Commonwealth Studies.

Nieboer, H.J. 1971. *Slavery as an Industrial System*. New York: Lennox Hill.

North American Congress on Latin America. 1976. *Oil in the Caribbean – Focus on Trinidad*. North American Congress on Latin America.

November 17th Research Group. 1978. *The Real Story of Tobago*. St Augustine: November 17th Research Group.

Obika, Nyahuma. 1983. *The Life and Times of T.U.B. Butler*. Trinidad: Caribbean Historical Society.

O'Brien, Patrick. 1982. "European Economic Development: The Contribution of the Periphery". *Economic History Review* 35, no. 1: 1–18.

O'Brien, Philip. 1975. "A Critique of Latin American Theories of Dependency". In *Beyond the Sociology of Development*, edited by Ivaar Oxaal, Tony Barnett and David Booth, 7–27. London: Routledge and Kegan Paul.

Ohlin, Bertil. 1933. *Inter-regional and International Trade*. Cambridge, Mass.: Harvard Univ. Press.

Oilfields Workers' Trade Union. N.d. *Memoirs of Uriah Butler 1937–42*. San Fernando, Trinidad: Oilfields Workers' Trade Union.

_____ . 1937. *Rules of the Oilfields Workers' Trade Union*. San Fernando, Trinidad: Oilfields Workers' Trade Union.

_____ . 1963. *Annual Conference of Delegates 1963: Addresses of President General and Economic Adviser*. San Fernando, Trinidad: Oilfields Workers' Trade Union.

_____ . 1966. *General Council's Report to the Twenty-sixth Annual Conference of Delegates*. San Fernando, Trinidad: Oilfields Workers' Trade Union.

_____ . 1969. *Oilfields Workers' Trade Union 1937–1969*. San Fernando, Trinidad: Oilfields Workers' Trade Union.

_____ . 1977a. *Oilfields Workers' Trade Union 1937–77*. San Fernando, Trinidad: Oilfields Workers' Trade Union.

_____ . 1977b. *Trade Union Conference, 20/21 July, 1977*. San Fernando, Trinidad: Oilfields Workers' Trade Union.

_____ . 1978a. *International Policy and the OWTU*. Oilfields Workers' Trade Union Special Conference of Delegates, 1978. San Fernando, Trinidad: Oilfields Workers' Trade Union.

_____ . 1978b. *The Development of the State in Trinidad and Tobago*. San Fernando, Trinidad: Oilfields Workers' Trade Union.

_____ . 1978c. *In Defence of Our Members and the People of Trinago against Global Texaco – Exploiter of Our Labour and Our Natural Resources*. San Fernando, Trinidad: Oilfields Workers' Trade Union.

_____ . 1978d. *The Industrial Labour Court and the OWTU 1971–1978*. 2 vols. San Fernando, Trinidad: Oilfields Workers' Trade Union.

_____ . 1982. *Our Fight for Peoples' Ownership and Control of the Oil Industry*. San Fernando, Trinidad: Oilfields Workers' Trade Union.

_____ . 1986a. *46th Annual Conference of Delegates*. San Fernando, Trinidad: Oilfields Workers' Trade Union.

_____ . 1986b. "Towards United Trade Union Activity". In *46th Annual Conference of Delegates*, 12-22. San Fernando, Trinidad: Oilfields Workers' Trade Union.

_____ . 1987. *Memorandum to the Government of Trinidad and Tobago*. San Fernando, Trinidad: Oilfields Workers' Trade Union.

_____ . 1987. *Fifty Years of Progress 1937–1987*. San Fernando, Trinidad: Vanguard Publications.

_____ . N.d. "Some Highlights in Broad Outlines on the History and Development of the Trade Union Movement from 1938 to the Present Time". Unpublished paper.

Okpaluba, Chuks. 1975. *Essays on Law and Trade Unionism in the Caribbean*. Port of Spain: National Union of Government and Federated Workers.

_____ . 1980. *The Evolution of Labour Relations Legislation in Trinidad and Tobago*. St Augustine, Trinidad: Institute of Social and Economic Research, Univ. of the West Indies.

Orde Brown, G. St J. 1939. *Labour Conditions in the West Indies*. Cmd. 6070, 216, London: HMSO.

Oxaal, Ivar. 1968. *Black Intellectuals Come to Power: The Rise of Creole Nationalism in Trinidad and Tobago*. Cambridge, Mass.: Schenkman.

_____ . 1971. *Race and Revolutionary Consciousness*. Cambridge, Massachussetts: Schenkman.

_____ . 1975. "The Dependency Economist as Grassroots Politician in the Caribbean". In *Beyond the Sociology of Development*, edited by Ivar Oxaal, Tony Barnett and David Booth, 28-49. London: Routledge and Kegan Paul.

Oxaal, Ivar, Tony Barnett, and David Booth, eds. 1975. *Beyond the Sociology of Development*. London: Routledge and Kegan Paul.

Palmer, R.W. 1979. *Caribbean Dependence on the United States Economy*. New York: Praeger.

Panday, Basdeo. 1979. *Address of the Party Leader to the Convention of the United Labour Front*. Couva, Trinidad: United Labour Front.

Pantin, Dennis. 1986. "A Theoretical Perspective on Trinidad and Tobago's Export Drive". *Asset* 5, no. 1: 10–21.

_____. 1987a. "Long Waves and Caribbean Development". *Social and Economic Studies* 36, no. 2: 1–20.

_____. 1987b. "The Lessons of the Global Debt Crisis for Trinidad and Tobago's Domestic Debt Crisis". *Asset* 6, no. 1: 9–19.

_____. 1989a. "The Adjustment of Imperatives: Appropriate Balance of Payments Policy for Trinidad and Tobago". *Asset* 7, no. 2: 20–51.

_____. 1989b. *Into the Valley of Debt*. St Augustine, Trinidad: Univ. of the West Indies.

Parris, Canute. 1976. "Political Dissidence in Post Independence Jamaica and Trinidad: 1962–1972". PhD diss., New School for Social Research.

Parris, Carl D. 1976. *Capital or Labour? The Decision to Introduce The Industrial Stabilization Act in Trinidad and Tobago*. Mona, Jamaica: Institute of Social and Economic Research, Univ. of the West Indies.

_____. 1981. "Joint Venture 1: The Trinidad–Tobago Telephone Company 1968–72". *Social and Economic Studies* 30, no. 1: 108–26.

_____. 1981. "Joint Venture II: The National Flour Mill of Trinidad–Tobago 1972–79". *Social and Economic Studies* 30, no. 1: 127–45.

_____. 1985. "Power and Privilege in Trinidad and Tobago". *Social and Economic Studies* 34, no. 2: 97–109.

Parsons, Talcott, Robert F. Bales, and Edward A. Shils. 1962. *Working Papers in the Theory of Action*. London: Collier–Macmillan.

Patterson, Orlando. 1975. *The Sociology of Slavery*. London: Associated Univ. Press.

Paul, Cecil. *c*.1986. "Collapse of Collective Bargaining in Trinidad and Tobago". CPTU position paper.

_____. 1987a. "Trade Union's Contribution to the Nation". Oilfields Workers' Trade Union document.

_____. 1987b. "Labour Unity post-PNM". CPTU position paper.

_____. N.d. Trade Unions and Politics. CPTU position paper.

Payne, Anthony. 1984. "Dependency Theory and the Commonwealth Caribbean". In *Dependency under Challenge*, edited by Anthony Payne and Paul Sutton, 1–11. Manchester: Manchester Univ. Press.

Payne, Anthony, and Paul Sutton, eds. 1984. *Dependency under Challenge*. Manchester: Manchester Univ. Press.

Pearce, Jenny. 1982. *Under the Eagle: US Intervention in Central America and the Caribbean*. London: Latin America Bureau.

People's National Movement. N.d. *Major Party Documents*. Port of Spain: PNM Publishing.

_____ . 1956. *The People's Charter*. Port of Spain: PNM Publishing.

_____ . 1961. *Election Manifesto: General Elections 1961*. Port of Spain: PNM Publishing.

_____ . 1963. *Constitution: Adopted by the Special Constitution Review Convention on 20th January 1963*. Port of Spain: PNM Publishing.

_____ . c.1964. *The Party in Independence*. Port of Spain: PNM Publishing.

Petras, James. 1978. *Critical Perspectives on Imperialism and Social Class in the Third World*. New York and London: Monthly Review Press.

Phelps, O.W. 1960. "Rise of the Labour Movement in Jamaica". *Social and Economic Studies* 9, no. 4: 417–68.

Phillips, Daphne. 1984. "Class Formation and Ethnicity in Trinidad". MSc thesis, Univ. of the West Indies, St Augustine.

Pierre, Lennox. 1975. *The Ideology of the Working Class*. San Fernando, Trinidad: Oilfields Workers' Trade Union.

Pierre, Lennox, and John La Rose. 1955. *For More and Better Democracy: For a Democratic Constitution for Trinidad and Tobago*. Port of Spain: West Indian Independence Party.

Post, Charles. 1978. *Arise Ye Starvelings! The Jamaican Labour Rebellion and its Aftermath*. The Hague: Martinus Nijhoff.

_____ . 1979. "The Politics of Protest in Jamaica 1938: Some Problems of Analysis and Conceptualisation". In *Peasants and Proletarians: The Struggle of Third World Workers*, edited by Robin Cohen, Peter C.W. Gutkind, and Phyllis Brazier, 198–218. London: Hutchinson.

_____ . 1982. "The American Road to Capitalism". *New Left Review*, no. 133: 30–51.

Post, Ken. 1981. *Strike the Iron: A Colony at War – Jamaica 1939–45*, 2 vols. Atlantic Highlands, New Jersey: Humanities Press.

Potter, David, ed. 1987. *Society and the Social Sciences*. London: Routledge and Kegan Paul.

Poynting, Jeremy. 1987. "East Indian Women in the Caribbean: Experience and Voice". In *India in the Caribbean*, edited by David Dabydeen and Brinsley Samaroo, 231–63. London: Hansib.

Prebisch, Raul. 1959. "Commercial Policy in the Underdeveloped Countries". *American Economic Review*, no. 44: 251–73.

Ramdin, Ron. 1982. *From Chattel Slave to Wage Earner: A History of Trade Unionism in Trinidad and Tobago*. London: Martin Brian and O'Keeffe.

Rampersad, Frank. 1962. *Growth and Structural Change in the Economy of Trinidad and Tobago 1951–1961*. Mona, Jamaica: Institute of Social and Economic Research, Univ. of the West Indies.

Ramsaran, Dave. 1989. "Trade Union Organization: A Comparative Study of Trade Unionism in the Oil and Sugar Sectors". MSc thesis, Univ. of the West Indies, St Augustine.

Ramsaran, Ramesh. 1985. *US Investment in Latin America and the Caribbean*. London: Hodder and Stoughton.

_____ . 1989. *The Commonwealth Caribbean in the World Economy*. Basingstoke: Macmillan.

Reddock, Rhoda E. 1979. "The Working Class Woman and her Work Situation in Trinidad and Tobago". Unpublished paper.

_____ . 1980. "Industrialisation and the Rise of the Petty Bourgeiosie in Trinidad and Tobago". Master of Development Studies thesis, Institute of Social Studies, The Hague.

_____ . 1984a. "Women, Labour and Struggle in Twentieth Century Trinidad and Tobago: 1898-1960". PhD diss., Institute of Social Studies, The Hague.

_____ . 1984b. "Women and Garment Production in Trinidad and Tobago, 1900-1960". Institute of Social Studies Working Paper, The Hague.

_____ . 1985. "Women and Slavery in the Caribbean: A Feminist Perspective". *Latin American Perspectives*, no. 44: 63-80.

_____ . 1986. "Indian Women and Indentureship in Trinidad and Tobago 1845-1917: Freedom Denied". *Caribbean Quarterly* 32, nos. 3/4: 27-49.

_____ . 1987. "Women and the Sexual Division of Labour: Historical and Contemporary Perspectives – the Case of Trinidad and Tobago'". Unpublished paper, Univ. of the West Indies, St Augustine.

_____ . 1988. *Elma François, the NWCSA and the Workers' Struggle for Change in the Caribbean*. London: New Beacon.

_____ . 1989. "Caribbean Women and the Struggle of the 1930s: A Pyrrhic Victory". *Caribbean Affairs* 2, no. 1: 86-102.

Rennie, Bukka. 1974. *History of the Working Class in the 20th Century: Trinidad and Tobago*. Toronto: New Beginning Movement.

_____ . 1975. *Revolution and Social Development – A Direct Address to the Unemployeds*. Tunapuna, Trinidad: New Beginning Movement.

_____ . 1976. *Don't Stop the Strike*. Trinidad: New Beginning Movement.

Report of the Trinidad and Tobago Independence Conference, 1962. 1962. Cmd. 1757, 13, London, HMSO.

Ricardo, David. 1981. *Principles of Political Economy*. Cambridge: Cambridge Univ. Press.

Richardson, David. 1987. "The Slave Trade, Sugar and Economic Growth". In *British Capitalism and Caribbean Slavery*, edited by Barbara L. Solow and Stanley L.Engerman, 135-62. Cambridge: Cambridge Univ. Press.

Richter, Andrew S. 1979. "Multinational Corporations, Local Businessmen and the State in a Small Developing Country: A Case Study of Trinidad and Tobago". PhD diss., Yale Univ.

Riviere, Bill. 1972. "Black Power, NJAC and the 1970 Confrontation in the Caribbean: An Historical Interpretation". Unpublished paper. Univ. of the West Indies, St Augustine.

Roberts, B.C. 1964. *Labour in the Tropical Territories of the Commonwealth*. London: Bell.

Rodney, Walter. 1969. *The Groundings with My Brothers*. London: Bogle L'Ouverture.

———. 1981a. *A History of the Guyanese Working People 1881–1905*. Baltimore: Johns Hopkins Univ. Press.

———. 1981b. "Guyana: The Making of a Labour Force". *Race and Class* 22 no. 4: 331–52.

Rostow, Walt W. 1948. *British Economy of the Nineteenth Century*. Oxford: Clarendon Press.

———. 1960. *The Stages of Economic Growth: A Non-Communist Manifesto*. Cambridge: Cambridge Univ. Press.

Rotterdam Univ. Press. 1972. *Towards a New World Economy*. Papers and proceedings of the fifth European conference of the Society for International Development. Rotterdam: Rotterdam Univ. Press.

Roxborough, Ian. 1979. *Theories of Underdevelopment*. London: Macmillan.

Rubin, Vera, ed. 1971. *Caribbean Studies: A Symposium*. Seattle: Univ. of Washington Press.

Rubin, Vera, ed. [1960] 1978. *Social and Cultural Pluralism in the Caribbean*. Reprint, Millwood, New York: Kraus.

Ryan, Selwyn. 1974. *Race and Nationalism in Trinidad and Tobago*. Toronto: Univ. of Toronto Press and the Institute of Social and Economic Research, Univ. of the West Indies.

———. c.1978. *The Disunited Labour Front*.Unpublished paper. Univ. of the West Indies, St Augustine.

———. 1988a. "New Directions in Trinidad and Tobago". *Caribbean Affairs* 1, no. 1: 126–60.

———. 1988b. "One Love Revisited". *Caribbean Affairs* 1, no. 2: 67–127.

———. 1989a. "The Disillusioned Electorate". *Caribbean Affairs* 2, no. 1: 19–50.

———. 1989b. *Revolution and Reaction: Parties and Politics in Trinidad and Tobago 1970–1981*. St Augustine, Trinidad: Institute of Social and Economic Research, Univ. of the West Indies.

———. 1989c. *The Disillusioned Electorate*. Port of Spain: Inprint Caribbean.

Ryan, Selwyn, ed. 1988. *The Independence Experience 1962–1987*. St Augustine: Institute of Social and Economic Research, Univ. of the West Indies.

Ryan, Selwyn, and Richard Jacobs. c.1979. *The Politics of Succession: A Study of Parties and Politics in Trinidad and Tobago*. St Augustine, Trinidad: Univ. of the West Indies.

Safa, Helen I. N.d. "Women and the Economic Crisis in the Caribbean". Mimeo.

Samaroo, Brinsley. 1972. "The Trinidad Workingmen's Association and the Origins of Popular Protest in a Crown Colony". *Social and Economic Studies* 21, no. 2: 205–22.

———. 1987. "The Trinidad Disturbances of 1917–20: Precursor to 1937". In *The Trinidad Labour Riots of 1937*, edited by Roy Thomas, 21–56. Univ. of the West Indies, St Augustine.

Sandbrook, Richard, and Robin Cohen, eds. 1975. *The Development of an African Working Class*. London: Longman.

Sandoval, José Miguel. 1983. "State Capitalism in a Petroleum-based Economy: the Case of Trinidad and Tobago". In *Crisis in the Caribbean*, edited by Fitzroy L. Ambursley and Robin Cohen, 247-68. London: Heinemann.

Schatan, Jacob. 1987. *World Debt: Who is to Pay?* London: Zed Books.

Sebastien, Raphael. 1979. "The Development of Capitalism in Trinidad 1845-1917". PhD diss., Howard Univ.

_____ . 1981. "The Political Economy of Capitalism of Trinidad and Tobago: An Overview". *Tribune* 1, no. 1: 41-65.

_____ . 1985. "State Sector Development in Trinidad and Tobago, 1956-1982". *Contemporary Marxism*, no. 10: 110-27.

Seers, Dudley. 1964. "The Mechanism of an Open Petroleum Economy". *Social and Economic Studies* 13, no. 2: 233-42.

_____ . 1969. "A Step Towards a Political Economy of Development: Trinidad/Tobago". *Social and Economic Studies* 18, no. 3: 217-53.

Serve the People – Organ of the National Movement for the Total Independence of Trinidad and Tobago (NAMOTI). 1980.

Sewell, William G. 1862. *The Ordeal of Free Labour in the British West Indies*. London: Sampson Low.

Shah, Raffique. 1976. Interview, in *Caribbean Dialogue* 2, nos. 3/4: 22-5, 41.

_____ . c.1978. *An Open Letter to Brother 'K' and other Brethren of the Panday Political Clique*. Trinidad: United Labour Front.

_____ . 1988. *Race Relations in Trinidad*. Trinidad: Classline Publications.

_____ . 1990. "The 1970 Army Mutiny". Mimeo.

Shaikh, Anwar. 1979. "Foreign Trade and the Law of Value". *Science and Society*, no. 43: 281-302.

_____ . 1980. "Foreign Trade and the Law of Value: Part Two". *Science and Society*, no. 44: 27-57.

Simpson, Joy M. 1973. *Internal Migration in Trinidad and Tobago*. Mona, Jamaica: Institute of Social and Economic Research, Univ. of the West Indies.

Singh, Kelvin. 1979. "The Roots of Afro-Indian Conflict in Trinidad in the Indentureship Period". Unpublished paper. Univ. of the West Indies, St Augustine.

_____ . 1987. *Bloodstained Tombs*. Basingstoke: Macmillan.

Skocpol, Theda. 1977. "Wallerstein's World Capitalist System: A Theoretical and Historical Critique". *American Journal of Sociology*, no. 82, 1075-90.

Smith, M.G. 1965. *The Plural Society in the British West Indies*. Berkeley: Univ. of California Press.

Smith, Neil. 1984. *Uneven Development*. Oxford: Blackwell.

Smith, Sheila, and John Toye. 1979. "Three Stories about Trade and Poor Economies". In *Trade and Poor Economies*, edited by Sheila Smith and John Toye, 1-18. London: Frank Cass.

Smith, Sheila, and John Toye, eds. 1979. *Trade and Poor Economies*. London: Frank Cass.

Solow, Barbara, and Stanley L. Engerman. 1987. Introduction to *British Capitalism and Caribbean Slavery*, edited by Barbara Solow and Stanley L. Engerman, 1–35. Cambridge: Cambridge Univ. Press.

Solow, Barbara, and Stanley L. Engerman, eds. 1987. *British Capitalism and Caribbean Slavery*. Cambridge: Cambridge Univ. Press.

SOPO. 1990. *Programme*. Trinidad: SOPO.

Southall, Roger, ed. 1988. *Trade Unions and the New International Division of Labour*. London: Zed Books.

Spackman, Ann. 1965. "Constitutional Development in Trinidad and Tobago". *Social and Economic Studies* 14, no. 2: 283–320.

———. 1967. "The Senate of Trinidad and Tobago". *Social and Economic Studies* 16, no. 1: 77–100.

Spalding, Hobart A. 1988. "US Labour Intervention in Latin America: The Case of the American Institute for Free Labour Development". In *Trade Unions and the New International Division of Labour*, edited by Roger Southall, 259–86. London: Zed Books.

Spraos, John. 1983. *Inequalising Trade?* Oxford: Clarendon Press.

Stern, Steve J. 1988a. "Feudalism, Capitalism, and the World System in the Perspective of Latin America and the Caribbean". *American Historical Review* 93, no. 4: 829–72.

———. 1988b. "Reply: 'Ever More Solitary' ". *American Historical Review* 93, no. 4: 886–97.

Stone, Carl. 1972. *Stratification and Political Change in Trinidad and Jamaica*. Beverly Hills: Sage.

———. 1973. *Class, Race and Political Behaviour in Urban Jamaica*. Mona, Jamaica: Institute of Social and Economic Research, Univ. of the West Indies.

Sturmthal, Adolf. 1973. "Industrial Relations Strategies". In *The International Labour Movement in Transition*, edited by Adolf Sturmthal and James G. Scoville, 1–33. London: Univ. of Illinois Press.

Sturmthal, Adolf, and James G. Scoville, eds. 1973. *The International Labour Movement in Transition*. London: Univ. of Illinois Press.

Sudama, Trevor. 1979. "The Model of the Plantation Economy: The Case of Trinidad and Tobago". *Latin American Perspectives*, no. 20, 65–83.

———. 1980. "Class, Race and the State in Trinidad and Tobago". *Latin American Perspectives*, no. 39, 75–96.

Sutton, Paul. 1983. "Black Power in Trinidad and Tobago: The 'Crisis' of 1970". *Journal of Commonwealth and Comparative Politics* 21: 115–32.

———. 1986. *Dual Legacies in the Contemporary Caribbean: Continuing Aspects of British and French Dominion*. London: Frank Cass.

Tapia. 1969 (28.9), 1970 and 1973. (Organ of the Tapia House Movement.)

Tardanico, Richard, ed. 1987. *Crises in the Caribbean Basin*. Beverly Hills/London: Sage.

Thatcher, M.H. 1979. Foreword to *History, Capitalism and Freedom*. London: Centre for Policy Studies.

Thomas, Clive. 1968. "A Model of Pure Plantation Economies: Comment". *Social and Economic Studies* 17, no. 3: 339–48.

———. 1988. *The Poor and the Powerless*. London: Latin America Bureau.

Thomas, Hugh. 1979. *History, Capitalism and Freedom*. London: Centre for Policy Studies.

Thomas, J.J. [1889] 1969. *Froudacity: West Indian Fables by James Anthony Froude*. Reprint, London: New Beacon.

Thomas, Roy Darrow. 1969. *The Adjustment of Displaced Workers in a Labour Surplus Economy: A Case Study of Trinidad and Tobago*. PhD diss., Cornell Univ.

———. 1971. "The Regulation of Industrial Relations in Trinidad and Tobago — The Next Step". Unpublished paper. Univ. of the West Indies, St Augustine.

———. 1975. *Bargaining for Wage Increases*. San Fernando, Trinidad: Oilfields Workers' Trade Union.

———. 1984. *Labour Law in Trinidad and Tobago*. St Augustine, Trinidad: Univ. of the West Indies.

Thomas, Roy Darrow, ed. 1987. *The Trinidad Labour Riots of 1937*. St Augustine, Trinidad: Univ. of the West Indies.

Thomas, Tony, and John Riddell. 1972. *Black Power in the Caribbean: The 1970 Upsurge in Trinidad*. New York: Pathfinder.

Thompson, E.P. 1978. "Eighteenth Century English Society: Class Struggle without Class". *Social History* 3, no. 2: 133–65.

———. [1963] 1988. *The Making of the English Working Class*. Reprint, Harmondsworth: Penguin.

Tinker, Hugh. 1974. *A New System of Slavery: The Export of Indian Labour Overseas 1830–1920*. London: Oxford Univ. Press for Institute of Race Relations.

Transport and Industrial Workers' Union. 1976. *Towards the Founding Congress of the ULF*. Laventille, Trinidad: Transport and Industrial Workers Union.

Tribune. 1980, 1981. (Organ of the February 18 Movement.)

Trinidad Chronicle. 1958 (27.6).

Trinidad Guardian. 1956 (22.6).

———. 1957 (23.3).

———. 1969.

———. 1970.

———. 1971a (2.7).

———. 1971b (3.7).

———. 1971c (25.9.

———. 1971d (28.9).

———. 1971e (20.10).

———. 1975.

———. 1976a (25.4).

———. 1976b (19.9).

———. 1977.

_____ . 1978 (1.4).

_____ . 1984 (24.5).

_____ . 1987 (29.11).

_____ . 1988.

_____ . 1989a (6.3).

_____ . 1989b (7.3).

_____ . 1989c (9.12).

_____ . 1990a (5.1).

_____ . 1990b (18.3).

_____ . 1990c (19.3).

_____ . 1990d (25.3).

Trinidad and Tobago. 1950. *Administration Report of the Commissioner of Labour for the Years 1947 and 1948*. Port of Spain: Government Printing Office.

_____ . 1951. *Administration Report of the Commissioner of Labour for the Year 1949*. Port of Spain: Government Printing Office.

_____ . 1952. *Administration Report of the Commissioner of Labour for the Year 1950*. Port of Spain: Government Printing Office.

_____ . 1952. *Annual Statistical Digest 1935–51*. Port of Spain: Central Statistical Office.

_____ . 1954. *Administration Report of the Commissioner of Labour for the Year 1951*. Port of Spain: Government Printing Office.

_____ . 1957. *The Size and Structure of the Labour Force*. Port of Spain: Central Statistical Office.

_____ . 1958. *Quarterly Economic Report* (Oct.–Dec. 1958).

_____ . 1960a. *Population Census 1960*. Vol. II, Part A. Port of Spain: Central Statistical Office.

_____ . 1960b. *Population Census 1960*. Vol. II, Part B, Port of Spain: Central Statistical Office.

_____ . 1965. *The Industrial Stabilisation Act 1965*. Trinidad and Tobago.

_____ . 1966a. *Debates of the Senate, Official Report (Hansard) March 19, 1965*. Port of Spain: Government Printing Office.

_____ . 1966b. *First Annual Report of the President of the Industrial Court of Trinidad and Tobago*. Trinidad and Tobago.

_____ . 1967. *Second Annual Report of the President of the Industrial Court of Trinidad and Tobago*. Port of Spain: Government Printing Office.

_____ . 1969. *Third Annual Report of the President of the Industrial Court of Trinidad and Tobago*. Port of Spain: Government Printing Office.

_____ . 1970. *Debates of the House of Representatives, 4th Session, Second Parliament*, Vol. 13, no. 26, *Official Report (Hansard), April 29, 1970*. Port of Spain: Government Printing Office.

_____ . 1973. *Debates of the House of Representatives, Official Report (Hansard), June 14, 1972*. Port of Spain: Government Printing Office.

_____ . 1975. *Social Indicators*. Port of Spain: Ministry of Planning and Development, Central Statistical Office. 202

Trinidad and Tobago, Republic of. 1984. *Review of the Economy 1984*. Port of Spain: Central Statistical Office.

———. 1985. *Review of the Economy 1985*. Port of Spain: Central Statistical Office.

———. 1986. *Review of the Economy 1986*. Port of Spain: Central Statistical Office.

———. 1989a. *Review of the Economy 1989*. Port of Spain: Central Statistical Office.

———. 1989b. *Annual Statistical Digest 1988*. Port of Spain: Central Statistical Office.

Trinidad and Tobago, The Demas Task Force. 1984. *The Imperatives of Adjustment: Draft Development Plan 1983–1986*, vols. 1 & 2. Port of Spain: Government Printing Office.

Trinidad and Tobago Labour Congress. 1966. *Constitution*. Trinidad: Trinidad and Tobago Labour Congress.

———. 1986. Draft Discussion Documents on Labour Unity. Unpublished documents.

———. 1987. "Adjustment Mechanisms for Assisting the Government in Turning Around the Economy". Labour Congress paper.

Trinidad and Tobago — Laws and Statutes. 1972. *The Industrial Relations Act 1972, Act No. 23 of 1972*. Trinidad and Tobago.

Trollope, Anthony. 1968. *The West Indies and the Spanish Main*. Reprint, London: Frank Cass.

Trotsky, L. 1936. *The History of the Russian Revolution*. London: Victor Gollancz.

Turner, Terisa Elaine. 1972. *Political Mobilisation in a Satellite Society: A Study of the 1970 Rebellion in Trinidad*. MA thesis, Oberlin College.

ULF. 1977. *ULF Crisis Bulletin*. Nos. 10, 12, 15, 16, 19.

ULF News. 1980.

UNESCO. 1977. *Race and Class in Post-Colonial Society*. Paris: UNESCO.

United Labour Front. 1975. *Resolution passed at Mass Rally at Skinner Park, 18 February 1975*. San Fernando, Trinidad: United Labour Front.

———. 1976a. *Policy Statement Presented to a Conference of Shop Stewards and Branch Officials, January 3 and 4, 1976*. San Fernando, Trinidad: United Labour Front.

———. 1976b. *Constitution of the United Labour Front*. San Fernando, Trinidad: United Labour Front.

———. 1976c. *Policy and Programme of the ULF*. San Fernando, Trinidad: United Labour Front.

———. 1976d. *Election Manifesto 1976*. San Fernando, Trinidad: United Labour Front.

———. 1977. *Minutes of a Meeting of the Central Executive of the United Labour Front, February 12*. San Fernando, Trinidad: United Labour Front.

———. c.1977. *Answers Now! Mr. Panday*. San Fernando, Trinidad: United Labour Front.

United National Independence Party. 1970. *All for One, One for All: Basic Philosophy and Objectives*. Curepe, Trinidad: Moko Enterprises.

Vanguard. (Organ of the Oilfields Workers' Trade Union.) 1947, 1969, 1970, 1971, 1983, 1984, 1985, 1986, 1987, 1988, 1989, 1990, 1991.

Wallerstein, I. 1974/1980. *The Modern World System*, 2 vols. New York: Academic Press.

_____ . 1980. *The Capitalist World Economy*. Cambridge: Cambridge Univ. Press.

_____ . 1983. "Capitalism and the World Working Class: Some Premises and Some Issues for Research and Analysis". In *Labour in the World Social Structure*, edited by I. Wallerstein, 17–21. Beverly Hills: Sage.

_____ . 1988. "Comments on Stern's Critical Tests". *American Historical Review* 93, no. 4: 829–72.

Wallerstein, I., ed. 1983. *Labour in the World Social Structure*, Beverly Hills: Sage.

Walton, J., and D. Seddon. 1994. *Free Markets and Food Riots*. London: Blackwell.

Warren, Bill. 1988. *Imperialism: Pioneer of Capitalism*. London: Verso.

Waterman, Peter. 1990. "Social Movement Unionism". Mimeo.

Waterman, Peter, ed. 1984. *For a New Labour Internationalism*. The Hague: International Labour Education Research and Information Foundation.

Watson, Beverly. 1974. *Supplementary Notes on Foreign Investment in the Commonwealth Caribbean*. Mona, Jamaica: Institute of Social and Economic Research, Univ. of the West Indies.

Watson, Hillbourne A. 1980. "The Political Economy of US–Caribbean Relations". *The Black Scholar* 11, no. 3: 30–41.

Weber, Henri. 1981. *Nicaragua: The Sandinista Revolution*. London: Verso.

Weekes, George. [N.d.] 1965. *High Treason: The Trades Union Congress and the Sugar Workers' Strike – Why I Resigned*. Reprint, San Fernando, Trinidad: Oilfields Workers' Trade Union.

_____ . 1986. *George Weekes Speaks on Economic Crisis, Apartheid and the Struggle for Justice*. San Fernando, Trinidad: Oilfields Workers' Trade Union.

_____ . 1973. *The Real Gangsters and Whitemailers*. San Fernando, Trinidad: Oilfields Workers' Trade Union.

West India Royal Commission 1938–39: Recommendations. 1940. Cmd. 6174 London: HMSO.

_____ . 1945. Cmd. 6656. London: HMSO.

West India Royal Commission Report. 1945. Cmd. 6607. London: HMSO.

West Indian Census. 1946. *Census of the Colony of Trinidad and Tobago, 9 April 1946*. Port of Spain: Government Printing Office.

West Indian Independence Party. 1952. *Statement and Fundamental Programme of West Indian Independence Party of Trinidad and Tobago*. Port of Spain: West Indian Independence Party.

We the People. Journal of the Workers and Farmers Party. 1966.

Williams, Eric. 1955. "Economic Problems of Trinidad and Tobago". Teachers, Economic and Cultural Association, Public Affairs pamphlets.

_____ . 1956. *Federation*. Port of Spain: PNM Publishing.

_____ . 1958. *Perspectives for Our Party*. Port of Spain: PNM Publishing.

_____ . c.1960. *The Approach of Independence*. Port of Spain: PNM Publishing.

_____ . 1960a. *Perspectives for the West Indies*. Port of Spain: PNM Publishing.

_____ . 1960b. *Our Fourth Anniversary . . . The Last Lap*. Port of Spain: PNM Publishing.

_____ . 1960c. *Responsibilities of the Party Member*. Port of Spain: PNM Publishing.

_____ . 1961. *Massa Day Done*. Port of Spain: PNM Publishing.

_____ . 1964. *History of the People of Trinidad and Tobago*. London, André Deutsch.

_____ . 1965a. *Reflections on the Industrial Stabilisation Bill, Trinidad*. Port of Spain: PNM Publishing.

_____ . 1965b. *An Address to the Ninth Annual Convention*. Port of Spain: PNM Publishing.

_____ . 1966. *British Historians and the West Indies*. London: André Deutsch.

_____ . 1969. *Inward Hunger: The Education of a Prime Minister*. London: André Deutsch.

_____ . 1970. *From Columbus to Castro: The History of the Caribbean 1492–1969*. London: André Deutsch.

_____ . 1987. *Capitalism and Slavery*. London: André Deutsch.

Wong, David C. 1984. "A Review of Caribbean Political Economy". *Latin American Perspectives*, no. 42: 125–40.

Wood, Donald. 1968. *Trinidad in Transition*. London: Oxford Univ. Press.

Workers and Farmers Party. 1966a. *What the WFP is and What the WFP is Not*. San Fernando, Trinidad: Stephen Maharaj.

_____ . 1966b. *1966 Election Manifesto*. Port of Spain: Workers and Farmers Party.

Workers Tribune. 1980 & 1981. Journal of the February 18 Movement, nos. 1(1) & 2(2).

Worrell, DeLisle. 1987. *Small Island Economies: Structure and Performance in the English Speaking Caribbean since 1970*. New York: Praeger.

Worsley, Peter. 1972. "Frantz Fanon and the Lumpen-Proletariat". *The Socialist Register 1972*: 193–230. London: Merlin.

_____ . 1980. "One World or Three: A Critique of the World System of Immanuel Wallerstein". *The Socialist Register 1980*: 298–338. London: Merlin.

Wright, Erik Olin. 1985. *Class, Crisis and the State*. London: Verso.

Yelvington, Kevin. 1987. "Vote Dem Out". *Caribbean Review* 15, no. 4: 8–33.

_____ . Forthcoming. "Trinidad and Tobago, 1988–89". In *Latin American and Caribbean Contemporary Record*, edited by James Malloy and Eduardo A. Gamarra, vol. 8. New York: Holmes and Meier.

Young, Joe. 1976. "The Politics of the Labour Movement". In *Butler versus the King*, edited by W. Richard Jacobs, 161–67. Port of Spain: Key Caribbean.

Interviews

Abdulah, David. 1990. Political leader of the Movement for Social Transformation (MOTION). 25 April.

Aberdeen, Albert. 1990. President of the Transport and Industrial Workers Union. 26 April.

John, Selwyn. 1990. President of the National Union of Government and Federated Workers. 30 April.

Maharaj, Sam. 1990. General Secretary of the All Trinidad Sugar and General Workers Union. 12 April.

McLeod, Errol. 1990. President of the Oilfields Workers' Trade Union. 30 March.

Millette, James. 1990. General Secretary of the United Labour Front . 2 March.

Panday, Basdeo. 1990. Leader of the United Labour Front and the United National Congress. 16 March.

Paul, Cecil. 1990. General Secretary of the Council of Progressive Trade Unions. 28 March.

Pierre, Lennox. 1990. United Labour Front Central Committee member. 31 March.

Rabathaly, Patrick. 1990. General Secretary of the Bank Employees Union. 3 May.

Ramnanan, Frank. 1990. General Secretary of the Trinidad and Tobago Unified Teachers Association. 10 May.

Rennie, Kenrick. 1990. President of the Public Services Association. 7 May.

Shah, Raffique. 1990. Parliamentary Leader of the United Labour Front. 20 April.

Singh, Gajraj. 1990. Senior Labour Relations Officer, Ministry of Labour. 8 May.

Tull, Carl. 1990. General Secretary of the Trinidad and Tobago Labour Congress. 1 May.

Index

Day of Resistance (1989): and joint union protest, 163

Debt peonage: among Indian immigrants, 56

Democratic Labour Party (1956), founding of, 93; 111

Dependency theory, 17; and the Caribbean as satellite of Britain, 22; on class formation, 23; critique of, 20; and role of external vs internal forces, 20; weaknesses in, 23

Devaluation, 154

Development: impact of labour and race, 172–173; impact of oil price increase in Trinidad (1970s), 134

Development theory, task of, 13

Dispute Settlement Ordinance, 67

Dualist theory, critique of, 12

Durkheim, Emile: on changing nature of society, 7

❑ .... **E**

East Indian National Association, 64, 68

Economic crisis, as result of oil dependence (1980s), 153

Economy: crisis (1980s), 152; decline (1960s), 98; devaluation, 154; development strategies, 106; impact of industrialization, 105–110; statistics (1980s), 154; in Tobago, 62; in Trinidad in 1930s, 69–70

Education, as agent of social mobility, 57

Elections: in 1950, 88; in 1956, 91; and the race question, 93, 96, 97, 140; in 1958, 93; in 1946, 8; in 1976, 140; 1961 and TTUC support of PNM, 95

Employers' Consultative Association (ECA), 13

Employment: impact of industrialization strategy, 108; postwar increase resulting from US base and oil boom, 83; statistics (1980s), 155, 157

Encomienda, 44

External control, 19

❑ .... **F**

February 18 Movement: Millette faction, in ULF conflict, 144

February Revolution: causes of, 113; features of, 119; role of working class, 105

Foreign invesment: ownership, 106; strategy for development in the Caribbean and Latin America, 35–37; weakness as development strategy, 107

Functionalist theory, weaknesses inherent in, 11

❑ .... **G**

Gomes, Albert: and self-government, 85

Granger, Geddes. *See* NJAC

❑ .... **H**

Habitual Idlers Ordinance, provisions of, 66

Henry, Zin: and industrial relations in the Caribbean, 10

❑ .... **I**

Immigration Ordinance (1870), 51

Income distribution, 108; gender and race issues in, 109

❑ .... J

❑ .... K

❑ .... **R**

❏ .... U